LITERARY MONOGRAPHS · Volume 3

LITERARY
MONOGRAPHS

Volume 3

EDITED BY

Eric Rothstein

Published for the Department of English by

THE UNIVERSITY OF WISCONSIN PRESS

Madison, Milwaukee, and London 1970

Published 1970
The University of Wisconsin Press
Box 1379, Madison, Wisconsin 53701

The University of Wisconsin Press, Ltd.
27–29 Whitfield Street, London, W.1

First printing

Printed in the United States of America
The Heffernan Press Inc., Worcester, Mass.

ISBN 299-05780-1; LC 66-25869

Publication of this volume has been made possible in part by a gift to the University of Wisconsin Foundation from the estate of Beatrice T. Conrad, Davenport, Iowa.

PREFACE

The Department of English of the University of Wisconsin continues with this volume a series of monographs in English and American literature. The series was inaugurated in 1967 to serve scholars whose work might take a form too lengthy for journals but too brief for a separate book.

For future volumes of *Literary Monographs* we invite works of high quality, scholarly or critical, that contribute to English or American literary studies. We welcome any promising contribution, from the United States or from abroad. We welcome not only conventional literary essays but also those involving experimental critical theories and methods whenever they are eloquent and persuasive. And we will be flexible enough to welcome monographs involving comparative literature or comparative aesthetics, so long as they significantly illuminate literature in English.

The editorial board of *Literary Monographs* would like to express its appreciation to the University of Wisconsin Foundation for making possible the publication of this volume through a gift from the estate of Beatrice T. Conrad, Davenport, Iowa.

Eric Rothstein

Madison, Wisconsin
June 1970

NOTES ON SUBMISSIONS

Manuscripts should be from 15,000 to 35,000 words in length. They should be submitted, with return postage and self-adressed envelope enclosed, to

The Editor
Literary Monographs
Department of English
University of Wisconsin
Madison, Wisconsin 53706

Manuscripts should follow the *MLA Style Sheet*, with a few exceptions or amplifications included in the specific instructions given below.

1. Paper should be 16-pound or 20-pound weight bond in normal quarto size; do not use highly glazed paper (sold under such trade names as "Corrasable"). To make satisfactory photocopying possible, the paper should be white and the typewriter ribbon black. Handwritten corrections may be made in pencil or washable ink; avoid ballpoint pen. Leave margins of 1 to 1½ inches on all sides.

2. Manuscripts should be double spaced throughout, including notes and all excerpts, prose or verse. Do not indent prose excerpts, but mark them with a pencil line along the left margin to the full length of the quotation and allow an extra line of space above and below.

3. Brief references should be inserted in the text (see *MLA Style Sheet*, Sec. 13f). In notes, first references should be cited in full. Succeeding references to books should use short titles rather than *"op. cit.";* e.g., Taylor, *Problems*, p. 12. Short references to journal articles should use author's name, journal name, volume, and page; e.g., McKerrow, *RES*, XVI, 117.

As can be seen from this volume, *Literary Monographs* reserves the use of footnotes for information that is needed in order to follow the argument of the text or to understand a system of in-text citation. Endnotes supply documentation, or they may extend or parallel the text discussion. Contributors are requested to organize their manuscripts so that endnotes and footnotes are on separate pages, with separate numbering sequences.

CONTENTS

HOROLOGICALS TO CHRONOMETRICALS: THE RHETORIC OF THE JEREMIAD

Sacvan Bercovitch

Now in an artifical world like ours, the soul of man is further removed from its God and the Heavenly Truth, than the chronometer carried to China, is from Greenwich. And, as that chronometer, if at all accurate, will pronounce it to be 12 o'clock high-noon, when the China local watches say, perhaps, it is 12 o'clock midnight; so the chronometric soul, if in this world true to its great Greenwich in the other, will always, in its so-called intuitions of right and wrong, be contradicting the mere local standards and watch-maker's brains of this earth. . . . And yet it follows not from this, that God's truth is one thing and man's truth another; but—as hinted above, and as will be further elucidated in subsequent lectures—by their very contradictions they are made to correspond.

Melville, *Pierre*

Jeremiah and the Two Covenants

Let it be such a Dial, not as the dead face of a clock . . . but rather such a Dial as is the garden itself, in whose leaves and flowers and fruits the suddenly awakened sleeper is instantly apprised not what part of dead time, but what state of life and growth is now arrived and arriving.

Emerson and Margaret Fuller, *The Dial*, I (1840)

On board the *Arbella*, on the Atlantic Ocean, John Winthrop set forth the principles of the infant New England church-state in a provisional but sweeping prophecy of doom. Because the passengers had entered into a marriage-bond with God and he was condescending to dwell among them as his own people, therefore,

3

charged Winthrop, they must beware of swift and harsh affliction.
Henceforth the Lord would survey them with a more strict and
jealous eye. At the slightest shortcoming, for the neglect of the "least"
stipulation in their "speciall Commission," he would surely break out
in wrath against them and be avenged. The forecast sounded a familiar
note. Before they had embarked on the voyage, John Cotton had
similarly instructed them in the grave perils of their commitment. The
"same God that planted you," he observed, recalling the ominous
precedent of Israel, may "also roote you out againe." Men generally
succumbed to carnal intentions, tended toward profits and pleasures,
permitted their children to degenerate. Should the emigrants fall prey
to such temptations he would at once withdraw their "special appointment," pluck them up, and cast them irrevocably out of his sight.[1]

These threats, which represent an effort to cope with the practical
difficulties of the new settlement, clearly derive from the notion of
national covenant: the conditional pact whereby the community
volunteers to serve God to its immediate, earthly advantage and
whereby, on his part, "God writes his *severe truths* with the *blood* of
his *disobedient Subjects*." But the rhetoric that conveys the threats
implies a radically different outlook. Winthrop's allusions and figural
correspondences betoken an "extraordinary" "worke and end," based
on an unalterable pledge and locating the venture within a configuration which extends beyond Sinai and Pisgah to the Mount Zion of
Revelation. With this intent, too, Cotton chose for his text the
momentous prophecy in 2 Sam. 7:10. America, he suggests, the Land
of Promise, is the antitype of Canaan, espied and reserved by God for
his saints in fulfillment of his predestined plan. *A Model of Christian
Charity* hints that all history is converging upon "the cosmic climax of
Boston's founding"; more cogently still, *Gods Promise to His Plantations*
"reveals . . . the Puritans' hopes that their plantation would become
the scene of Christ's triumphant descent to His New Jerusalem."[2]

The two sermons, then, embody a conflict between literal content
and prophetic form. Their Janus-like analogy to Israel identifies the
settlers at once with a fallen people and with an irreversible movement toward redemption. They seem to alternate between the provisional and the predetermined, or in the words of Melville's Plinlimmon
between the horological, the imperfect time of mankind, and the
chronometrical, the "original Heaven's time" unaffected "by all terrestrial jarrings." Plinlimmon introduces the dichotomy in order to

point out the unbridgeable chasm that separates God's permanent and universal Truth from "relative, worldly, human truths," and so to caution against confusing the New Jerusalem with "the general Jerusalem of this world." In particular, he inveighs against the destructive self-deception of otherworldly idealists: "the absolute effort to live . . . according to . . . the chronometrical is, somehow, apt to involve those inferior beings eventually in strange, *unique* follies and sins, unimagined before."[3] It is precisely this effort, I believe—this determination to impose chronometrical upon horological—that motivates the rhetoric of Cotton and Winthrop. Their overt insistence on the possibility of failure asserts a distinction between the two levels of time; their language, by incorporating that possibility within the broader framework of the absolute, implicitly affords a synthesis of the human and the divine. This synthesis—formulated by the men who became the chief spokesmen for church and state in Massachusetts and sustained as the context within which the orthodoxy defined its errand in the New World—marks a vital and enduring aspect of the colonial imagination.

In part, the evolution of New England vindicates the nonbenevolent philosopher: within the first decade the clergy already begins to record the betrayal of the vision. The first election sermon we have warns the settlers against their apparent desire to choose a captain back to Egypt; two years earlier, and only six after the *Arbella* arrived, Thomas Shepard moaned that "We never looked for such days in *New-England* . . . Are all [God's] kindnesses forgotten? all your promises forgotten?" During the sixteen-seventies Increase Mather bitterly recalled that "*Our Prophets have foretold us of these dayes . . . Renowned Hooker would many times express his fears,* that God would punish . . . *New-England,*" and John Norton "*saith,* Now our . . . Lights are gone," and "blessed Mr. *Cotton,* did in his time . . . testify against such a spirit of worldliness and Apostasy [as we see at present], even in those dayes prevailing in this Country." As the century progressed, the ministers more and more vehemently sounded their fears, in a "melancholy dirge," an "unending monotonous wail" that came increasingly to acknowledge that their enterprise was "sick unto death."

[By] the end of the century, the . . . preachers [in "something of a ritualistic incantation"] . . . would take some verse of Isaiah or Jeremiah, set up the doctrine that God avenges the iniquities of a chosen people, and then run down the twelve heads [of the land's "enormities," as set forth by the synod of 1679], merely bringing the list up to date by inserting the new and still more depraved practices an ingenious people kept on devising. . . . In the whole literature of the world, including the satirists of imperial Rome, there is hardly such another uninhibited and unrelenting documentation of a people's descent into corruption.[4]

All this is well known. It is almost too well known; for students of the period, taking the theme of declension for granted, have neglected the far more powerful, and distinctive, countertheme of exultation and affirmation. As they have described the Puritans' long lament, it represents not a New World phenomenon ("the one literary type which the first native-born Americans . . . developed, amplified, and standardized"), but an imported community ritual, an immemorial formulaic refrain which sounds loudly in the medieval and Renaissance pulpit and continues through the sermons of moral complaint in late seventeenth-century England, when the Anglican Gilbert Burnet, for one, thundered that "the wrath of God hangs over our Heads . . . the whole Nation is corrupted . . . we may justly look for unheard of Calamities." What is in this respect peculiar and essential to the New England orthodoxy lies in its unshakable optimism. In deliberate opposition to the traditional mode, its rhetoric all but submerges the prognostications of disaster and builds upon the founders' deepest aspirations, their dream of a society in which "fact could be made one with the ideal," toward a strange, unique triumph. Even while invoking the specter of national covenant, the ministers retain the dream and amplify its meaning; as fact and ideal veer further apart, they restructure experience in terms of the one reality where horological and chronometrical can be made to synchronize, the realm of the imagination. The development may be traced through many forms of the literature. Most dramatically and forcefully it appears in the procession of political sermons—the discourses on public problems and prospects tendered at every ritual-communal occasion (on days of fasting and prayer, humiliation and thanksgiving, at covenant-renewal and artillery-company ceremonies, and for election-day gatherings, the "greatest solemnity that the colony afforded")—which we designate as the jeremiad.[5]*

---

* I use the term "political sermon" here synonymously with "jeremiad." First employed by the ministers to convey the duality of their calling, as practical and as heavenly guides, "political sermon" also came in their exhortations to imply the

Seen in this double perspective, the designation is an apt one. Jeremiah, we recall, both laments an apostasy and heralds a restoration; though he may often "lift vp his voice like vnto a *Sonne of Thunder* . . . eftsoones [he] . . . change[s] the same, vnto the still, and soft voice of a . . . *Sonne of consolation,* (for their sakes whom the Lord had appointed to bee heires of salvation)." As a son of thunder, he expounds the articles of the national covenant and of providential historiography. The Israelites had begged favor at God's hands and engaged themselves to keep his laws—"*Which my Covenant they brake, although I was an husband unto them* (31:32) . . . [wherefore] the Lord cast them off," to "laugh at their Calamities until He has *consumed them utterly, so that there shall be no Remnant, nor escaping.*" Yet there *was* to be a remnant, a chosen number who would escape the calamities. As a son of consolation, Jeremiah holds up to the Jews of the captivity the future which God has in store for them as "a new Exodus, of which the earlier one was the type," their return from Babylon to a more bountiful and blessed Canaan, a Jerusalem renovated and "rebuilt, after the pattern of the Jerusalem which is above." And to consecrate the promise, this "sublimest of the prophets" announces—in the verses immediately preceding and following the denunciation (31:31, 33)—a new covenant between God and the house of Israel, now established *in aeternum.* "Though their sins were such as deserved utter extirpation . . . yet [his] clemency and goodness . . . should appear in the preservation of a remnant," to be his "Holy *Seed,* forever." To the Puritans, these "predictions of good things [seemed far] greater than his predictions of punishment," for they embodied the "essence and substance" of the covenant of grace, here "*more cleared by* [Jeremiah] *then any before.*" In this capacity, the Prophet does not speak as formerly to an immediate audience about a temporal situation. He addresses himself rather, *sub specie aeternitatis,* to all true believers (the *spiritual* Israel) "*touching Christ the Messiah, his Kingdome, Priesthood, Benefits* . . . and their eternal deliverance . . . Typicall from Babylon."[6] By the figures and types of the original heaven's time, he enunciates the terms of the history of redemption: the everlasting pledge, unchanged from the *proto-evangelium* through the Incarnation, that Christ's Church would

---

unity of the two spheres, to demonstrate (rhetorically) that, within their church-state, theology was wedded to politics and politics to the progress of the Kingdom of God.

triumph over Satan; whatever their horological blemishes, his saints
would in the end rejoice in Zion.

Stated thus, the two covenants stand as sharply divided as
Augustine's two cities, and upon the basis of this division the Elizabethan Protestants erected the doctrines of congregationalism and
of national election. The adherents of both movements identified
themselves to some degree with the blessed remnant, and both
selected as their main text Jeremiah's description (50:5) of a group
which at the close of the seventy-year exile "shall ask the way to
Zion . . . saying, come, let us join ourselves to the Lord in a perpetual
covenant." Their essential difference lay in two divergent emphases
on the meaning of the Babylonian captivity, each deeply ingrained in
Reformation thought. For Calvin, the captivity signified the bondage
of sin. Following Augustine, he denied the possibility of a temporal
commitment on God's part, and explicated Jer. 50:5 (as he did also
Jer. 31:32) purely in terms of grace, as a release from the *regnum
satanae* into the *regnum spirituale*. His exclusively Christological
eschatology, precluding hope in any radical improvement of the
earthly state, treated the return from exile as a promise outside time
and the *civilis ordinatio* of *profectus* for the believer, his "growing up
into the perfect manhood of Christ." Luther, however, attached a concrete, worldly import to the captivity. Seeking a correlation between
prophecies and contemporary events in order to answer the Roman
Catholic objections to the Reformation, he found in the New Covenant
an adumbration of man's temporal progress. Jeremiah, chapter 31, he
claimed, "instructs us in what manner the end of the world is approaching": the captivity foretold the dark night of Catholicism; the
deliverance prefigured the Reformation (the Church's exodus from
slavery to the seven-headed Monster of Rome), the "vengeaunce . . .
to be powered forthe upon this Babylonish beast," and the saints' now-
irreversible march toward the millennium. For all its apocalyptic
Sturm und Drang, Luther's interpretation does not fundamentally
contradict Calvin's. Because both assume the disparity between
"geistliches und weltliches Regiment," they both pertain finally to the
history of redemption. But their differing perspectives—Calvin's personal Eucharistic outlook, Luther's developmental-historical bent—
opened in seventeenth-century England into two mutually opposed
concepts of a visible people of God.[7]

The more popular of these concepts, that of national election, stems
from the identification of Babylon and Rome. Though English
theologians agreed that "mystically" Babylon signified the postlap-
sarian world, they eagerly adopted Luther's position. Buoyed up by a
high tide of nationalism, they discerned in their own past the dawning
of the Reformation (its "first small beginnings" in Wycliff and the
Lollards) and, rewriting Britain's history to correspond with the
apocalyptic timetable, they proclaimed their "noble and puissant
Nation" destined to head the universal battle against "the malignant
church, with antichrist and his kingdom, prefigured afore in . . .
Jeremy." This millennial fervor, we know, spread steadily from the
period of the Marian exile to become a motive of revolution, and reflected at all stages a belief in the imminent end of natural history;
nonetheless, the very fact of a national impulse rooted the movement
per se in external, political reality. The New Jerusalem, after all, be-
longed to the saints, and not even the extreme patriot-chiliasts doubted
that in Britain as elsewhere many were called but few chosen. The
martyrologist John Bale, for example, who inspired a generation of
his countrymen to expect "now in our time" Babylon's fall and the
recovery of Zion, followed "the true opinion of St. Austin" concerning
the two cities, limited atonement, and the need to seek justification "in
the solitary heart, and not in the outward" social framework. So, too,
Oliver Cromwell's schoolmaster reminded his "happy favoured
brethren" that the final conflict ultimately meant the destruction of
sinners, among whom he numbered most Englishmen. From Foxe to
Fuller every historian who extolled the prospects in store for England's
green and pleasant land hastened to add that in the "higher" sense "it
is not fit that good men should live long on earth. . . . God knows
[that the world, including Britain, is] too bad, for his servants to live
in."[8]

Inevitably, therefore, the adherents of national election turned to
schema relevant to the *civitas terrena.* When they boasted of being a
"new chosen people" or an "army of saints" they spoke metaphorically,
supposing at most a vague analogue to the ineluctable progress of the
Invisible Church. Their specific associations were with the institutions
of the historical past, such as the medieval state-compact and the
covenant of Jer. 31:32. "The sum" of our duties, Robert Dowglas told
the members of Parliament in 1651, is *"To walk after the Lord & keep*

his commandments," in the hope of at last establishing "Peace and
Safety" and with the "terrible liberty" to defy God and so justly to *"be
divided and cut in pieces,"* as his "sword is now devouring Germany."
Accordingly, they appealed to natural law and secular reason, in explicit antipathy to *"Church-oath"* with its pretensions of assurance about
grace. What they offered differed only in degree from the condition of
other nations: an exemplary community in direct relationship with
God concerning the people's outward "happinesse or misery." Accordingly, too, their providential view of history centered upon terrestrial affairs. In asserting that God manipulated every event, they
meant no more than to explain in Christian terms the vicissitudes of
fortune. Openly affirming a double standard in their treatment of
human and sacred history, they acknowledged, as historians, that the
latter transcended their "impaired resources," and in their writings
they focussed upon the "vagaries of . . . mundane happenings" or the
patterns of rise and fall in the story of men and nations. What morals
they drew from their investigations applied to visible rewards and
punishments, teaching "for what vertue . . . God made prosperous; and
for what vice . . . he made wretched," for what "secondary causes" he
would "[en]courage and discourage, raise and throw down kings,
estates, cities."[9]

The English Congregationalists took the contrary course; they
linked their movement solely to the City of God. To be sure, they
frequently equated Babylon with Rome, anxiously awaited "the year
of the great Revolution," and, for a time, accepted the idea of
England's calling. But fundamentally they sought separation from the
Kingdom of Sin. They came out of Babylon as a remnant fleeing from
spiritual exile, "not by bodely remooving, but vnlikeness of maners."
Like the apostolic Christians, for whom the earth was "the sphere of
uncleanness," they gathered into small vineyards of Christ as into
oases in the wilderness of the world. They acknowledged the fallibility
of their methods, but hoping at least externally to approach perfection
they deemed it necessary to stand as a tiny minority outside all "agreements of the people." Before 1640, as Brethren of the Separation,
they condemned the Anglicans for their indiscriminate church-membership policy. After 1640, as proponents of the Congregational Way,
they suspected the state church of being a "popish device." "The
prophet Jeremiah," they pointed out,

speaking [of] . . . the new covenant . . . testifieth that [God would] . . .
remember [the chosen ones'] iniquities no more, Jer. xxxi. 31, 33, 34. . . .
But your national church never came within the compass of this promise.
It is [therefore] . . . Babylon, though much purged and repaired. . . . Now
as the people of God in old time were called . . . to come to Jerusalem
and there to build anew the Lord's temple . . . so are the people of God
now to go out of Babylon spiritual . . . [and] as lively stones couple them
selves together by . . . covenant [so as to constitute] a spiritual building,
the Lord's temple . . . [having] for an inheritance . . . the kingdom of
heaven.[10]

The images of temple and kingdom in this passage not only lie
beyond the domain of providential historiography but in a sense
stand deliberately opposed to it. They militate directly against any
attempt "to bring the church out of the desert, [in order] to make her
triumphant in the . . . councils of nations," and offer instead a *Heils-
geschichte* viewed against eternity, a pattern working itself out inde-
pendently of the recurrent cycles of human "repair" and deterioration.
In this perspective, the New Jerusalem cannot be built in England or
anywhere else, not even as an "analogy to that blessed state." Indeed,
it is precisely that blessed state which conclusively reveals the "fair
field of England, of whose beauty all the Christian world is enamored,"
to be a weed patch with a "few kernels of wheat scattered among the
tares here and there"—"a small sprinkling of good men amongst the
great retchless rout of wicked and graceless persons"—and hence
merely another form of the captivity from which Jeremiah summoned
the people of God. It may be, as these arguments suggest, and as the
Presbyterians expressly charged, that the Congregationalists (con-
founding "pollucyon by sinne" with what really referred to "Rome's
punishment") came to place an undue trust in their sense of election.[11]
But if so, they carefully divorced that personal assurance from the
providence guiding the mass of mankind. Insofar as church covenant
intimated sainthood their kingdom was not of this world. It had to
do with the journey to redemption, with chronometricals.

The Great Migration owes its unique character to its inheritance
of both these strains in its English background. The settlers—children
of an improbable mixed marriage—were Congregationalists on a
historic mission. They took with them when they left both a providential and a divine historiography: both their sense of election and
their expectation of great things to come on earth. On the one hand,

they conceived of their flight (with the Plymouth Pilgrims) in spiritual and inward terms, as a means of self-improvement. Your goal, President Chauncy told his Harvard flock, is to build "the Temple" in defiance of "Babylonish practice. . . . The God of Israel hath separated you . . . to bring you neer unto himself." On the other hand, they saw themselves leaving a real Babylon, in another (and final) stage of the Exodus motif that defined the temporal meaning of the Reformation. Unlike their Plymouth brethren, they were determined from the beginning not to withdraw from the world but to reform it. If they looked "upon [their] departure to these parts," in Shepard's and Allin's words, "to be . . . a heavenly translation from corrupt to more pure churches," they also thought of it as "the establishment of the Holy Commonwealth . . . preparatory to the great event." England had forfeited her calling; her leading ministers, men like Preston and Brightman, were forecasting as well-nigh "inevitable" an "apocalyptic . . . lamentable calamity." For their part, the emigrant leaders viewed the prospect with a grim joy. "Truth," declared Thomas Hooker immediately before his departure, was being "driven out of Europe altogether . . . [and] God had chosen New England as her residence"; "I am veryly perswaded," Winthrop wrote his wife in 1629, that "God will bringe some heavye Affliction upon this lande, and that speedy-lye." He also, in the same year, reasoned out the migration in traditional Separatist language, by reference to the woman in Revelation, chapter 12, forced to fly the world's "coldness, carnality, contention." That rationale for him and his colleagues complemented and enforced the other; together they demonstrated (as Winthrop further noted in his 1629 "Conclusions for the Plantation in New-England") that "It appeares to be a worke of god . . . he hath some great worke in hand wch he hath revealed to his prophets among us." Thus, clad in "the mantle of Israel, lost by England's Stuart kings," they set out as the "*spirituall* remnant" God "meanes to save out of this generall callamitie" in order to complete a "Super-humane . . . [and] predeterminate Design."[12]

Nowhere does this dual legacy show itself more lucidly than in the prototypic jeremiads of Cotton and Winthrop. Puritan scholars have analyzed the *Arbella* sermon as a model of social discipline, the great class hierarchy it extols "knitt together" like some ideal English squirearchy or medieval "Citty" by authority, "charitie," and reasoned "consent." And so, clearly, it is. Yet the same terms apply with equal clarity to the ecclesiastical order. A city is the "Title given to the Church," as Richard Mather observed, and specifically to "a Church by Covenant," "knit together by a voluntary consent" according to the reach of "rationall charitie." Such "Fellowship . . . is a *City set upon a Hill*" as an immediate "Shelter" for the soul rescued out of Babylon, a "model" of heaven to come, and a present-future image of the millennial *"Throne of the Lord* [when] . . . *all Nations shall be gathered unto it."* The nationalist John Milton, using the concept in its social sense only, spoke in 1643 of England "holding up, as from a Hill, the new Lampe of *saving light* to all Christendome." Somewhat earlier, the Separatist John Robinson maintained, from his spiritual viewpoint, that the saints must "resort to the place where [God] hath put his name, for which they need not go either to Jerusalem, or to Rome, or beyond the seas; they may find Sion the Lord's mountain prepared on the top of every hill." Winthrop and Cotton use both aspects of the concept simultaneously; and the double meaning they thus invest in the New World city on a hill pervades their discourses. It recurs in their blessings and threats and in the scriptural allusions that thread their argument: to the colony's "grand Charter" which embodies the eternal covenant, to the "ends of the earth" which signifies the Second Coming as well as a specific locale, to the "Spirit [acting] upon the drie bones" which refers at once to civic harmony, personal adoption in Christ, and the Church's liberation from the "Prison of *Babylon.*"[13] More largely, their rhetoric opens out into a literal-prophetic historiography which unites the Reformation thrust and the history of redemption.* The elect nation remained earthbound

---

* Both Cotton and Winthrop explicitly apply the same images in both a temporal and an absolute sense, as when Cotton, speaking of the new plantation, explains that God "plants us when he gives us roote in Christ" (John Cotton, *Gods Promise to His Plantations* [London, 1630], in *Old South Leaflets* [Boston, [1874–76]], Vol. III, no. 53, p. 15), or when Winthrop sets forth the necessity for mutual love in a group of men who have joined together as members of the Body of Christ (John Winthrop, *A Model of Christian Charity* [1630], in *Puritan Political Ideas, 1558–1794,* ed. Edmund S. Morgan [New York, 1965], p. 87). Secondly, both men discuss the colony's prospects through scriptural texts familiar for their doctrinal value in terms of the covenant of grace. Thus Winthrop's closing reference (*Model,* p. 93) to Moses' "Farewell Exhortation" signifies the Hebrew's prophetic plea with "the remnant of *Israel* to praise God for their deliverance from . . . *Mystical Babylon,* that had detained them in spiritual bondage; and especially for the expiation of their sins by Jesus Christ" (Urian Oakes, *New England Pleaded With* [Cambridge, 1673], p. 3). Finally, both Winthrop and Cotton deliberately employ texts noted for their messianic-historiographic meaning, as in the case of Winthrop's argument from the "drie bones" of Ezekiel, chapter 37—an argument central to the view of society he

because the final rights to the millennium rested with the Church;
the Congregationalists held their church-states aloof from the world.
It was reserved for the American Puritans to give the kingdom of God
a local habitation and a name.

I have tried elsewhere to show how this impulse informs the major
narratives of early Massachusetts, and, in a highly representative way,
Cotton's polemic against Roger Williams. To Williams, as to other
conscientious Calvinist-Congregationalists, the emigrant's soteriological
self-concept seemed nothing short of blasphemy. What if God *once*
summoned the patriarchs to a holy land? Those scriptural events, considered as precedents for Christians, were simply, overwhelmingly, the
"spiritual shadows" of a new dispensation. Christ's offer of eternal life
to each believer meant "the *Cessation of . . . Holiness of Places*" in
this life. It meant that "America (as Europe and all nations) lies dead
in sin," and that "we are all, in all places, strangers and pilgrims."
How then, Williams demanded, could the colonists "propose the . . .
Nationall State of the *Jewes*"—the type of heaven—"as the Type of the
. . . [American] Kingdome of *Christ Jesus*," counting "the very Land
of *England* literally *Babel* . . . and the Land of New England, [a
sanctified] *Judea, Canaan*?" How dared they "mingle *Heaven* and
Earth, the *church* and *worldly state* together," making the "garden and
the wilderness, the church and the world all one," as though the Incarnation had not separated those areas once and for all? John Cotton
in his replies confirmed Christ's antitypical role, but he refused therefore to relinquish the actual parallel. Indeed, it was exactly by form-
ulating a synthetic "middle way" that he defended the theocracy.* As
a "Nationall Civil State," he wrote, adhering to the "judaical laws of

---

advances—which points to a "Prophecy . . . yet to be fulfilled" pertaining to
events *"preparatory* to . . . the *Millennium*," such as the Calling of the Jews and
the final triumph of the New England church-state (Peter Bulkeley, *The Gospel-
Covenant* [London, 1651], pp. 16–17; John Davenport, "Epistle" to Increase
Mather, *The Mystery of Israel's Salvation* [London, 1669], sig. A3ᵛ).

  * The term "theocracy'" has been criticized, cogently, by a number of recent
historians. I retain it here partly as a convenience and partly because the New
Englanders themselves repeatedly used it, meaning thereby to indicate *not* "the
rule of the priesthood" but the harmony, the mutually sustaining compatibility,
of minister and magistrate in church and state affairs, emblemized by "Moses and
Aaron kissing on the Mount." So conceived, the term seems to me to express, as
an ideal, the confluence of horological and chronometrical concerns which this
study tries to examine.

Moses . . . *out of Faith*" in Christ, the colonists "fulfill[ed] the type of
Israel materially." As the remnant designated to inaugurate the millennium they revealed the spiritual dimensions of that fulfillment, in
terms of "the on-going, governing, redeeming purpose in history."
Upon this conviction, Cotton acclaimed the church-state a terrestrial
entity which yet conformed to the nature of the antitype, specified the
"current events in God's chronological scheme," and expounded his
"eschatological expectation of New England."[14]

Upon this conviction, too, his contemporaries and successors built
their political sermons. To be sure, they stressed God's particular
providences and urged each man to search into the minutest details
of his life. But they also insisted upon the overarching plan which
explained the corporate pattern of their lives, and so allowed them to
fuse the particular and the universal into an organic whole. The Old
Testament promises, they cried, "belong unto . . . us"; the predictions
about *"the remnant of Israel"* and the "full and final deliverance and
restauration of the Church" justly "may be applied to us"; in fact, "We
may with astonishment behold how literally it is [all] fulfilled at this
day." From one election day to the next, on one day of humiliation
after another, the colonists heard how for them Jeremiah came with
a "comfortable Vision . . . [and] with milk and honey in his mouth," to
say that God would allure them "in a way of wonders and mercy and
grace" from *"the streets of Rome,"* and so "declare the *Removal* of the
Glory and of his Kingdom from them [the Hebrews] to *another*
People," in America. Through them, his visions ("agreeing with Those
in the Revelation") were being realized. Their "Mountain of Holiness"
attested to the correspondence of the human and the "Super-humane";
in a celestial dialectic, it proved that *"Prophesie* is Historie *antedated;*
and History is *Postdated Prophecie."* And prophecy now disclosed, in
the "sober sense of many of our Divines," "a certain Prognostick that
happy times are at hand, even at the Doors." Now that the last days
were approaching, "No changes no injuries of Time can stop the
course. . . . *For the set time to favour Sion is come* . . . the time prefixt
by the Prophet Jeremiah."[15]

The concept of destiny thus formulated marks a significant extension of traditional exegetical and eschatological views. For Augustine,
and for the early Calvinists, the biblical promises outline the pilgrim-
age to God. In Book XI of the *Confessions,* which anticipates Plinlimmon's distinction between the two realms of time, Augustine directs

man away from the horological towards a vision of the "permanent and stable unity" of creation, perceptible through an indivisible present that engulfs past and future. The history of nations here reduces to a series of meaningless moments in a drama of the absurd; time in its absolute sense, as it conforms to the heavenly chronometer, opens into the "true order of Reality," where each instant affords the prospect for the choice of eternity, where the *itinerarium mentis* subsumes the literal journey, and where every object or event translates into an emblem which illuminates the full meaning of existence since the believer may now see through it to "the true image of the timeless." In this light, the prophecies type out an essentially private eschatological experience: the reconstructed Zion means the "dominion of God in the conscience" and the reclaimed wilderness is the heart flowing with the waters of salvation. As in Bunyan's *Pilgrim's Progress*—or its many contemporaneous equivalents (Stephen Crisp's *Travels from Babylon to Bethel,* Herbert's *The Temple,* Thomas Green's *Journey out of Aegypt into Canaan through the Wilderness*)—the whole story of Israel becomes the background, as it were, for the liberating, self-transcending act of will "which gave the Reformed movement (including Puritanism) its special cast," and which transformed theology itself, in William Ames' words, into "the doctrine . . . of living to God, or . . . working towards God."[16]

The New England settlers of course retained the Augustinian framework. But they deliberately adopted a double focus—personal *and* social—on the kingdom of God. The Bishop of Hippo was "almost totally unconcerned with history"; their enormous interest in history directed the colonists perforce to other modes of exegesis, in an effort to reconcile Luther's "futurist eschatology" with Calvin's "realized eschatology," Augustinian piety with institutional reformism. To this end they invoked (alongside their numerous references to Ames and Perkins) the writings of early Christian progressivists, like Eusebius and Joachim of Floris, and especially those of Twisse, Brightman, and "famous Dr. Owen," all of whom—speaking for the millenarian movements in seventeenth-century England—interpreted the Prophets in practical social terms to explain current upheavals. For the emigrant leaders, the two approaches fused into alternative perspectives on the work of redemption. In effect, they remolded the "mystical apocalypse" into a historiographical analogue to the private, spiritual movement of grace. If Jeremiah's denunciations and prophecies adumbrated the morphology of conversion (as Calvin, Ames, and Perkins taught), they also came to stand in the political sermons as a preview of "the larger ordering of human history, which God was enacting," with specific emphasis on the "role of New England in fulfillment of God's universal plan." For the Congregational saints of New Canaan, that is, the remnant chosen to consummate the Reformation, the antitype shadowed forth not only the progress of the saint but equally that of the settlement at large. Their biographies repeatedly assert the identity of the exemplary life and the colonial errand; both explicitly and implicitly (through the metaphors, for example, which bind the ocean crossing to the rites of baptism and the wilderness trials to the temptations of the soul), the individual becomes a "representative man" in a way which attests at once to his own and his society's divine calling.* And their jeremiads from John Cotton to Cotton Mather, reversing this technique, proclaim the colony to be (like the saint *profectus* in Christ) "the antitypical fulfillment of all Biblical types," in an attempt to show how "New England was a . . . prefiguration of the Second Coming." "Others," said Cotton in 1630, "take the land by Providence, but God's people take it by promise"; his grandson over half a century later elucidated the promise in terms of a corporate, terrestrial enterprise, formed and crowned by a *"great end always in view,* even the *Generall Restoration of Mankind from the Curse of the Fall,* and the opening of [the last stage in] that Scheme of *the Divine Proceedings,* which was to bring a blessing upon all the *Nations of the Earth.*"[17]

* E.g., from Cotton Mather's *Magnalia Christi Americana; or, The Ecclesiastical History of New England* (1702), ed. Thomas Robbins (Hartford, 1853): "I shall now invite my reader to behold at once *the wonders of New-England,* and it is in one *Thomas Hooker* that he shall behold them" (I, 303); "Mr. MITCHEL . . . was a circle, whereof the centre was at Cambridge, and the circumference took in . . . all New-England" (II, 105); "the New-English principles and practices . . . are found in the character of our celebrated Eliot. . . . In one Eliot you see what a people it is . . . [that inhabits] New-England" (I, 526–27, 578, 580). The pervasive plea in the jeremiads that "the heart of this people might be moved, as the heart of one man" is generally accompanied by the explanation that "Israel are often called collectively God's son . . . as if the whole multitude of them were one person . . . one vine," since Christ, the antitypical vine, adumbrates the elect in the plural as well as in the singular person, at once in terms of spiritual biography and of historical narrative (Samuel Torrey, *Exhortation Unto Reformation, Amplified* [Cambridge, 1674], p. 35).

THE BLESSINGS OF TIME AND ETERNITY

I have been anxious to stand on the meeting of two eternities, the past and
the future. . . . In eternity there is indeed something true and sublime. But
all these [blessings] . . . are now and here . . . in the present moment. . . .
[Therefore, be] not a Nilometer [living "by the ticking of a clock"] . . .
but a Realometer [living by] . . . a truer sacrament, that is, . . . [an]
"outward and visible sign of an inward and spiritual grace" [which shows
your every action to be] . . . originally inspired directly from Heaven.

Thoreau, *Walden*

The growth of this social-historiographical concept of eschatology
finds its parallel in the theory of church covenant. All accounts now
indicate that before their arrival the settlers had not worked out the
details of Congregational polity; had not, that is, practically confronted the dichotomy of demonstrable calling and invisible adoption,
of appearance and reality. Their immediate solution met the challenge
of their historiography. To some extent the solution may be gleaned
from their uneasy doctrine of nonseparation, in which on the one
hand they affirmed their solidarity with the Reformation movement,
and, on the other hand, asserted their unique purity to the point of
making themselves suspect of hypocritically "practising separation
here" while "preaching and printing against it" as dogma. In
general, their solution manifests itself in the New England Way of
church-state (or state-church), a community at once purer and more
political than its Old World counterparts, effecting a social cohesion
more profound than that of national groupings and, simultaneously,
raising the church's spiritual authority beyond the limits of the most
militant English congregations. Both these developments have received attention from recent scholars. Larzer Ziff has shown how the
church covenant "served as the basis of a new cultural identity . . .
broader than religious practice and deeper than political rights."
Edmund Morgan has traced the orthodoxy's effectual transformation
of the idea of visible sainthood into a union of the seen and the unseen,
wherein the outward act reliably evidenced the interior inception of
grace. In both cases, "social philosophy [was] inseparably connected
with the ecclesiastical polity," and ecclesiastical polity itself elevated
as "a necessary condition of salvation." In our American churches, announced Richard Mather, "Church-Covenant . . . is not another
Covenant contrary to the Covenant of Grace . . . but an open profession of a mans subjection to that very Covenant": it signifies

nothing less than that "solemne Covenant" in which "God tooke [Abraham] and his seede to be his Church and people . . . separating *Ishmael* from *Isaac* . . . *Esau* from *Jacob*," those under "the law [from] . . . the children of promise," and, to speak plainly, the damned from the elect.[18]

The English national covenanters were bound to object (as, from the opposite perspective, Roger Williams had decried the colonists' concern with the literal and historical). Samuel Hudson, for one, protested that "Mr *Cotton* tels us, that a *visible Church is a mysticall body, whereof . . . the Members* [are] *Saints . . . and united together . . . by a holy Covenant*," whereas this definition obviously belongs to the *"invisible Church"*; and John Owen, expostulating against Thomas Hooker with all the high authority at his command, denounced even more emphatically the new-fangled New World attempt to "make particular Churches to be a species of the Universal Church." But the emigrant divines stood fast. In their eyes "the New England design was precisely to make visible that which [others] admitted was invisible." Hypocrites would now and then deceive them, yet as a rule, they maintained, " 'The Covenant of Grace is cloathed with Church-Covenant in a Political, visible Church-way.' . . . To swear to the obligation of membership 'is an evidence that God hath chosen us . . . & taken us to be his.' " Expressly joining Jer. 50:5 and Jer. 31:31–34 (including 31:32), they proceeded as though godliness could be truly detected, institutional forms could guarantee eternity, and the covenant of fraternity could be made one with the covenant of heaven:

[In] *Jeremiah, L, 5* . . . be the words which . . . foretold [that] . . . the people of God returning out of captivity of Babel should . . . bind themselves in church covenant with the Lord. . . . Here is the covenant itself, that is perpetual . . . *let us join ourselves to the Lord in a perpetual covenant that shall never be forgotten.* You read the like expression, Jer. xxxi, 31, 32, 33, 34. *This shall be my covenant with the house of Israel . . . I will forgive their iniquities and remember their sins no more.* . . . The use of this point in the first place, may shew us . . . the necessity of a *church covenant.* . . . The covenant of grace doth make a people, a joined people with God, and therefore a church of God . . . therefore look at the covenant by which you have entered here. . . . You come and resolve to walk in all ordinances, and undertake to reform both church and commonwealth; in such a covenant the Lord is content to take you by the hand and become a husband to you, Jer. xxxi, 32. . . . You have [thus] entered into such a covenant, wherein Christ is yours, and all the promises yours, and all the blessings yours, and the whole world yours.

Although that which is foretold [in Jer. 50:5] . . . was in part fulfilled
when the people of God returned from Captivitie in *Babylon* at the end of
seventie yeares: yet we must not limit the place to that time onely. . . . For
as some passages in this Scripture were never fully accomplished . . . so
many things that literally concerned the Jewes were types and figures,
signifying the like things concerning the people of God in these latter
dayes . . . [in] their returne from [the new] Babylon to [the new] Sion. . . .
And this may be added further, that this place seemes not onely to be
meant of the private or personall conversion of this or that particular
Christian, but also further, of the open and joynt calling of a company . . .
so noting the joyning of a company together in holy Covenant with God
. . . [namely, in] Church-Covenant . . . [by] *publick promise.* . . . [And our]
good warrant for it, [is, first,] that . . . the Prophets do foretell it . . . [as
in] *Jer.* 50.5 . . . [and second, that] God hath promised . . . [it,] *Jer.*
31.33.[19]

Experience later modified the theory, but this implicit yoking together of cultural identity and the claim to election left a vivid imprint
on the political sermons. One of its most remarkable aspects is the
expansion of Cotton's and Winthrop's ambiguities into a cultural commonplace. Again and again the colonial Jeremiahs describe the settlers
as "God's peculiar people" in terms of "the *seed of Jacob*" and of a
political body whose order of government is (in turn) an "*Example
and shadow of Heavenly things.*" Their portrayals of the "Temple-
worke" in progress refer simultaneously to the elect soul, to the actual
flourishing of plantations, and to the overall design of mankind's salvation; without losing its import as a model of each believer's conversion and rebirth, it becomes the prophetic "type [of] . . . *Good
things to come,*" and the historical "pattern" for "the very work we are
engaged for in this *Wilderness* . . . that which is written upon the
forehead of *New-England,*" as upon the forehead of the regenerate
individual (see Exod. 28:38; Ezek. 3:8, 9:4) and of the "servants of our
God" who "shall walk in the light" of the New Jerusalem (Rev. 7:3, 9:4,
21:24, 22:4). In the same way, their numerous allusions to the "wilderness" and the "vineyard," to "Canaan," "the watered garden," and
"Zion," recurrently blur the distinction between the concrete and
spiritual levels of meaning. They blur them further still by equating
the material and mystical blessings for sainthood. The theocracy, said
William Hooke in 1643, will "beautifie" the land with "not onely a
spirituall glory . . . but also an externall, and visible glory."[20] He did
not mean that prosperity rewards piety. Individually, he knew, saints

might suffer as much or more than others; in accordance with the ways of divine providence, even the holiest of New Englanders might expect private reversals for a variety of reasons, not all of them comprehensible to him. But collectively, as a historic enterprise, God's American people had his pledge that the desert would bloom like the rose.

Calvin had written that its Christological significance superseded the material import of the Hebrew Bible, as did European Puritans of all convictions after him. If Canaan was *really* (as the Good Book said) a land of earthly abundance, "What is this," cried the Separatist John Robinson, "but to make the Lord's people an herd of oxen which are promised to be brought into a fat pasture, there to feed at ease?" So too, Thomas Brightman and Joseph Mede, the authorities on apocalyptic historiography, stressed over and again that for Christians Jeremiah's predictions pertained exclusively to the realm of the soul. "The enjoying of these *outward* things, unto the *Jews* was a pledge of the *Spiritual* as it were inwrapped in them . . . according to the oeconomy of that time": a pledge of "*Everlasting Life* . . . not deliverance from Temporal enemies, worldly prosperity, nor the land of *Canaan*, nor long life in the land the Lord hath given us." The case was different for the New Canaan. Here, as nowhere else, "the *Wheels of Providence* [and] . . . the *Wheels of Grace*" revolved in harmony; here, "the Gospel . . . hath brought . . . in its right hand . . . Eternal Salvation . . . And in its left hand, Riches . . . with Protection and Deliverance from Enemies," "according to that great Promise [in] *Jer*[emiah]." At every kind of public occasion, the ministers stood "amazed" that heaven and earth should so "deck themselves [for us] in their best Attire," "loading us with His Benefits." Lest any "be possessed with doubts . . . because they are suffered to prosper so much," they reiterated that "these outward blessings are the blessings of *grace*." What king, after all, "was ever able to reward his faithful Subjects . . . as Christ can *his*"? And here—because "God is in Covenant with our whole man" and would fit us for our calling "both in *this* and in *another* world"—he had granted "a sanctified use of all . . . [proper worldly] Enjoyments," had "blessed his poor people . . . with an addition of many earthly comforts . . . townes & fields . . . habitations & shops . . . great encrease in the blessings of the Land & Sea." In short, through the "Mercy of the *New-Covenant*" New England fell heir to "Promises of Converting and Sanctifying

Grace; and thereunto . . . an addition of Promises respecting *Temporal Blessings* . . . the Blessings both of the *upper and nether Springs*, the Blessings of Time and of Eternity."[21]

As these statements indicate, the mixture of upper and nether blessings emanates not only from church-covenant but from the covenant of grace, enlisted in part by the American Puritans as a vehicle of social control. It seems evident that they never abandoned the cardinal tenets of Calvinism; what they did insist on—what appeared to "strict predestinarians . . . a veritable doctrine of works"—was their concept of preparation. According to Norman Pettit the concept contained a "conscious ambivalence," acknowledging as it did the sovereignty of God's will while stressing the efficacy of human participation. Yet insofar as preachers regarded their audience as a "Species of the universal Church," as a gathering of the elect, their attitude is entirely consistent. Grace, they pointed out, has a twofold nature. "The promise was made to Christ before the foundation of the world, but there is a Covenant also made in time." On the former level, "in the mind and will of God," justification antecedes faith in an unconditional decree whereby "No number of sins doth exclude us from salvation." On the horological level, "as applyed unto us," justification depends on faith and works. In these imperfect human terms, "Christ is not actually ours till he be received by us" and our receptivity entails a *"mutua obligatio"* which binds on both parts. On our part, grace can offer at most provisional security. "In time," we will stray from its demands or "actually" forsake it: "Consider how we are said sometime to *keep* Covenant, sometimes to *break* Covenant." It establishes a "way of tryall by conditionall promises" that "provokes us . . . to be faithfull . . . least we be deprived of the condition"[22] and so leads us to the right conduct which will in some small measure repay our debt.

As they developed this concept, it served the colonists as a crucial justification of their New England Way: provided them with a middle ground not only between right- and left-wing Protestants but more broadly between the Arminians and the Catholics. Against the former they argued that God "giveth himselfe first in order of nature, before he giveth any thing else accompanying Salvation"; the "Papists," they charged, "who build upon their works," wrongly "teach a doctrine of doubting; No man (they say) can come to be assured . . . of his own salvation." Their own position was in effect less an effort to steer clear of either extreme than a means to draw in both, precisely as the idea of theocracy encompassed both day-to-day discipline and a prearranged goal. Thus Thomas Hooker in a characteristic passage describes God's role in the colony's affairs through the *"type"* of Canaan's conquest: "it was the lord's power and gift that gave [the Israelites] possession of the land. . . . Yet notwithstanding they were fain to fight for it, before the Canaanites were dispossessed." The synthesis lent itself to a variety of uses. It allowed the ministers, as we shall see, to threaten their straying congregations with making "the Covenant of Grace voyd unto themselves," and to assure them that although our "temptations, [or] discouragements . . . are so many, [and] so violent . . . God will give [a triumphant] issue to all": indeed, at just those times "when wee breake our Covenant . . . he takes a faster bond." Finally, by harmonizing threat and consolation, it allowed them to combine idealistic motive with utilitarian means in enunciating New England's "special appointment."[23]

It was in accordance with the latter outlook—from what they explicated as a partial perspective (rather than with unintentional ambivalence)—that the ministers urged preparation. Eschewing Arminianism, they never forgot that the difference between the decree and the *"mutuall* confederacy" was merely in manner of expression, that "the elect seed . . . *have* the covenant, although they break it," that "God calls a man *actually* in time, *as* he hath chosen him in his *eternal* decree," that ultimately "the absolute and conditionall promises are both one in substance . . . both one and other springing from the same fountaine, even from the purpose of his grace." If for other Protestants Augustinian piety involved "the problem of time versus eternity," for the American Puritans the covenant idea merged the two in organic unity. Within this framework only did they resort to what has been misconstrued as a "self-contradictory" emphasis upon works. The elitist nature of their preaching, and their very theory of church-state, made such emphasis all but unavoidable. When John Cotton, for example, argued with an apparently democratic zest for the layman's participation in government, he meant not "the liberty of the people" but the "rights of saints," who by public confession had let "all the World . . . know that [they] have made an Everlasting Covenant." When he and his colleagues taught gospel responsibilities, they did so not for the heathen but, demonstrably, within the confines of "a church designed . . . for the saved." They would probably not have admitted to what Professor Morgan calls their indifference about "the rest of the world go[ing] freely to Hell"; but they could scarcely have contested the fact that they intended their doctrinal sermons primarily to "protect themselves and their children." No tenet was more basic with them than that "grace may be interrupted in [the saint] . . . for a season"; no remedy for that dark period came more readily than Peter Bulkeley's in 1651:

conditionall expressions . . . have in them the force of a . . . quickening exhortation for every one that standeth [in Christ] . . . to take heed lest he fall; and so . . . they make us stand more cautiously and sure. . . . They serve to keep the Saints more watchfull, by which watchfulnesse they are helped to stand more firmely. . . . [Thus,] the same thing is promised both absolutely, because it shall certainly be fulfilled, and with condition, because it shall not be brought to passe but by meanes, in which mans care is required. . . . Truly, such is the mercy shewed us in making this Covenant with us, that . . . we might live unto eternity."[24]

The early Separatists acted as if they were saved while acknowledging that they might be damned; the New Englanders, in accenting the oneness of the conditional and the absolute, acted as if they were damned while presuming they were redeemed. To this end, the clergy instructed the settlers that, since "men plot and perfect their own ruine," they were "not to cast off [their] duties . . . but to cast them *down* at the feet of Jesus," as the "tokens and pledges of salvation . . . [which] follow such a man as shall be saved." And to make the lesson more graphic, they outlined two separate, though complementary, ways of trial. One was by way of threat and affliction. Should any of the Lord's chosen "make bold to abuse & imbeazle [his] treasures," "hee doth procure to himselfe [such] speciall, rare, choyse and extraordinary wrath . . . that hee that heares of it, both his eares shall tingle." The doctrine of works served as a schoolmaster to direct men to faith; the doctrine of grace served as a torture instrument to drive them to do well. With it, the ministers taught the tried and tested saint who stumbled in taking hold of his inheritance—who, "*Having these Promises*" was slow to "*cleanse* [himself] . . . *from all filthiness*"— about the nature of damnation. In their hands, the covenant became a "halter" to restrain "slippery and unstable . . . hearts," a "hammer" with which "the soul can be broken," an "Image . . . of fear" to make "thee see plainely, that . . . thou . . . art become the heire apparent of hell." At the same time, they offered a "kind, loving, easie" form

of provocation. God was also pleading for their repentance by unveiling his intention to heal and save his people. Such gratuitous love
could not but bring them gratefully to obedience. It turned his wrath
itself into an act of mercy, giving "encouragement to such as are
smitten downe with the terrors of the Almighty so as they dare not
approach neer unto God" to fly from despair to a "greater design." It
revealed within the greater design that precisely when "the soule
seeth the flashes of hell . . . [then] God intends to doe good to a
man," that though in the day of affliction "your faith may be . . .
exercised for a season, yet Gods promise is faithfull and sure," a
granite "rock . . . to stand upon [for] . . . comfort and help."[25]

The confluence of these opposite ways of trial (proving the fundamental sameness of the provisional and absolute perspectives on redemption) figured centrally in the settlers' idea of mission. In its
overall import, it gave sustenance to their historiography. In the
decree of grace, wrote Thomas Shepard, "we see with open face Gods
secret for time past . . . [and his] performances for [the] future, as if
they were accomplishments at present. . . . In that Covenant . . . two
Eternities (as it were) meet together." As the church covenant provided their venture with a sense of absolute confidence by (in effect)
raising the visible to the invisible, so conversely the eternal covenant
lent it a concrete significance by applying the continuity in the process
of redemption to the area of man's moral responsibility.

And for our selves here, the people of *New-England*, we should in a
speciall manner labour to shine forth in holinesse above other people; we
have that plenty and abundance . . . of grace, as few people enjoy the
like; wee are as a City set upon a hill, [in] the eyes . . . not only [of] the
Lord our God, with whom we have made Covenant, but heaven and
earth, Angels and man. . . . Let us [therefore] study to walk . . . that they
may be constrained to say of us, onely this people is wise, an holy and
blessed people; that all may see . . . that the name of the Lord is called
upon us; and that we are the seed which the Lord hath blessed.[26]

On this basis, the two ways of trial, by justice and by mercy, under-
lie the jeremiads' prescripts for a backsliding New England. Perry
Miller has defined the relation they assert between sin and affliction,
but characteristically the equation reaches further than this. Its more
comprehensive view is apparent in the overlapping of genres between
the political sermons and the treatises on grace. The latter often undertake to uncover and remedy present temporal ills, complaining "as

sometime *Jeremiah* did" that "you suffer Christ to lye in the street . . .
and will be at your own carving." The former relate the duties of fast
and humiliation to the meaning of redemption, and, explicating Jer.
31:31, teach how "we do all commit this cause [of our "suffering
country"] unto the Lord even in the same way as we do every one
commit unto him the Salvation of our Soules." In particular, they use
the concept of grace to recast the country's adversities into a confirmation of its mission, under the overriding metaphor of a period of trial
and *"solemn divine Probation."*[27]

TRIAL BY MERCY AND JUSTICE

> The problem of the future of America is in certain respects as dark as it is
> vast. . . . It seems as if the Almighty had spread before this nation charts of
> imperial destinies, dazzling as the sun, yet with many a deep intestine dif-
> ficulty, and human aggregate of cankerous imperfection—saying lo! . . . You
> said in your soul, I will be empire of empires, overshadowing all else, past
> and present—I alone inaugurating largeness, culminating time. But behold
> the cost. For you too the demonism of greed, the hell of passion, the decay
> of faith, the ceaseless need of prophets.
>
>   Whitman, *Democratic Vistas*

The ministers' description of New England's degeneracy reflects
God's merciful trial of the saints. The problem, as they expressed it,
related only superficially or symptomatically to overt misbehavior;
essentially it entailed the state of the soul. Richard Mather's *Farewel-
Exhortation* pictures a relatively upright community which must nonetheless fear for its salvation—"least *a promise* of eternal life . . . *being
left you* in Christ Jesus, *any of* you *should seem to come short of it"*—
and most political sermons echo his analysis. Though they detailed
and deplored a long list of carnal excesses, they acknowledged that
in their *outward* comportment New Englanders surpassed all other
peoples: that, in Richard Mather's words, "in this country [unlike
others] profession is somewhat common, Authority through the goodness of God countenancing Religion, and ministring Justice against
all known ungodlines"; or, in the words of his son and grandson (some
fifty years later), that *"New-England* [shows] . . . a measure of
Religion" and "Blameless Morality" so far "beyond what is to be found
with any other people," in "any Country upon the face of the Earth,"
that "there are Practices which . . . would [elsewhere] be a step

toward Reformation that [here] . . . would deserve the Name of great Degeneracy and Apostasy"—for "New England has one thing that will weigh down more than forty of the best things that other countries can brag of: that is, religion, religion, religion! . . . Imposters have but seldom got in and set up among us; and when they have done so, they have made but a short blaze, and gone out in a snuff."[28] But all three Mathers knew that there remained a more insidious form of fraud within their ranks: the outward show of godliness without a corresponding inner conviction. Ironically, indeed, the very "weight" of religion in the colony encouraged such imposture, and it was precisely the concern with "profession" and "practices" that the ministers most virulently denounced.

"*Because* the Word of God is plentifully and powerfully dispensed throughout this Land," said Richard Mather, and Increase after him, "You have *therefore* so much more need to take heed and beware, least your Religion reach no further [than the] . . . form thereof." The rest of the orthodoxy joined in chorus. "You are a Professing People . . . but all [this] . . . will signify and come to nothing, if this spirit be wanting." What "vain Confidence to rest on any external signs of Gods presence," to feel comfortable "when the Word is lodged onely in the Porch, and never cometh into the House"—as though it sufficed dutifully to "live under the Gospel, and enjoy the clear and convincing Dispensations of it!" "Do you think that God liveth on goat's bloud"? Others could aspire to no more than a "visible regular course of Obedience"; the elect distinguished themselves by their dread of failure, by continual contrition and repentance. Hence, as "*a people near unto the lord* . . . we have greater cause *not* to be secure." The ministers, in short, knew "how much weight he lays upon his fear, in that he hath made it one of the main grants of the Everlasting Covenant," and to that end they directed their appeal for reform. They showed, on the one hand, a people "grown customary, formal, superficial," "fawning upon God" with faces like "painted Sepulchres," carrying "Notions in their *Heads*" that had left no "suitable Impressions in [their] Hearts," a people "drudging and plodding on" like shadows without the substance, shells without a kernel, "meer Engines [with] . . . no internal principle of life in them." On the other hand, they drew the Lord "*pleading a controversy with this Land* . . . [for] *not prizing and accepting the Grace of Christ.*" They depict him in this guise as a rejected and supplicating lover: "*waiting that he may*

be gracious," longing to grant them "*a new heart and a new spirit,*"
encouraging them by a promise that "we shall tast the sweet of it,"
engaging himself to "give all suitable directions" for a "reall and
actuall turning" toward their "*perishing need of Salvation.*"[29]

In compliance with this traditional emblem of sainthood the ministers couched their appeal to a people on probation. Having pleaded
so long in vain, God was preparing to forsake them and leave their
"*Citie upon an hill* . . . like a *Beacon upon the top of a mountaine,*
desolate and foresaken." But he was offering a last chance. "God hath
set *New-England* between *Ebal* & *Gerazim*" and announced: "here is
life and death set before thee; choose which you will." As an omnis-
cient God he knew the outcome; on the human level, he left it to
them "what *exit* we shall make upon this trial." The jeremiads took
their direction from the discourses on grace. To the extent that they
"flourished in dread of success," the preachers were trying to stress
that the proper exit would be reached by *in*security. "The spirit of the
law," they knew, "fills a man with rejoycing . . . but the spirit of grace
will make us vile in our owne eyes"; and to the "*Children of the
Kingdom*" in the election assemblies they intoned: "Consider your
selves who you are, and of what consequence it is that *righteousness
be rained* down on you." The "awful, considerable" alternative was
firstly personal. "Though you may be *Justified,* yet . . . God will not
let you see that you are so. . . . God being sadly *Grieved* by your
Sins, will Retire from you . . . [and his] burning Indignation . . . [will]
break forth upon you"; he will "*change from a faithful* Monitor *into*
[an] . . . *Eternal furious Enemy, Avenger and* Tormentor," threatening
no "*escape if we neglect so great Salvation.*"[30]

Secondly (and in these sermons more importantly), the alternative
meant the collapse of the colony. Since the enterprise concerned
millennial history—since the meeting together of "two Eternities"
linked the community's future with that of the individual soul—the
progress of saint and society became identified: one reflected, and
verified, the other. This mutuality (intimated above in the connection
between personal and social eschatology and between American
Puritan biographies and histories) becomes crucial to the ministers'
plea for reformation. When he rebuilt Jerusalem after the Babylonian
captivity, Nehemiah could claim that what he had done for his people
would redound to his perpetual good. How much more should this
hold true for the inhabitants of the New Israel, of whom Nehemiah

(that "exemplary magistrate and *citizen*") was a type! If we would
have the privileges of heaven, should we not "be *found* already Initiat-
ing our selves at the works of that *Kingdom*" in America? Instead,
"*The land mourns and fades* . . . [because we] *have broken the everlasting Covenant.* . . . Wherefore if we would be recovered out of our
Condition, 'tis the *Covenant* . . . that must Recover us . . . [the]
Covenant of grace . . . [which does] most Explicitly *Apply* . . . unto
all the Designs" of our church-state. The obligation, so articulated,
had enormous implications: "Our *Everlasting Recompenses* will be
very much adjusted, by the Regards which we had for [New Eng-
land]." Those who came to the colony's aid would find their reward
both on earth and in the afterlife; those who failed the cause "shall
in the *other* World be Losers too." (So, too, by extension, with regard
to foes or fellow-travelers abroad: he "*whose heart doth indeed travel
with* . . . *the Lord Jesus in these Ends of the Earth*"—or who has
actually "fought the welfare of the [American] children of Israel"—
will share in the millennium; as for him who would harm it, "Woe
to that person, whoever he be": "it were better . . . that a mill-stone
were hanged about his neck, and he thrown in the midst of the sea.")
By this standard, Samuel Torrey in 1683 stated the orthodoxy's plea
in summary form:

May we not with fear and trembling apprehend our selves: even . . . this
whole People, New England, as it were standing before God, upon our
great Trial for *Life and Death* [?] . . . You have been set . . . in this your
day of Grace . . . in a way of *probation and trial* . . . O it is high time . . .
to make that great, comprehensive, unchangeable, eternal Choice, upon
which depends not only the Salvation of your own Souls, but even the
deliverance and salvation of this People, and these Churches: If you do
thus chuse Life, all will be well with *New-England,* but if you should refuse . . . you will be likely, not only to destroy your selves; but all. . . .[31]

The nature of the choice indicates a deep stubborn optimism in the
clergy's appeal. Though the facts tell us that by 1683 the country
had largely abandoned the founders' design, the rhetoric of probation
bespeaks a concerted attempt to retain it. The attempt becomes clearer
still in what must otherwise appear as a pervasive paradox: the
jeremiads' reiteration that God would ultimately *not* forsake his people. The assurance appears sometimes as an amelioration of the threat.
"God hath good things yet in reserve for New-England," and he "is
but waiting for an opportunity of our thankfulness . . . to turn his face

toward us that we may be saved." He "is not only ready . . . but
desirous"—"as willing as able"—to pardon all sins and inaugurate a
climactic movement whereby the "great Mountains standing before
you . . . shall become a Plain." The latter allusion recurs throughout
the century, in connection both with the leveling of the mountains in
Isa. 40:4—signifying "an everlasting deliverance . . . in which all the
nations will be involved"—and with Zerubbabel, the "typical" postexilic king of Israel who has a vision of the seven-branched candlestick that symbolizes the old-New Zion (Zech. 4:2). Often the ministers
fuse both meanings in affirming their expectations for the future:

It is our great hope, and will be our great rejoicing to *see the Plumes still
in the hand of Zerubbabel, with those Seven,* to see a powerful and prosperous progress of the Work of Reformation. . . . True it is, that there are
great Mountains standing before you, but . . . if the Lord Spirit you unto
the Work, they shall become a Plain; and although the work be much
declined, it shall be again revived.[32]

These promises, circumscribing the colonists' free will in their option
of "life and death," appear in every form of the literature. In the
poetry, as Kenneth Silverman notes, however bleak the picture of New
England "hope is held out. Although with the death of [Thomas]
Shepard Zion's brightest star has been set, Oakes sees reason [in his
elegy] to believe that the Wilderness Errand *will* be performed. . . .
[Similarly,] Benjamin Woodbridge . . . takes faith that while Cotton
. . . is gone, 'yet *Joshua* is not dead.' Norton 'worthy hee / Successor
to our MOSES is to bee.' " Indeed, even Michael Wigglesworth's *God's
Controversy with New-England,* usually cited as a prime instance of
clerical denunciation, ends with the promise that his "heart is with
you all / And shall be with you maugre Sathan's might." The prospect
of final success—often emblemized (as above) in the conquest of
Canaan under Joshua—becomes more formidable still in the sermons.
From the early 'sixties through the great synod of 1679, the clergy
chanted in unison that the Lord's very desire for the colonists' recovery
signified the outcome of their trials: testified that his urging upon
them the "Necessity for Reformation" was also his way of comforting
them. "Be strong, O Zerubbabel, and be strong all ye people . . . for
[God is] with you; according to the word that [he] covenanted with
you." Recall that "we . . . of these Ends of the earth have long since
made our choice"—that *"N-Englands* true & main Interest . . . is a
fixed unalterable thing"—and then "Consider how unwilling the Lord

is to leave . . . a People he hath owned to be his," a people that had the "Name of God written on their foreheads." If, therefore (as "the Lord expects"), "we stick to our choice," he will "surely measure out an Inheritance for . . . [his] precious Remnant . . . in this Wilderness," and thereby prepare us *to be partakers of the Inheritance of the Saints in Light* and to have the colony "betrothed *to the Lord for ever*."[33]

Finally, the prospect of salvation is made explicitly unconditional. Often in the same paragraph in which they formulate the terms of trial, the ministers observe that God may "*chasten* us, yet he will not *kill* us," since he "hath engaged himself . . . to pardon us, to purge us, to convert us, to heal us." Thus Samuel Willard, John Oxenbridge, and Samuel Whiting, having recited the predictable catalogue of declension, proclaim that "no matter how far New England had declined . . . God would revive the country. . . . It [is] . . . darkest just before the dawn" wherein he "shall deliver [us]. . . . Such a promise was given the Prophet [Jeremiah] for his encouragement in his work. . . . The close of the greatest day of *Jacobs* trouble is, that he shall be saved out of it, *Jer.* 30.7." Would "the Lord that hath so marvellously distinguished this people for himself . . . [consent to] lose his propriety here"? Far from it: "The Lord will *not* forsake his people for his great names sake." Then "let this be our comfort," that amid "the Hurracano's of tempestuous times . . . the cause of God and Israel is Committed to the Lord himself that he would *maintain it*." Similarly, Samuel Torrey adds after his warning (cited above) that the Lord *will*

revive us. . . . Gods compassions are *moving*, his bowels are *sounding*, his *repentings* are kindling, his *heart is turning within him*, towards New England. . . . And therefore after all our backslidings . . . he is after all . . . crying after us . . . *I am married unto you* . . . *I will heal your backslidings*. . . . *Open unto me, my Love* . . . [and I will give thee] *a new heart, and a new spirit, Jer.* 31.33. . . . We may therefore comfortably believe . . . that God will keep Religion alive with us . . . in these ends of the Earth, which we believe God hath given to his Son *for an Inheritance* and for a firm Possession. . . . O, when God thus saves *New-England* . . . we shall rejoyce and triumph. . . . Then will be . . . fulfilled in us, and for us what is prophesied and promised.

So, too, Urian Oakes—who portrays New England as a sailor drowsing (like Melville's Ishmael) "*on the Top of a Mast in the midst of the Sea* . . . over-born by Security in the mouth of danger"—concludes for the assembly's "*Advantage and Comfort*" that "*God will not make*

an utter end of us." "All is well that ends well," he observes, and it is
"the Lords design in humbling and proving you that he may do you
good at your *Latter End.* Though *the Earth should tremble and reel
to and fro . . . yet . . . it shall be well.*"[34]

Other ministers, in much fiercer denunciations than Oakes's, reaffirm
and elaborate upon his conclusion. It was "obvious that God hath a
Controversy with us," and it had been their sad duty to communicate
his "wrath with his Inheritance." Yet they had "not spoken these things
that we should Despair, but that we might be *Awakened*" in our
"Gracious *Time* of *Visitation.*" For his visitation was for them also a
time of implantation: "when he hath prepared the Soyle . . . he will
cast in the precious Seed." And though preparation itself entailed
harsh measures—breaking up, overturning, remolding the dry earth—
it also signified the cultivator's loving care and the harvest to come.
Understand, then, that *"He knows not* how to give thee up . . . O *N.E.*"
Remember, that the Lord *"hath chosen this for his habitation,* He is
your God . . . and remember it is in a Covenant of Grace he is yours.
. . . If he seems as if he would be gone, it is but to try your love."
Remember, too, the great distance between a *"sinner foresaken and
a saint foresaken"*; in the latter case, God "withdraws himself . . . yet
so that he draws their hearts after him." Through his very threats,
therefore, he was reassuring New England of its destiny: *"Fear thou
not O my servant Jacob, and be not dismayed O Israel, for behold I
will save thee* [Jer. 46:25]" and "lift thee up . . . above all afflictions."[35]
Such passages form a persistent and significant thread in the jeremiads.
They disclose the full meaning of the clergy's appeal for reformation,
its *imaginatively* successful endeavor to control the colony by transforming the horological thunder into an instrument of chronometrical
consolation. They find their counterpart in the clergy's equally successful translation of God's severe judgments upon the colony into
an emblem of the afflicted saint.

The emblem is shadowed forth in the settlers' earliest writings.
They had known from the outset that their "special appointment"
would bring special troubles, that "the way of gods kingdome . . . is
accompanied with most difficulties" and that the "Priviledge of the
Covenant . . . was alwayes a . . . provocation of Gods wrath," "*for
unto whom much is given, from them shall much be required.*" They
knew as well that these difficulties were a badge of grace. The familiar

text read, "As many as I love, I rebuke and chasten" (Rev. 3:1); its meaning was plain enough:

So many as I love I rebuke earnestly, lest they should perish with the wicked. And those that I favour I chasten in this life, lest they should be damned forever. Who is that man that hath of me here neither chastisement nor rebuke, but is left without restraint, wallowing in the concupiscence and desires of his flesh? A great sign it is of the indignation of God; whereas the other is an evident token of love.

The divine wrath, in short, which lighted up the saints' way of trial, and so called attention to the disastrous pitfalls along the journey, also revealed the New Jerusalem at the end of the road. With this end in view, the ministers painted (alongside their images of a flourishing state and of a pleading God of Mercy) the picture of a chosen people castigated by a God of Justice. "Have you not observed," they asked after every setback—drought, Indian attack, outburst of dissension or crime or heresy—"that there have been more . . . tremendous dispensations of divine Providence in New-England than in any place where you have been?" Why was it that "no place under heaven . . . will so highly provoke and incense the displeasure of God as . . . New-England"? Why were there "no persons in all the world unto whom God speaketh as he doth to us [by his] . . . most awful Providences"? The reason was obvious. They were "a people near unto the Lord," a land wherein "the word of God is preached in the greatest power," a community "Of all Humane Societies on Earth" most set upon "highest Reformation." And because this "Jerusalems remnant are holy," it must expect his lash and dread his jealousy. He had said, "as many as I love I rebuke and chasten; And [those] . . . that I am now speaking unto, [have] experienced solemn Rebukes from him . . . for a long Time; yea from our first constitution . . . [when] the Foundation of this Temple was laid." Without any doubt, "God is terrible out of his holy places."[36]

As they expanded this concept, it meant not only that as a covenanted group they stood in greater danger than others, but that the danger made tangible the predetermined plan of their errand. In this sense, they distinguished between the lesser "vindictive" punishment meted out to other nations and their own unrelenting "corrective affliction." The former represented the wages of disobedience, the latter was a token of grace. In New England, God chastised his people more severely—"so as purely to Purge away their Dross"—and more lovingly, to draw them closely and firmly to himself. In either case, he was turning their suffering to his and their glory. Both aspects of his anger made it "*good* for [them] to be afflicted, crossed, disappointed," since that would "prevent greater evil," provide them (individually) with "the sweetest glimpses . . . of heavenly glory," and make them (collectively) "sure to conquer at last and have good Success . . . [in the colony's] general *Grand Design*."[37]

In short, not merely might their troubles "be a sign of God's loving help rather than of His wrath"; his aid and his wrath combined as a sign of election. The idea that "the word 'woes,' like 'judgments,' has an ambivalent meaning"—that it may connote either "punishments of evil" or "definitive victories"—had a long tradition which (through Foxe and others) made a considerable impression upon Elizabethan England. The New World clergy frequently strove to dispel the ambivalence by offering, as one of the "Things for [their] Distressed People to Think About," Calvin's strictures on the

need of many evils . . . *because* [God] would heal those wounds which he himself had inflicted. . . . As the Prophet [Jeremiah] saw that . . . the Jews . . . disregarded all God's promises, he added terror to the hope of mercy. Hence he said, "Ye shall perish, thou and thy people" [Jer. 27:13; cf. 31: 32]. He was, no doubt, constrained by necessity to speak in this severe way; for the kind of exhortation which he had used [previously] availed nothing; and yet God shewed at the same time by his threatening how much he loved the people; for he . . . willed not [their] death . . . but sought to induce [them thereby] . . . to repent that they might live.

Pointing out, accordingly, that New England's "dismall *Providence*[s]" were "decreed before the world began," the ministers urged the colonists to remain optimistic. Of course it was lamentable that "*Vile Things*" were being committed by "*a People that are obliged unto* [God], *above the rest of mankind*": "Our Lord Jesus Christ from Heaven may thus Argue with us; *If other People do Wound me by their Sins, 'tis not such a Wonderful and horrible Thing. But for you, O my People of* New England, *a People that . . . I have known above the other Families of the Earth*," it was heinous beyond expression. And yet the very wonder and horror of the crime, the very swiftness and terror of his retribution, afforded proof that God did *not* will their death. More than that: it allowed him more strikingly to display his purpose. Unfortunately, far too often "we doe by an *evill heart depart from the Living God*: Hence also . . . God will . . . make it marveilous in the eyes of the world . . . that grace should be shewed in pardoning such sins; that they shall say . . . *Who is like unto thee*[?]" And therefore, "Fore-warned," as Samuel Willard said on a day of humiliation in 1673, is "fore-armed"; from their standpoint divine "storms and tempests" could hardly be anything else than prods for the settlers "to seek a comfortable shelter" where they might "prepare *to meet with their God,*" confident in their "hope of mercy" both for themselves and for their enterprise.[38]

Thus it was with *pride* that the ministers noted how they had experienced his solemn rebukes from the very outset of their venture. Having consulted the divine will, they had a direct "Commission" from heaven to say that "All the Sorrows, and Afflictions, and Sufferings of the People . . . shall end in joy." By right of the commission, they explained the purpose of their season under the rod in the phrases of grace. Norton, Hooker, and Cotton, for example, had written that God visits sorrows upon the saint in order to "knocke off his fingers from base courses," thus "to do [him] good in the latter end": "that which God ayms at" in the "*blackness* of your *trouble*" is "to fit you for your [heavenly] Mansion-place," where he will "prove how *he hath loved* you and *mend all* . . . in glorious days." The jeremiads tell us of King Philip's War that "God is knocking the hand of New Englands people off from . . . new Plantations . . . [in order to] prove us, that he may doe us good in the latter end . . . when he hath performed his whole work upon our Zion." And they explain the witchcraft temptations by noting that since New England is a "country devoted unto the worship of the Lord JESUS CHRIST above the rest of the world . . . it is impossible that [it] . . . should not be exposed unto the bitterest enmity and calumny . . . until our Lord Jesus Christ do shortly 'make them [the devils] know, that he has loved' what they have hated"; therefore, "the Blacker you see the *Troubles* of the Age to grow, the . . . surer" you may be that you "shall have glorious daies" wherein "all will be mended." Such parallels persist from Chauncy's Harvard address of 1655 through the earthquake crises of the 1720s. Undoubtedly, they are meant to sustain and encourage the settlers during difficult times; basically, however, they are symptomatic of the teleology imposed upon tribulation. God was "*Proving* . . . and *trying*" the land because he "hath *taken up Great Expectations*

of us, and made great Promises to himself concerning us." Indeed,
"the reason why Jesus Christ doth not come immediately to judge
the world . . . is because of *his long suffering toward us Israelites"*;
they were not quite ready—not yet pure or contrite enough—and so
he was punishing them: "we are *judged of the Lord* that *we might
not be condemned with the World."*[39]

The jeremiads buttress this eschatology of affliction with a variety
of scriptural analogues. They present the settlers as a prodigal son
guided by a severe father who was spitting in his face to shame him,
and hedging his ways with thorns to confine his sinful inclinations. Or
they paint them as a patient receiving treatment from "the great
Physician of *Israel"* who had vowed to restore his health. Or again,
they render them as precious raw metal placed by a perfect refiner
into the furnace to purify. Or once again, they describe them as a
biblical hero in his moment of temptation: Moses at the rock, David
in adultery, Peter denying Christ, Christ himself in the wilderness,
and, repeatedly, "*Job* in the midst of his plunges," begging for pity,
though his "Deliverance out of trouble will not arise untill the Lords
Time be come." Perhaps the dominant comparison is to the rebuilding
of Jerusalem. Consider, said the ministers, the "faults, evils, and dis-
tempers" of the "Jews upon their return from *Babylon.* . . . You must
not think it strange, if you be tryed in the same manner," for your
mission at once resembles and supersedes theirs. Consider also that
"every *Tragedy* they passed through, had a glad *Catastrophe,* every
stress had a comfortable issue," and that, even "more universally and
gloriously" than then, "the Lord of Hosts will be gracious to His
remnant."[40]

The most complete statement of this position appears in Increase
Mather's *The Day of Trouble is Near.* Pronounced by the foremost
American Puritan in his bid for clerical leadership, and bringing
together as it does the various images of saintly affliction in an especially dark period of the country's history, it deserves to be cited at
length:

Christ himself was exposed to sufferings . . . [and] *David* speaking . . . as a
Type of Christ saith, *Thou hast showed me great and sore troubles.* . . .
[Thus] God hath Covenanted with his people that sanctified afflictions shall
be their portion . . . that they shall have Physick as well as Food . . .
[both] ordered according to the Covenant of Grace. . . .

[Indeed,] . . . *when glorious Promises are near unto their birth, we may
conclude that a day of trouble also is near* . . . dark and dismal dispensa-

tions are wont immediately to precede . . . [an] eminent Mercy [as] . . . *cries and travailing pains* must go before deliverance can be expected. . . . This is the usual method of divine Providence . . . by the greatest Miseries to prepare for the greatest Mercies. . . .

The Lord aimeth at the Probation of his people, in those troubles which befall them. . . . Hence the afflictions . . . are compared to a refining Furnace . . . wherein Metals are *Tried*. . . . [Moreover,] Afflicting times are not only Trying times, but also Teaching times. . . . Hereby the children of God *learn* . . . to know more of God, and of themselves too: as we see in Job. . . .

[Now, with respect to New England in particular,] . . . the Lord is carrying on the building of his own House . . . [and will effect] a glorious and happy deliverance out of all these troubles . . . *Jer. 30.7. It is even the time of Jacobs trouble, but he shall be saved out of it.* . . .

The Lord hath been whetting his glittering Sword a long time [over New England]. . . . The sky looketh red and lowring. . . . The clouds begin to gather thick in our Horizon. . . . *Without doubt,* [then,] *the Lord Jesus hath a peculiar respect unto this place, and for this people.* This is *Immanuels Land*. Christ by a wonderful Providence hath dispossessed Satan, who reigned securely in these Ends of the Earth, for Ages the Lord knoweth how many, and here the Lord hath caused as it were *New Jerusalem* to come down from Heaven; He dwells in this place: therefore we may conclude that he will scourge us for our backslidings. . . . It is not onely true concerning particular persons, but as . . . [to whole groups of men for whom] Christ hath a peculiar love. . . .

[And since he *has* scourged us] we may therefore hope that the Lord will not destroy us. . . . I am not at all afraid of that . . . [for as said] a Jewish Writer . . . who lived in the dayes of the second Temple [i.e., after the return from Babylon]; "the dealings of God with our Nation . . . and with the Nations of the World is very different: for other Nations may sin and do wickedly and God doth not punish them, until they have filled up the Measure of their sins, and then he utterly destroyeth them; but if our Nation forsake the God of their Fathers never so little God presently cometh up on us with one Judgement or other, that so he may prevent our destruction." So [with other places] . . . it may be he'll reckon with them once for all at last; but if *New-England* shall forsake the Lord, Judgement shall quickly overtake us, because God . . . is not willing to destroy us . . . [but on the contrary] will be gracious to the remnant of Joseph.[41]

The coherence of Increase Mather's statement—blending the theocracy's views on grace and church-state, history and eschatology, blessing and affliction—bears witness to the coherence of the founders' dream, and, particularly, to the force of the rhetoric marshalled to protect it.* In this respect, the jeremiads develop from year to year,

---

* Briefly, the stylistic strategy entails: (a) the interrelationship of types

and from one generation to another, in a conscious and self-perpetu-
ating tradition. In 1719 William Williams informed his election-day
audience that "This *Exhortation* has been many times urged from this
Place." Twenty years before, Cotton Mather buttressed his discourse
by invoking the whole range of election addresses, and a decade
earlier Samuel Torrey quoted "diverse of [God's] faithful Servants . . .
[who had spoken before] this General Assembly." More specific citations, mutual commendations, and allusions to arguments abound
throughout the political sermons. The latter respond, too, to local
issues and general concerns of the day, but as Charles Sanford notes,
they show a marked "inclination to devaluate the contemporary situation"—or, more accurately, to lift the situation out of its contemporary
setting into the framework of the ideal. They provide a kind of inverted
index to actual events, waxing more visionary with every major
setback. Darrett Rutman has pointed out that in a climate of declension, in face of mounting isolation and impotency, the leaders of the
orthodoxy grew "more and more adamant in . . . defense of their
unique 'New England Way.'" But it does not follow that their outlook
becomes irrelevant to the country's development (much less that the
setbacks compelled them to abandon their interpretation of the wilderness errand, as other historians have argued). Their intransigent recourse to the ideal is, on the contrary, intrinsic to the process by
which they managed to retain their hopes, and to shape and transmit
the beliefs or fantasies of their culture. The nature of this process—in
which fundamental social aims and prospects are defined in direct
opposition to historical realities—belongs essentially to the area of
symbol and imagination. Accordingly, what Professor Rutman and
others have seen as a sort of post-mortem ideological "hardening"[42]
meant in fact the flowering of the jeremiads' outlook from promise to
myth.

---

emanating from the first statement (Christ to David, Job, Jacob, and Joseph);
(b) the unity of disparate images (food and "physick," birthpains, refiner's
furnace, sword and sky), both through the logic of the argument and through the
interlinking biblical texts to which the images allude; (c) the sustained connection between the darkly "lowring" present and the approaching millennium,
which constantly looks forward to the climactic parallel between New England's
remnant and the remnant returned from Babylon—a climax prepared for earlier
by the emphatic reference to the New Jerusalem to come. It might also be observed that Mather deliberately and persistently interrelates the personal (absolute) level and the collective (temporal) level.

THE FLOWERING OF NEW ENGLAND HISTORIOGRAPHY

"Twelve o'clock reported, sir," says the middy.
"*Make* it so," replies the captain.
And the bell is struck eight by the messenger-boy, and twelve o'clock it
is. . . .
[Thus] Hand in hand we top-mates stand, rocked in our Pisgah top, the
whole long cruise predestinated ours. . . . [For] we Americans are a
peculiar, chosen people—the Israel of our time; we bear the ark. Seventy
years ago we escaped from the thrall; and God has predestinated, mankind
expects, great things from our race. We are the advance-guard, sent on
through the wilderness to break a new path in the New World that is ours.
. . . [The] Messiah has come in *us*.

Melville, *White-Jacket*

The jeremiads' view of history unfolds in successive stages through
the seventeenth century. It blossoms in an organic process of foliation
with every crisis, through the Pequot battles, the witchcraft trials,
and the Charter negotiations; it finds its sharpest focus in the mid-
century controversy over baptism. Historical scholarship has established the Half-Way Covenant as the *locus classicus* of the clergy's
acquiescence to the exigencies of an imperfect world. It seems evident
in retrospect that after the native-born colonists failed to qualify for
church-membership the theocracy had to shed much of its "holy
pretence": that its decision to grant provisional status to the visibly
still-unregenerate children—on the assumption that baptism conferred
certain inalienable covenant rights—proved in the long run a form of
self-betrayal. But the ministers themselves denied the notion of dis-
continuity. Whether or not they yielded out of practical necessity, they
impressively demonstrated their unity with their forebears. Increase
Mather's compilation of *First Principles* shows beyond a doubt that
Hooker, Norton, Cotton, and other luminaries had concurred in placing an immense significance on baptism in New England. Pointing to
the crucial passage in Genesis where God makes his pact with Abraham *and his seed*, they claimed that "[our] *Children . . . Confederate
in their Parents*, because to the Children of Parents in Covenant, that
promise *Gen. 17.7* doth belong." The promise, that is, assured those
children of membership by birth in the elect community. The assurance might not pertain to every child, but its overall probability permitted the elders to look upon baptism (restricted as it was to the

saints' offspring) as a reasonable guarantee of conversion, and hence as a valid premise for what came to be known as half-way participation in the church-state. "Even if [the saints'] children showed no visible signs of grace, there was still good reason to believe that they would finally be saved"—for, in Increase Mather's words, the

persons in Question are either belonging to the visible Church, or of the world only. The Scripture speaketh of those two terms, *Church* and the *world*, as opposite and Contradistinct. . . . [Now, our] visible Church . . . is gods house . . . [of which the Israelites'] Temple . . . was (as Divines conceive) a Type. . . . [Therefore, all those] within the Pale of the [New England] visible Church . . . have the right to Baptism, and consequently may transmit the right to their children. . . . [Furthermore, and most important,] *the Lord promised to* . . . give grace to our Children . . . that he should extend his Covenant, not only to Parents, but also their . . . Offspring [in accordance with] . . . Scripture Prophesies and Promises [which] predict the Calling of the Gentiles.[43]

This genetics of salvation—which links the notion of individual inheritance both with the internal cohesion of the Holy Commonwealth and with its historic thrust—is formulated in many early documents other than those Mather assembled. According to the majority of emigrant divines, because "the end and use" of church-covenant "is to confirm the covenant of grace," therefore "all the rich blessings of that Covenant shall be [our] *Inheritance for ever*," ours and our children's alike. The latter, in the light of "Scripture Promises," already "bear the name of God upon them . . . [as] a pledg . . . of salvation." "If God doe give himselfe to be a God unto *Abraham*, and to his seed . . . it must of necessity follow, that . . . he will perform both his owne part of the Covenant, and *Abrahams* part also . . . from one Covenant to another; by all which things it doth appear that the Lord will keep our part of the Covenant also." Such arguments in no way imply that the first settlers anticipated the problems of the 1660s. Their belief in the *"Prae-ingaged"* holiness of their infants reveals, on the contrary, the conviction that no problems would arise. In their view, no "Essential Alteration" *could* obtain between the generations; it could not be otherwise than that "the Branches would be answerable to the root." It is a conviction profoundly expressive of their sense of mission. Since they were called *en masse* to a historic undertaking, it followed that the spiritual legacy from father to son would continue to the final victory. Their sermons glow with visions of the parents and "their Off-spring with them partak[ing] of Eternal

Life and happiness"; in some cases, in fact, they suggest that the offspring, being nearer the victory than their "Godly Ancestors," may not
only "*Inherit* the *Glory* of their *Ancestors*" but shine with a "Double
Glory," since in temporal terms at least God "will do *more* for us than
ever He did for them": as history draws towards its close, the "*Cove-
nant-Mercy* of God unto [his people] . . . the *further* it Rolls, the
bigger it grows." Thus, while most English Puritans (despite the
enormous diversity of opinion) regarded baptism as a "seale prest
uppon water" or at most as a ritual which offered the individual the
"means of grace" (without any attendant claim upon salvation), the
New Englanders tended toward the idea of prevenient grace through
the efficacy of baptism. For them above all others, "this outward dispensation . . . served to bind the community through successive
generations to a unity of purpose." Their historiography could not
"take in the Parent, and *leave out the child*"; it demanded the "deep
truth" that "the line of Election . . . doth . . . for the most part run
through the loyns of godly Parents."[44] Their view of baptism, in providing that truth, secured the otherwise uncertain transition between
the second escape from Babylon and the Second Coming. If in so
doing it also fed into the semi-Presbyterian solutions of the Half-Way
Covenant, the orthodoxy took no notice of the irony. Instead, through
the jeremiads, it built upon those solutions a defiant affirmation of
the colony's Grand Design.

Most directly, the affirmation manifests itself in the legend of New
England's golden age. The ministers' diatribe against the unconverted,
expressed through the image of "the God of . . . *Godly Parents*"
rebuking a "degenerating Generation," actually proposes the latter's
redemption through its ancestry. In part, this takes the form of a plea,
repeated with almost formulaic persistency, that the children recall
their origins. "Scripture Prophesies & Promises"—bringing "advantages
for the obtaining Grace & Salvation . . . as others have not"—*require*
them to claim God as their own. "Ungainsayably Engaged are those
persons, to say . . . *He is my God*, who can say, *He is my Fathers
God*"; they fall under a "necessity to be *New born*."[45] More widely,
the jeremiads use the plea to elevate the founders to heroic stature.
Their intent here is obviously pragmatic: to shame the youth into
conformity (while insinuating the outcome all along through the bond
between the saint and his seed). But their descriptions transcend all

immediate concerns. As they evoke the saintliness of former days, they recreate a race of giants in an age of miracles, imposing on the tiny, barren American Strand of three decades before the archetypes of scriptural and secular antiquity.

"If my weakness was able to show you," said Higginson in 1663, "what the Cause of God and his People in *New-England* is, according to its *divine Originall* and *Native beautie*, it would dazzle the eyes of Angels, daunt the hearts of devils, ravish and chain fast the Affections of all the Saints." As a rule, the ministers overcame their weakness through the most florid stylistic flights in the literature. "Our Fathers were Clothed with the Sun . . . the Moon was under their Feet. . . . God Rode upon the Heavens for their help" and "ran to . . . fall on their necks and kiss them." No land under heaven saw "such rich overflowing of Compassions," such "Holiness . . . Humility, [and] . . . Exemplariness"; no state had possessed "men civil and ecclesiastical . . . of such weight and worth" or enjoyed "the uniting glory then manifest from the shine of mercy from the Throne, Grace Ruling and Ordering both Rulers and People under the Glorious Banner . . . of Love": "If we look abroad over the face of the whole earth, where shall we see a place or people brought to such perfection?" Never, in sum, had God so "wonderfully owned and exalted" a people as he did this "precious Remnant." Their city on a hill—a place "much nearer Heaven . . . than any place . . . heare[d] of in the world"— bodied forth the hopes and fantasies of mankind. It was a greater Latium, a dream of another earthly paradise made real, recovering from the "disguises of mythology" and the imaginary El Dorados of Renaissance writers the actual (and more splendid) benefits God intended for his peculiar people. "Such great Persons as *Budaeus*, and others, who mistook *Sir Thomas Moor's* UTOPIA; for a Country really existent . . . might now have certainly found a Truth in their Mistake; *New England* was a true Utopia."[46]

As a backdrop for this age of wonders the jeremiads delineate an apocalyptic history of America, built on Jer. 50:5 and related texts but bearing concretely upon contemporaneous events. Disappointment with Cromwell convinced English millenarians (including the Fifth Monarchists) that the Parousia was far less advanced than previously thought; the Restoration left English Puritans in general with a new realistic "sense of their identity as a nation." The very nature of their covenantal anticipations, rooted as these were in the things of this

world, must have facilitated their transition "to a more prosaic day"—
their renunciation of "any hopes of making England a holy community"—and so helped them to compensate for their lost dreams with
an increased emphasis on the believer's inward grace on the one
hand, and on the other, with a renewed pride in national origins and
antiquities. The New World ministers, already committed to a scheme
which could not admit of failure, compensated for their thwarted
errand by constructing a legendary past and prophetic future for the
country. America, they asserted, had remained unknown and under
Satan's total dominion so that Christ could more awesomely reveal
his power when, in "the fulness of time," he undertook the renovation
of the Church. Connecting Jeremiah's predictions with those concerning "the ends of the earth"—a phrase which through a variety of
Scriptural texts intimated the Second Coming—they observed that
God had vowed (Ps. 2:8) to give his remnant *the heathen for thine
inheritance, and the* Uttermost *parts of the earth for thy possession.*"
What else could He have meant by that decree but "a *New* Heaven in
the *New* World?"[47]

Moreover, America clearly denoted the fourth and last of the round
earth's imagined "ends." The apocalyptic number (see Rev. 6:2-8,
7:1) had been traditionally linked to "the four horsemen . . . as types
of the spread of the gospel," and to the Adoration of the Magi "as
signifying the acceptance of Christianity all over the world, each of
the Magi representing one of the continents then known"—and the
"fourth" continent in turn representing the last stage of time. In the
Reformation, it took on another level of meaning. If a fact "so great
and considerable as America is . . . was yet unknown . . . for so
many generations together," wrote John Goodwin, does not its discovery "in these last days" mean that new "secrets of the scripture
[will] see the light of the sun?" His colleagues in America were more
concrete. Following Bale's commentary on Revelation, chapter 21,
they pointed out that "*Asia, Afica,* and *Europe* have, each of them,
had a glorious Gospel Day (each "Prefigured . . . in the passage of
the children of Israel [coming] out of Egypt"). By the end of the
fifteenth century, therefore, the "Barrier *Solum*" to the millennium
lay across the Atlantic. Hence Columbus providentially called the
continent "ST. *SAVIOR,*" and the two highest achievements of modern
"*humane affairs . . . Literature* and [Reformed] *Religion* . . . dawned
upon the miserable world, one just *before,* the other just *after,* the

famed navigation hither"—a voyage directed by God for "the great issue . . . of the . . . *Hopes* of his people."[48]

Hence, too, the settlement which instituted "the *New* National [!] Covenant, Jer. 31.31," followed directly upon the awakened interest in the Book of Revelation: upon the Puritan's recognition (Calvin notwithstanding) that in "this heavenly book . . . all the universal verities . . . [are] under pleasant types and tropes decided," and "all the Mysteries of Divine Dispensation . . . in every Age and Generation . . . untill [our] last and utmost Prophetical Period" stand revealed. Ever since the turn of the century, English Protestants had argued that as history advanced more light would be thrown on the Apocalypse, that "the nearer the *Kingdom* is . . . the more *unsealed* . . . will be the *Sayings of the Prophecy*." Now in retrospect the colonial clergy realized that, specifically, "Mr. *Medes Clavis* [*Apocalyptica*] was first published in the year, 1627, which was a notable means to revive the thinking and Speaking of *New Jerusalem*. And this was the year wherein the Design for . . . *New England*, began to be ripened." The meaning of this correspondence could hardly be mistaken. "When the *Seventy years*, for the Churches confinement in *Babylon*, were almost out, Good men might have *Known* that they were so: Holy *Daniel* did *Know* it," as did Jeremiah. It was so also before the deliverance from Egypt and before the Incarnation. Surely, then, the recent and multiplying speculations on the vision of St. John—who, the emigrants underlined, was like them exiled, like them "carried away into the wilderness that he might see more clearly not only the judgment of the great whore but also the coming down from heaven of . . . the New Jerusalem" (for "such of us as are an exiled condition . . . shall know what God is doing, and about to do in the world, though others know nothing of these matters")—surely those speculations proved that "the *Twelve Hundred & Sixty years* assigned unto the Reign of the *Antichristian Apostasy*, draw towards *their Period*." Considered together with the other aspects of American history, it constituted "not meer *Conjecture*, or *Opinion*, but . . . Demonstration [that] . . . an *Age of Miracles* [is] now *Dawning* upon us," one in which the inhabitants of "this *New-English Israel* . . . are concerned more than any other men Living."[49]

From this vantage point, the jeremiads portray the colony through a mirror reflection of past and future. The new dawning verified the pristine age of miracles and its imminency was made apparent by virtue of the original divine beauty, for that beauty was "not the *business of one age*" but part of a schematically implemented program. Seen as an isolated phenomenon, to be sure, the New World venture simply repeated the biblical Exodus, as Cotton Mather indicates in the playful-serious introduction to his election sermon of 1700: "A people there has been of whom that Account may be given, *O Lord, Thou has brought a Vine, thou has cast out the Heathen, and planted it: Thou didst cause it to take deep Root, and it filled the Land. . . .* My Hearers all this while know not, whether I am giving an Account of *old Israel,* or of *New-England:* So Surprising has been the *Parallel!*"

But his hearers did know: as Mather goes on to acknowledge, the jeremiads had long since been clarifying not only the similarities but the crucial difference between the two. Insofar as both the biblical event and its present-day counterpart were *either* horologically *or* chronometrically considered they were indeed parallel. Considered horologically, the vine of Israel provided the definitive *exemplum* of the provisional scheme whereby God rewards righteous men or communities, including (in this immediate and secular way) his New World theocracy. "Jerusalem was, New England is, they were, you are . . . it is [all] so much the same that . . . [we may] put . . . in New Englands name instead of Jerusalem." God's "Outward Providence," in this regard, his "voluntary Presence" or "*common* love" which alters as he finds alteration among men, applied to all alike, saint and sinner, David as well as Saul. It applied, moreover, to any locale, by any name, even one that "smelled so sweetly *unto His nostrils*" as did Jerusalem or, more recently, Boston, "our little *outcast Zion*" and "city of salvation."[50]

In this literalist sense, the parallel dramatically called attention to the colony's present degeneracy and could only bode worse evils to come. "We are very stupid, if we do not read an *Admonition* to our selves, in this Ancient and Famous Providence," for it gives "us a Sign and an Example of Vengeance," teaching as it does the immemorial lesson of mutability and decay ("cracking and sinking," "blinding, hardening, ruining") and of man's inability to stand by his works. "We must acknowledge, God planted us . . . a noble vine: but we see a generous vine subject to a degenerate vine, *Exod.* 32, 7, 8," and then festering till it stank worse than weeds. Mather's hearers understood this prospect, but they knew, too, that it represented but

one aspect—"the *narrowest acceptation*"—of the parallel. Considered
chronometrically (as the clergy rarely failed to do at these occasions),
the flourishing vine emblemized a greater present moment: that
"permanent point, without succession, parts, flux or division," in which
the believer becomes implanted in Christ. On this "inward and *invisible*" plane, "*the Lord planted us a Noble Vine, wholly a right
Seed* . . . [and] will *continue to be gracious unto . . . His Remnant.*"
Whatever his interim retributions (no matter what "fiery Serpents, and
Scorpions, and droughts" his saints encountered) ultimately he would
give them the means to overcome their natural creeping degeneracy,
by placing them, like another Children of Israel, "under the hands
of *Moses*, which was a type of the Law, and *Joshua* a type of *Jesus.*"
Again, therefore, as in its literal rendering, the parallel bespoke a
development in time. As the vine must needs first be planted and then
take root before it could fill the land, so, too, the divine meanings behind the story of Israel—though all inevitably "tending unto one
ende . . . [namely,] Jesus Christe the parfait some [i.e., sum] & ful
conclusion of al the Lawe & Prophets"—had to be revealed gradually:
since "we cannot comprehend the unspeakable justice of Christ or his
wisdom, hence God, that he may *by degrees* lead us to knowledge of
Christ shadows him forth to us under . . . types."[51] And so, too, finally,
the elect must labor, step by struggling step, towards the Good Land
that is by heaven's time already theirs.

Mather and his predecessors stressed neither of these two meanings
in their jeremiads; or rather, they used both of them so as to stress
their interdependency. They vindicated their failing communal errand,
that is, by interweaving its "outward" and its divine attributes, by affirming at once the human dimension of the absolute and the spiritual
context of the political reality. In its "correspondence with the
heavenly," the parallel helped them more clearly to unfold the temporal process of universal history: the growth in time, through a succession of human agents from Adam through Moses to the present
age—and in this age from Wycliff through Luther and Calvin to the
Bay emigrants—of the Work of Redemption. In its "narrow" providential
aspect, the parallel enabled them to assign God's palpable chastisement its due place within "New-England's design in this vast undertaking" (a place comparable, as we have seen, to that of works in the
design of the saint's life). And from the vantage point of this double
significatio, they could avoid or explain away the disturbing signs of

the concrete present. Looking to past and future, they could, for all collective and historical purposes, impose "heaven on earth," in John Eliot's words, by positing a "theory of . . . successive revelations," a "parenetic" linear-spiritual progression *a minori ad maius*, from *old* Israel to *New* England. In these terms, they "would *not* be understood, as if the Dispensations of God now did exactly quadrate with his Dispensation to the Jews" then. The two events reflected one another not (as modern commentators have maintained) as a redundant "reliving . . . of the Exodus" in "reproduction of Bible history" but, in William Tyndale's phrase, as a gradual unveiling of "promises rehearsed" by promises performed,[52] as a movement from the type to its realization.

Literally, then, *or* allegorically—as "a humane action . . . done by a humane agent" *or* as an "action above Humane Efficiency . . . carried on . . . from all Eternity"—the relationship of Israel to the colony was paradigmatic and archetypal; historically, for the clergy from Cotton to Mather, it was (in their special sense of the term) typological.* Jeremiah himself had emphasized that the exodus to come would excel that of the past, and Christian thinkers reiterated that, although it would have all the features of the old deliverance (as Mather and many others outlined them), yet "it is not a case of simple repetition. The 'new wonders' will cause 'the things of old' to be forgotten" in a teleological dialectic between the static and the dynamic, analogue and contrast, temporal process and atemporal plan—a dialectic which incorporates the past in the act of superseding it, or (conversely) which leads "to a goal, and constantly bears within itself this goal as prophecy or promise." In this perspective, "historical Prophesie or Propheticall history" disclosed a constant "advancing and growing": from Israel under Solomon through Jerusalem under Nehemiah to New England under the founding fathers. Moses left the "patern of the Temple" to David who "left the patern therof to his Son *Solomon*: And lo we have the patern!" Unmistakably, "the wonderful appearance of God in carrying on the work of *Reformation* . . . in the latter ages . . . [already] displayed in many signal steps [hitherto, contains] . . . Hints . . . of present use to *us*." For here, where God has "*set His Hand again . . . to recover the Remnant of his People*," we are witnessing "the great issue . . . of the *Promises* and *Prophesies* of his Word."[53]

* These various forms of colonial rhetoric are more fully documented in Appendix A.

Whatever the ebb and flow of external circumstances, therefore, it was incumbent upon New Englanders to *"observe Christs Dispensations . . . so as to be encouraged."* You must comprehend the present, urged the orthodoxy, not in the light of what is "literally understood of *Israel* . . . according to the Type" but "more fully" according to "the Antitype" embodied in the theocracy as it *was*—a people "separated from the . . . world (as it is prophesied of Jacobs remnant . . . Mic. 5.7)," for whom "the Lord did more . . . then for any people in this world"—and consequently as it *would be,* in a "more Glorious manner than ever." In sum, Cotton Mather explained, "the Triumph of Israel was but a Figure and Shadow of the Churches more illustrious Triumph" here, of "the *matchless* favours of God unto New England" with which he has dealt "as not with *any* [other] nation." How well his listeners would have comprehended his meaning—the momentous distinction between the two Israels which emerges from his "parallel" —is suggested by the intensity and persistence of the theme through the political sermons. More explicitly the concurrence of populace and pulpit appears in certain nonclerical utterances: in the impassioned tracts of Samuel Sewall and Joshua Scottow, for example, or in the celebration of Massachusetts' mission, some fifteen years before Cotton Mather's birth, by Captain Edward Johnson, "representative of the rank and file" settlers:

As it was necessary that there should be a Moses and Aaron, before the Lord would deliver his people and destroy Pharoah lest they should be wildered indeed in the Wilderness; so now [in the early seventeenth century] it was needfull, that the Churches of Christ should first obtain their purity, and the civill government its power to defend them [as has been manifested in the New England theocracy], before Antichrist come to his finall ruine: and because you shall be sure the day is come indeed, behold the Lord Christ marshalling . . . these N[ew] E[ngland] people. . . . What the issue will be is assuredly known in the generall already. Babylon is fallen. . . . The poor remnant of Gods people [in America] . . . have heard the noyse of the great fall. . . .

> The noble Acts Jehova wrought his Israel to redeem,
> Surely this second work of his shall far more glorious seem.[54]

The New World plantation, then, paralleled *and* built upon the scriptural patterns of Exodus. As the story unfolds in the political sermons, the migration opened with a "Divine Call," in an "incomparable Minute," to a group sifted like choice grain from the European Ur-Egypt-Babylon, "a people separated and set apart by God to be the Subject of a very great and glorious Work of Reformation" which would accomplish (what the Hebrews had failed to do) "a decisive and irrevocable break with Antichristian corruptions." These "chosen instruments" the Lord "brought . . . by a mighty hand and an out-stretched arm over a *greater* than the Red Sea," and—in accordance with his numerous prophecies to his elect (Ps. 72:8–9, 98:3; 1 Sam. 2:10; Isa. 43:16; 45:20–25; Zech. 9:9–15; Luke 1:46–55)—he gave them *"these Ends of the Earth . . .* for the *Bounds of their Habitation."* How he had subsequently preserved and prospered them there was a matter of common knowledge. "Ask now of many of the Ages that are past, and ask from one side of Heaven unto the other, whether there hath been any such . . . almost unexampled unparall[el]ed mercy" shown to man. The desert had flourished into another Garden of God. He "hath instructed us, as he did *Israel*" and, having led and fed us "by the hands of *Moses* and *Aaron*," he "turned this Wilderness into a *Canaan*" —not the lost land of milk and honey but the miraculously rejuvenated home of the redeemed remnant. In phrases drawn from Isaiah, Psalms, and Jeremiah (interwoven with those from Revelation and from the Pentateuch) the jeremiads exult in a miraculous and instantaneous transformation. "When he planted these Heavens and laid the foundation of this Earth," his vow to create in "Sion . . . *a Tabernacle not* [ever to be] *taken down*" and to *"make the Wilderness a Pool of Water* . . . hath in an eminent degree [been] fulfilled before our eyes." "In a day"—with a "wonderful alteration" such "as was never heard of"—the "remote, rocky, bushy, wild-woody wilderness" became "for fertilness . . . the wonder of the world," a more resplendent Promised Land or second Eden, physically *"rejoycing and blossoming as a Rose,"* and spiritually *"Beautiful as* Tirzah, *Comely as* Jerusalem, *Terrible as an Army with Banners."* Its inhabitants God had guarded as *"the Apple of his Eye"* and "dandled in the lap of his providence." He drove out the heathen to make room for them and shielded them from enemies within and outside the plantation: from the Indian "Bear that *would have rooted up this Vineyard of the Lord*" and from the heretical "Foxes which [hoped to] . . . eat up the Vines and the tender Grapes." Against these and all schemes of Satan, "God himself hath been a Wall of fire to us . . . *he hath fenced us . . . about as his peculiar garden of pleasure*" and "enclosed [us] . . . to be a *City of Righteousness*" and a *"Valley of Vision."*[55]

The jeremiads project this heroic era into the universal reign of the saints. As, parenetically, the New Canaan encompassed the old, so in turn it served as "prototype of the millennium": all three states were "not only . . . typologically interconnected but also in part overlapping," in accordance with the divine historiography which, as we have seen, allowed the American Puritans to anticipate the future on the basis of analogy to related events in earlier ages, stretching back to the Promised Land and to Creation itself. "The flourishing beauty of . . . heavenly grace," as William Hubbard put it, "which did so strangely metamorphose the visage of the face of things at first in the world . . . was the [same] verdant lustre . . . that turned the rough and barren [New England] wilderness . . . into a fruitful Carmel or fragrant Sharon." And the New Jerusalem, by extension, would bring that luster to a more brilliant glow. It was an intrinsic part of the country's history, the culmination of the founders' achievements. In fact it still remained on the horizon; in the larger progressivist-dialectic view it was already present, its "scope and end" indelibly "stamped on this People," as the harvest is implicit in the planting or as the antitype is embedded in the *figura*. "Though there be in special one grand accomplishment of Scripture Prophecies," William Adams pointed out on a fast-day in 1678, "yet there hath been a *glorious* accomplishment of it already," albeit a "partile accomplishment . . . wherein those . . . promises are fulfilled in their measure and degree." His outlook was characteristic of the orthodoxy at large. In urging John Davenport to follow him to America, Cotton wrote that "the order of the churches and the commonwealth [here] . . . brought into his mind the new heaven and the new earth"; and his "description of the millennium," as a recent scholar has observed, "sounds very like the holy commonwealth already established in Massachusetts . . . [a sort of] thousand-year extension of the New England Way."[56]

The second and third generation ministers made the identification still more detailed. When they called in the 1660s and 1670s for a history of New England they were only partly motivated by the hope that "the deeds of the fathers would arouse the emulation of their sons." More largely, they wanted the history as a "Monument" in its own right, one which would attest to "the glorious works of God, for this people in the past," and which *as such* would presage the glories to come. In transforming the American wilderness, God, they explained, provided through his church-state "a type and Embleme of New Jerusalem," "a *First Fruits* of that which shall in due time be accomplished in the world throughout," "a specimen of the new heavens and a new earth . . . which shall ere long be seen the world over." Urian Oakes' often-quoted remark on "our great duty to be the Lords *Remembrancers* or *Recorders*" derives from Isaiah's proclamation that the God who delighted in his people "as the bridegroom rejoiceth over the bride" had announced "unto the end of the world . . . [that] thy salvation cometh" (Isa. 61:2–12). Earlier in the same sermon, Oakes had applied the test at length to the colonists' accomplishments. "As a City upon a hill," he recalled, "you have, to a considerable Degree enlightened the [world] . . . as to the pattern of Gods House." Indeed,

if we cast us the Accompt, and Summe of all our mercies, and lay all things together, this our Common-wealth seems to exhibit . . . a *little model of the Kingdome of Christ upon Earth* . . . wherein it is generally acknowledged and expected. This work of God set on foot and advanced to a good Degree here, being spread over the face of the Earth, and perfected as to greater Degree of Light and Grace and Gospel-glory will be (as I conceive) *the Kingdome of Jesus Christ so much spoken of. When this is accomplished,* you may then say [with St. John] . . . *the Kingdoms of this World are become the Kingdome of our Lord* . . . [and you may then fully understand how] you have been . . . *as a Candle in the Candlestick that giveth light to the whole House.*

On these grounds, Oakes and his colleagues confirmed "Dr. *Twiss* his Opinion that when New Jerusalem should come down from Heaven *America* would be the seat of it" and urged prayer to hurry its descent. "'Tis the prerogative of New-England above all the Countries of the world" because "the *New English* Churches are a preface to the New Heavens."[57] It was a prerogative that enabled the preachers decisively to turn the Janus-like vision of their predecessors into the two-handled engine of literal-prophetic historiography.*

* Twisse set forth his opinion—one which was upheld, he added, by many other divines—in a famous letter (March, 1635) to Joseph Mede, who suggested in reply that the New World might have been reserved instead for Gog and Magog. Mede's conjecture rankled the American Puritans throughout the century because (among other more obvious reasons) it seemed to echo their opponents' analogy between the New Englanders and the "unprofitable servant" whom Christ condemned to "outer darkness" (Matt. 25:30), that image of hell prefigured by the desert to which Abraham banished Hagar and Ishmael. In general, the settlers countered with a barrage of contrary images: "Sion the outcast," the woman of Revelation, chapter 12, the patriarchs and the exiled prophets, "light in darkness," and, of course, the Israelites and the blessed remnant).

THE NEW ISRAEL AND THE JEWISH PROBLEM

> *New England* they are like the *Jews,*
> as like as like can be.
>   Peter Folger, *A Looking Glass* (1676)

> And these Watchmen upon seeing the Messengers from afar, lift up
> their Voice to give Notice to the Jews of the actual Coming & speedy Motion
> of these most welcome Bringers of good Tidings; and they sing forth Joy
> in their lifting up their Voice. . . . How *beautiful* do the *Messengers* and
> *Ministers* appear . . . on Account of their good Tidings sent unto Zion!
>   Thomas Frink, *A Sermon Delivered at Stafford* (Boston, 1757)

The means of this transformation had been afforded them long
since in the sermons that framed the voyage of the *Arbella.* With the
demise of the Good Old Way they drew out its full implications. Perhaps most conspicuously their achievement stands forth in their use of
the parallel with Israel. The emigrants had circumvented its ominous
historical aspect, as we have seen, by accenting its developmental-
typological connotations. But they took with them from England
another and equally far-reaching notion about Israel, the doctrine of
the National Conversion. According to this view, Jeremiah's forecast
included the entire literal house of Israel as well as the gentile remnant. Although its transgressions had caused "stiff-necked Israel"
centuries of persecution, God's righteous indignation would eventually
abate. Directly before the Parousia, a forgiving Deity would heal the
"obdurate blindness" of Abraham's descendants and restore them *in
toto* as his chosen people once again: "*Then* should we see the *Veil*
taken off the Minds of the *Jewish Nation* . . . and the [redeemed]
Gentiles would *walk* [together with *all* the Jews] *in the Light* of the
New Jerusalem." "As their captivitie in *Babel* resembled their . . .
captive condition now," wrote Bulkeley, describing "the present miserable forsaken condition of the *Jewes,*"

so their deliverance out of *Babel* then, typed out their [collective and eter-
nal] deliverance . . . *by the bloud of the Covenant* [i.e., by grace] . . . *The
Jewes though for the present they be as prisoners in the Pit, yet they shall
be againe delivered out of it, by vertue of the Covenant made with their
Fathers.* . . . This . . . is foretold in that place of *Jeremie* . . . [where he]
tells us, that *the City (Jerusalem) shall be builded* [again] . . . and *Israel*
. . . called upon to returne. . . . And from all this concludes, *that all Israel
shall come in and be saved.*[58]

The Hebrews' apostasy and downfall, then, did not signify a broken national covenant after all. It was only a surface lesion in a "special branch of the Covenant of Grace," a sort of unhappy horological interlude between two divine acts: their call through Abraham and their salvation through Christ at the close of history. The idea gained authority from a long tradition beginning with the Church Fathers; it found indirect support in the rabbinical commentaries which the clergy cited often and with respect. From Akiva through Rashi and Maimonides to Manasseh ben Israel (who helped secure Jewish emigration to Cromwell's England as "a condition precedent to their Redemption") Hebrew theologians laid particular stress upon eschatological prophecy—and especially upon those favorite Puritan texts concerning the return to Zion "in which the restoration of Israel to dominion and glory was a central motif." In the decades immediately preceding and following the Massachusetts venture, their exegeses provoked a widespread messianic-Zionism which was comparable to, and inextricably bound up with, the Reformers' apocalyptic view. On their part, the rabbis were deeply affected by the Reformation and the "proofs [it offered] of the near approach of the Messianic era." Cabbalistic calculations ever since the *Zohar* had fixed upon 1648 as the *Annus Mirabilis*; during the first half of the seventeenth century the Ottoman conquests, the religious wars, the great Cossack rebellion, all intensified "the national fervor . . . from Morocco to Poland."[59]

The fervor had a decided impact in its turn upon the Reformation. Through the influence of continental and English luminaries—Reuchlin, Pico, Scaliger, the Buxtorfs, William Gill, Henry More, and others—the study of Hebrew, along with the wide circulation of Hebrew literature in translation, facilitated the "free exchange" between Jewish and Christian scholars of their mystic and apocalyptic hopes. The exchange is attested to by the Christians' expectation "of a mass conversion of Jewry as soon as Jews could be convinced that the Cabbalistic writings in reality taught the Christian doctrine of the Logos." More strikingly still, it is manifest in numerous correspondences between Hebrew and Christian eschatology: in the concept of the fifth monarchy, for example, which according to rabbinical estimates would come upon the fall of Rome; or in the importance assigned to the study of the "Book of Mysteries" (Revelation and the *Zohar*, which the famous seventeenth-century exegete Abraham Azulai declared would be "unsealed" in the last days by "all those who . . . merit Redemption"); or again, and perhaps most dramatically, in the belief (shared alike by Jews and Puritans of all convictions) that a momentous change was at hand, for the Hebrew people first and then mankind at large. In the disillusionment of his last years, Milton wrote of the still "unreform'd" Israelites:

> Yet he [God] at length, time to himself best known,
> Rememb'ring Abraham, by some wondrous call
> May bring them back, repentant and sincere.[60]

For most of the pre-Revolution Puritans, the conditional tense was an absolute future, and for many of them, too, the *Annus Mirabilus* devolved upon the year 1648.

From all these various sources, the doctrine of National Conversion received virtually unanimous approval in the colony. Samuel Gorton complained in 1646 about the settlers "looking after, and foretelling so much . . . the calling of the Jews," and Increase Mather could say in 1710 (the year after he published his popular *Essay Upon the Jews Conversion and the Millennium*): "That the Church of God shall have a glorious time on Earth, after the Conversion of the Jews . . . has ever been received as a Truth in the Churches of *New-England*." It was a truth celebrated throughout the political sermons as the marriage of Christ and his church, foreseen by Moses and heralded by St. John: "the great Iubile" or "illustrious Epithalamium" set upon the "*Apocalyptical Stage*," whereby "the Earth shall be marvellously filled with *Heavenly Influences*." Long after 1648 had come and passed, the ministers discussed and prayed for the event; at times they even undertook themselves to convert the Jews: to persuade the "antient people of Israel [to] look out of [their] prison grates, [and] let these [American] Armies . . . of Jesus provoke [them] to acknowledge he is certainly come . . . that [together we] . . . may enjoy that glorious resurrection-day." They shared in the excitement through the 1660s (the crest of Shabb'tai Zvi's career) at the "constant reports from sundry places and hands" about an influx of Jews to the Holy Land, "carried on with great signs and wonders by a high and mighty hand of extraordinary providence"; and during the height of Eliot's missionary work they seriously contemplated the possibility that the natives "were descendants of the lost Ten Tribes of Israel," so that every conversion carried further assurance "that the work of Christ in the destruction of the Beast was well under way"— or, according to Thomas Shepard's 1648 tract on the Indians, that that "brighter day" was dawning "wherein East & West shall sing the song of the Lamb." But the main effect of the belief upon their thought lay in its relevancy to the New England venture. First, they used it to support the concept of the settlers' period of trial. Were not the "People of Israel . . . like us, the poor People of *New England*, brought into sad circumstances"? Clearly, since we know that "the unbelieving Nation of the *Jews* shall be converted and saved" we should "Hence . . . be encouraged" about our own prospects. Second, they found in it a lesson for their unconverted-but-baptized offspring. "They who make nothing of the Covenant of God with faithful Ancestors," they cried, "will see their error if ever they see the *Jews* converted." More positively, they brought a

consolation to such parents as have entered into a Covenant with the Lord. . . . They may be assured, that the vertue, the blessing, the efficacy of the Covenant shall never be disanuled, but it shall go on to your children forever; by your Covenant, you have such hold of God, that you may be assured, he will be a God, not to you onely, but . . . your seed [also] shall stand before the Lord, to serve him for ever. This you see fulfilled in the people of the Jewes . . . [and] what mercy *Abrahams* seed have belonging to them, the same doth belong to yours also; therefore . . . this your Covenant shall draw in your children to partake of . . . blessing and grace . . . with you, never to be broken off.

It may also serve for a consolation unto such children . . . that they may goe to God, and plead the Covenant of their fathers. . . . The people of *Israel* . . . ordinarily used to plead the Covenant which God made with *Abraham*. . . . The Lord himselfe [furthermore] lays this foundation of comfort for such children, *Esa.* 51. 1, 2. . . . The oyle that is powred upon the head, will run down to the rest of the members.[61]

Most important, the jeremiads identify National Conversion with their anticipations for America. Did not Isaiah promise, directly after reminding the Israelites to "Look unto Abraham your father," that "the Lord . . . will make [the] wilderness like Eden, and [the] desert like the Garden of the Lord," and that he would bring his nation triumphantly into that golden time when "the heavens shall vanish away like smoke, and the earth shall wax old like a garment"? Because, therefore, the ministers saw signs of the approach of the Conversion of the Jews they felt more secure in their success, and (primarily) because they felt secure—or spoke as though they did—they watched intently for the event. In his preface to Shepard's *Parable of the Ten Virgins* (1636–40), Jonathan Mitchell tells us that many applied the parable "to the

times about the expected calling of the *Jews* (and if so, the substance
of the work may be accounted to be . . . seasonable for these times)."
Shepard's contemporary, John Cotton, claimed that since New England enjoys "such fellowship as the Church of the Jewes had with
Christ coming out of Romish Babylon," therefore we may "expect a
powerfull and glorious calling of the Jewes," and Edward Johnson,
noting in the early 1650s these views of "Mr. John Cotton, among
many others," found in the Pequot defeat evidence that "the overthrow of Antichrist, and calling of the Jews . . . in all likelihood is very
suddenly to be performed. . . . The glorious harvest is hard at hand."
Cotton's stepson, in his first exposition of prophecy, wrote the colony's
major tract on the subject upon the premise that "there is reason to
hope that the salvation of the Tribes of *Israel* is near to be revealed
. . . because the Scripture saith that this work must be brought to pass
in the last dayes . . . *Jer.* 30." In 1692 Cotton's grandson reiterated the
prediction in a work whose title, *A Midnight Cry*, derives from the
parable of the ten virgins, and whose message, taken from the chiliastic
prophecy of Isaiah 52—and based upon the tradition associating the
Bride in Canticles and in Jeremiah 31 with the Wife of the Lamb in
Revelation 19—joined the old and the new Israel in exultation:
"*Awake, Awake* . . . O New-English *Zion,* and put on thy *Beautiful
Garments,* O American *Jerusalem.*"[62]

Within this continuity, the jeremiads of the last quarter of the
century employ the doctrine as a supernatural cure-all for the country's spreading disease of worldliness. Like the early American paradise,
observed the ministers, the Jerusalem of Nehemiah "doth admit of a
Typical and Partial . . . Accomplishment" of God's "more plenary"
aims; its "destruction . . . may be applied to the troubles of the last
times" and thus, by extension, to his gratuitous redemption of the
whole people. This pattern foretold the story of America in general—
which "hath been desolate and unmarried for numerous ages" only to
receive "a greater salvation than that out of *Egypt* was"—and as such
it provided a symbol of the destiny of mankind. But it had particular
meaning for the present. Addressing their backsliding audiences, they
announced that it carried a "Hint" of "the special design" to "be verified and accomplished . . . upon *you.*" God was not so much depending
on them as waiting to pour his lasting blessings upon them precisely as
he would upon Israel. The "surprising parallel" now seemed applicable

above all in terms of the future. "New England they were like the Jews" as that transgressing people would be once again, miraculously, irreversibly, the chosen of the Lord, in that day which (as in the 1630s) would see "a whole Nation . . . *born at once.*" Like his New World instruments, "the *Jews* were . . . grown a little too secure and careless . . . neglecting of His Ordinances for the sake of their own Secular Accomodations"; like them, they "that were the *only people of God in the world,* [became] involved in the most Awakening and Horrible Calamities; and [were shown the] . . . prospect of . . . a Speedy . . . *Ruine* before their Eyes." And like the Israelites, they might now, "in the days of the Messiah," expect that "God will remember his Covenant with their Ancestors, and will again receive them into favour and . . . [grant them] Salvation . . . *Jer.* 31." Accordingly, it was no longer only a question of trial. Above all, it was a matter of patience and faith, of "*quiet Expectation* for the performance of all the Great things he hath promised to do for his People."[63]

This figural association of Israel and New England—which changes the biblical parallel entirely from horologicals to chronometricals— stands as the ministers' supreme effort to unite the absolute and the human, or in any case to prevent the latter from interfering with their design. As such, it is one of the distinguishing traits of their jeremiads after 1675 and especially in the 1690s. It did not lead them, of course, to look passively or smugly upon their flocks' erring ways. Their lamentation persists, along with the threats and the pleas for reformation. They warn as before that "the eyes of *God* and of his holy *Angels* are upon you to see . . . how you Manage . . . this Trust," and they even lecture, at least once or twice, *against* presuming "upon Sovereign Grace, which we are apt and (I fear we begin) to doe." The growing emphasis upon the Jew's Conversion merely brings to the fore a hitherto subdued or minor ingredient, a relatively neglected "saving device," inherent in their complex historiography. It is a historiography which (as we have seen), by yoking together the disparate notions of human responsibility and of an absolute calling (whereby "He will make us able to do it, and willing to do it, and so to do it"), comes almost *sui generis* to incorporate a diversity of historical approaches: the providential concern with moral *exempla* alongside the "predestinate" view of mankind's redemption, the apocalyptic fixation upon the coming Kingdom as well as the antiquarian appeal to origins and precedents (which "is the very opposite of apocalyptic thinking for it stresses the past rather than the future").[64] From this viewpoint, the apparent contradiction in the later jeremiads—their juxtaposition of lament and the idea of unmerited National Salvation—arises simply from the fact that the clergy, without discarding former concepts, continually draws out the implications of its intrinsically ambiguous rhetoric.

The nature of the ambiguity appears in sharper relief when set against the historical background from which the rhetoric itself derives. The postexilic Hebrew prophets, as modern commentators have noted, avoided nihilism or despair—opened "a door of escape from cataclysm"—by linking God's past mercies to Israel with those to come, when he would pour out his Spirit upon the remnant destined to restore the Holy City. But as the prophets themselves explain the term, the remnant is simultaneously a conditional and an unconditional entity. Though it exists by miracle, its deeds must justify the miracle; its redemption does not depend upon works, but "the ends of that act of forgiveness include service." For example, "no other prophet emphasized the value of repentance for the whole nation as did Jeremiah," and yet none so fervently affirmed a gratuitous "*complete revolution* in the spiritual life of Israel." The result of this tension, Professor Alan Charity has demonstrated, was a reliance upon miracle that grew in proportion to the nation's horological deterioration. "The failure of Israel to do this service . . . led almost inevitably to the doctrine" that the community's true purpose and meaning lay not in the present, but, paradoxically, in pointing, *despite* the present, towards a supernatural salvation still to come, "the unique divine initiative at the end of history." It was a solution which fed into the Christian notion of the Conversion of the Jews, and which precisely mirrors the solution developed, just as "inevitably," in the political sermons. Like the prophets with whom they identified, the ministers "in an apparently hopeless situation" turned to "the promises made to . . . Abraham." "The covenanted nation," they taught, "was like the ripe, unreaped field whose members stood waiting for the sickle of grace," or, more accurately, like a field "much run to ruine . . . and gone beyond man," so that "it must be . . . God alone in some more than ordinary way of working that can retrieve" it. And like the prophets of old they instructed the people "*to know and discern the times*" not in order to dwell upon "*present* accomptings" but to "Con-

sider what Scriptures are now fulfilling" and so to place all trust in the
"future . . . kingdom of Yahweh" where "the law will be written . . .
upon their hearts (Jer. 31:33)." Putting the theocracy's name where
Jeremiah had written that of Israel, they cried to the mocking
"Ishmaelites of the world"—"the banterers and scoffers who jeered at
New England as the self-styled New Jerusalem"—that "AMERICA
is legible in these Promises."[65]

In this light, the political sermons show a remarkable unity of form
and content. By precedent and association, their rhetoric became
fundamentally a means to adjust human action to heaven's standard,
to imply the inadequacy of all pleas for reformation even while voicing
those pleas, for within the context stylistically established (by metaphor and allusion, type and trope) reformation *per se* could mean "at
best a temporary halt on the road to destruction." Rooted as it was in
the interpenetration of horologicals and chronometricals—in the transformation of "service" into "miracle"—their rhetoric carried within
itself the assurance of the thousand years' paradise to which the
Jeremiahs conditionally summoned their flocks, posited as New
England's ultimate goal a "complete and enduring reformation . . .
[which] would *require* divine aid," and provided a framework for
corporate self-definition in which "the discomforts and imperfections of
America dropped away." At least in part, then, the orthodoxy's
argument, including their outlook on history, evolved in accordance
with the logic of their distinctive eschatological language. Yet in part,
too, the history of the last quarter of the century stimulated or ac-
celerated the development of the rhetoric. Indeed, it seems possible to
trace that effect specifically to King Philip's War, the "holocaust" of
1675–76 which threatened the entire Bay settlement with "total an-
nihilation." From the security of a later decade, the ministers gloried
in "the Evident Hand of Heaven" that "Extinguished whole Nations of
Salvages" as once God had "made room" for the first settlers (and
now, moreover, "at such a rate, that there can hardly any of them
. . . be found . . . upon the face of the Earth").[66] But during the war
itself the terror they shared with all other New Englanders expressed
itself in a discernible shift of rhetorical strategy, a movement (so to
speak) from Jer. 31:31–32 to Jer. 31:33, from threat and commination
to concerted invocation of "the unique divine initiative."

The shift may be seen in the very titles of their discourses: *Right-*

*eousness Rained from Heaven; Man's Extremity, God's Opportunity;
The Soveraign Efficacy of Divine Providence; The Times of Man are
in the Hand of God; The Necessity of the pouring out of the Spirit
from on High.* It appears in concrete detail in their interpretation of
the Indian conflict. Increase Mather, for instance, like all his colleagues anxious to rouse and rally the settlers, informed those who
might despair in a "narrow" providential view of their disasters—who
"perhaps will say, did not God in the . . . War seem angry with [our]
prayers?"—that "those direful imprecations . . . are rather prophecies,"
revealing that the afflicted "indeed . . . are his delight." Many of his
New World people had of late received "the saddest tidings. . . . This
is true, yet know" that thereby "the Lord, who doth redeem Israel out
of all his troubles, hath graciously and gloriously begun our Salvation.
. . . Let him [now] bring . . . cure unto this *Jerusalem,* and reveal the
abundance of peace and truth [he holds in store for us]: And it shall
be unto him a Name of Joy, a Praise and an honour before all the
Nations of the earth, which shall hear all the good that he will doe
unto us." More blatantly still, the shift toward reliance upon the
divine is manifest in the covenant-renewal ceremonies. Instituted in
March, 1675, apparently in direct response to the war, the ceremonies
called the settlers to reaffirm their commitment to God and his New
Israel almost as a token (if heartfelt) gesture, a sign of grateful
acquiescence to what was "graciously and gloriously" already well on
its way. Since, they explained, the "people of *New-England* are (if
any under heaven are so) *a Covenant-People,*" the Lord certainly intended to remove all dangers now oppressing them and grant them
victory in this as in their other trials. What was demanded on their
part amounted to their collective sincere acceptance (or rather, reacceptance) of his once and future aid, their *"solemn profession that
we* [again] *fly for refuge to the . . . grace and mercy that is set before
us."*[67]

The clergy liked to point out that such reacceptance was embedded
in the scriptural relationship between God and his people on the
"mystical as well as *historical"* plane. Historically, the Israelites employed it "whilst yet in the Wilderness . . . being [about] to engage
with their Heathen Enemies"; they did so later, with equal success, in
"solemn assembly" under Nehemiah upon their return from captivity
in Babylon (Neh. 8, 9). Spiritually, it was an act incumbent on the
elect who "had as it were lost the work or effect of former Conversion."

The preachers reminded their audiences in this regard that "renewal" pertained not to works but to that absolute "Covenant wherein men profess themselves *unable* to doe any thing of *themselves*"—and that precisely such men must periodically rededicate themselves. Although the new birth occurs once only, "the practice of Saints" (Peter "after Satan sifted him," Jacob "in time of his distress," David praying for *"a clean heart"*) shows that "it may so decay as to need to be done over again." The twin reasons for covenant-renewal applied with unique force to New England. There, where the spiritual and the historical crossed, where the personal covenant of grace visibly fused with the linear Work of Redemption, it became incontrovertibly the duty of every believer seeking release from mystical Babylon to join in "open profession" with the chosen community in its time of distress, when it "had *as it were* lost the effect" of divine protection. And it seemed just as incontrovertible, to "those who have any right understanding of our present *State*," that the efficacy of such profession was a foregone conclusion. Early in 1675, the colonists were promised that the Lord would not "disappoint those [of us] who doe indeed put their trust in him." Two years later Urian Oakes triumphantly recalled to the Bay militia that "the People of God in this Country have had great Experience of this. What Deliverances hath God commanded! . . . The Salvations of *New-England* have been most apparent by the Lord's Governing *Time*, and *Chance*." Thus, privately lamenting our sins, we publically "ascribe unto *Grace*, Free *Grace* . . . the Honour of it all," because the God who redeems our souls, *"working by himself in Soverign Mercy,"* has similarly ordained "a general work of Conversion . . . to save his People by himself," so to vouchsafe *"the Successes of their Undertakings and Affairs."*[68]

Beginning with this period, accordingly, Jer. 31:33 and Jer. 50:5 (the texts which half a century before served to differentiate the individual from the national calling) become avowedly interwoven. According to the covenant-renewal jeremiad, participation in the ceremony meant that the colonist formerly "in the way to Hell . . . *is* [now] in the way to Heaven." It meant, in the same breath, that the theocracy, the Lord's people relying on "the Aids of Grace, for Self-Reformation," *"renew their Faith, . . .* are everlastingly in Covenant," and "are helped unto the performance" of their mission by "their saving *Conversion* to GOD" and his subsequent "intercession for . . . his [American] ISRAEL." The ceremony, that is, attested to "that

Engagement made by God in the Covenant of Grace, *Jer.* 31.33," and by that token it demonstrated, as a community ritual, that "the generality of them" were "walking in the way to Zion with their faces hitherward, *Jer.* 50.4, 5," "sure of spiritual . . . and temporal Blessings," certain "to be a *great* People, yea the greatest upon the Face of the Earth." The "Sum of the Covenant [we renew] is expressed by . . . his being *the God of his people, Jer.* 31.33 . . . [and as such it is] a *sure Covenant. Jer.* 50.5. *come let us joyne our selves to the Lord.*" This interlacing of covenants had of course been anticipated and to some extent applied long before. Covenant-renewal does not add to the jeremiad tradition but, with the doctrine of National Conversion, comes to fulfill it. As such it highlights various aspects of the rhetoric: the union of material and spiritual blessings, for example; or the concept of trial, which renders the verdict through the statement of choice ("Beware, O our *Evangelical* People, Beware" of "out-standing your day of Grace, lest" you "be guilty of New-Englands ruine"); or, once again, the mobilization of "preparation" into the service of corporate errand: "plead with Him to remember His holy Covenant-promise . . . unto us," so that "this Renewal of Covenant may be [not only] for . . . your everlasting comfort," but, further, for "all the Designs of *Reformation,*" from "the beginning, when God first laid the Foundations of Gospel work in these *Ends of the Earth,*" to "the Day when Jerusalem shall Rejoice [and] we shall be glad and rejoice with Her: Even in that [great] Day, which is not farr off."[69]

Most dramatically, the covenant-renewals highlight the jeremiads' rhetorical technique by their pervasive, proto-revivalist call for prayer. The ministers had always insisted that "*Prayer* is eminently the Duty of the *People of God.*" During the war, as their insistence intensified— and as in response the "prayers of many thousands . . . poured out with the greatest solemnity"—they began increasingly to stress that that duty, though apparently reflecting momentary crises, presupposed at bottom a sense of his secret design. For God's people, it represented less a reaction to temporal need than a response to the absolute, a desire to become the human vehicles of his intentions. When we cry out for his "intercession" against Philip, the clergy explained, we do it so that what was predetermined might come to pass; expecting the Father's will to be done, not altered, we raise our supplications like "*Under-Rowers*" on the ark of faith chorusing the Pilot's directions. The "motives to excite us in our prayers" lie wholly in "the promises

and prophecies of the Scriptures." Do we not find there "the predictions of [our] future glory" (as, indeed, we have seen "pledges of it
beforehand [in that] . . . the churches of New England . . . have been
and are yet the vineyard of the Lord of hosts")? It follows "from
thence [that we must] . . . plead with God for a more general effusion
of his Spirit": our pleading depends upon his pledges and he makes
good his pledges upon our pleading. "*As the Lord hath made promises
of great Blessings to his People; so he will be enquired of them . . . in
the way of Prayer and Supplication in order to the performance of that
which he hath promised, that he may do it for them.*"[70]

In conformity with this circular doctrine (and not as Arminians in
Calvin's robes) they assured the embattled settlers that their appeals
for victory "*must* now be fulfilled." From this perspective, they pointed
out in postwar sermons that "*New-Englands* late Deliverance from
the Rage of the Heathen, is an eminent Answer of Prayer." And with
this assurance, finally, throughout the period and beyond, they expanded covenant renewal into a titanic recruiting effort to bolster
their fading theocracy. We have seen how the jeremiads transmuted
the apologies for the halfway covenant into an affirmation of the New
World enterprise; the nature of the change is sharply illustrated in the
entreaties for mass conversion. Rededicating oneself to the Lord, said
the clergy, called to mind his promise to the chosen "seed," so that
on such occasions "*Godly Parents ought earnestly to pray . . . that he
would give Grace to their Children.*" By the same token, the still-
unconverted children (now only partial participants in the ceremony)
ought "prayerfully . . . *to make choice* of the Great GOD for *Our God*,
and [thereby] *make sure* of His being so." In both cases, the outcome
had long since been sealed in "*the Hand-writing of God.*" His decree
to "be a blessing to your posterity, as well as to yourselves," provided
an invincible " argument to plead in prayer for your children. . . . You
are the Lords people. . . . Beg therefore that God would fulfill his
own promise": that he would "*send us* . . . a general, plentiful dispensation of converting grace upon . . . this whole people, both the
standing and the rising Generations," and so complete "the work of
Christ in the promotion of his Kingdome" in New England.[71]

In 1680, when such mass "begging" had established itself as an
institution of the colonial Way—"a joyous feature of New England
life, usually attended . . . by a 'vast confluence of neighbours' "—
Increase Mather admitted that some Calvinists abroad regarded the

procedure—rededication, conversion, supplication, and all—with "evil surmisings, and censures." But they mistook its motive: neither he nor any member of the orthodoxy ever questioned the insufficiency of "means," and all of them punctuated their directions with reminders that God "will be gracious to whom he will be gracious, and will have Mercy upon whom he will have Mercy." What they meant was that those now asking for mercy were also "those whom he will in favour and mercy look to." If they gloried in the efficacy of their methods ("Remember, O *New-England,* how often that cry went up from thee to the Lord, *Return* . . . And now, behold, He is *Returned!*"), the reason lay in the confluence so demonstrated of their ends and those of the divine will. As though to italicize that rationale, they weighted their exhortations with collective entreaties of a more general kind. "Pray for . . . *The Calling of* . . . [all] Israelites"; cry "with earnest Expectation, Oh that the Jewish Nation were Converted!" Precisely because "Glorious Prophecies and Promises are come to Birth," we, *"the Servants of God, ought with Faith and Fervency"* to "pray for the accomplishment of all prophesied to be done," and "not cease Praying, 'till [we] . . . have obtained of God the Destruction of *Antichrist"* and *"he establish Jerusalem a praise in the Earth."* Such displays of concern, they contended, were twice blessed. They blessed those who pleaded and that which was pleaded for, serving as they did as midwife to the "birth" of the prophecies ("You may hasten them, by fervent Prayers"), to the new birth of the unconverted children, and to the rebirth of their "godly parents": "watch and Pray always, that we may be counted worthy to stand before the Son of Man. . . . The glorious king will take notice of it . . . [and] we shall reap plentifully," and, to conclude, *"New-England* shan't fail to be happy." What could more authoritatively underwrite the colony's stake in the "Times that are hastning"—as well as its role "in erecting and advancing his Kingdom"—than this supernatural harmony of self-interest and God's design? And conversely, what could better guarantee joyous issue of their prayers than this prearranged identity of the provisional and the promised?[72]

The call for prayer, in these terms which all but transfer human obligation to heavenly prerogative—which in Torrey's scriptural epigram render "man's extremity God's opportunity"—extends well beyond King Philip's War and echoes through the whole range of political sermons. Like the emphasis upon the Calling of the Jews, it marks a high-point of the jeremiad tradition, or better of the inter-action between rhetoric and history in the development of the jere-miad. If the appeals of covenant renewal followed upon the external threat of holocaust, and if (as we have seen) the language of National Conversion was prompted by the internal trend toward worldliness, so also both these elements embody *in extremis* the dominant patterns of the founders' rhetoric, and both represent the broadest reach of the ambiguous application of scripture (personal-social, temporal-abso-lute, linear-vertical) to the American experience of the New Israel. Accordingly, in the last decades of the century, the rhetorical forms which were designated to involve prophecy in history come to form a kind of colossal dyke against the flow of actual events. The nature of this achievement has already been sketched in outline. It emerges vividly through the contrast of any of the political sermons after about 1680 with those of the 1660s or early 1670s. To select the two most optimistic (and perhaps most influential) jeremiads of the latter period, the election speeches of John Norton (1661) and Samuel Danforth (1670) promise eventual triumph for the colony by invoking the need for works within the figure of Zion the outcast healed of her wounds:

Jeremiah looking at his sufferings, he will speak no more; but looking at Gods promise, and it is as fire in his bones, he cannot but speak. . . . If we look at *Sion* [i.e., New England] in the glass of the Promise, this Out-cast is both *Marah* [bitter], and *Hephzibah* [joyful], both a *Widow*, and *Beulah* [married]. . . . Gods touching an impenitent Out-cast with repent-ance, is a signal of Gods having mercy thereon. *Sions* recovery by re-pentance from her backsliding is an effect of grace, and a fore-runner of the set time of Sion's mercy. . . . [Thus we must] accept of Gods plaister . . . [so that] the set time of mercy . . . [may] come.

Now that . . . the Lord [hath] smitten us . . . [it] is high time for us to *remember when we are fallen, and repent*. . . . [It is true,] *we are feeble and impotent*. . . . [Yet] Remember the man that had a withered hand: Christ saith unto him, *Stretch forth thy hand . . . and it was restored whole . . .* Mat. 12.13. How could he stretch forth his hand when it was . . . shrunk up? The Almighty Power of Christ accompanying his Command enabled the man. . . . [So, too, in our present circumstances] Jesus, the Great Physician of Israel hath undertaken the Cure. *I will restore health unto thee, and I will heal thee of thy wounds, saith the Lord*, Jer. 30.17.[73]

Both passages intimate, of course, that God *will* cure the patient

(Danforth's, significantly, more forcefully than Norton's): the "Riddle of grace" which the text itself advances is that the physician will heal the "incurable." But both place due emphasis on acceptance, on man's conditional role in his recovery, his probationary participation in his blessing or affliction. Though Danforth accentuates "the promise of divine protection and preservation," he speaks at length of God's just wrath and of his demand that we "redress our faintings and swervings." More vehemently, still, John Norton, "that *Iudicious* and *Eagle eyed Seer*" of a former time, thunders the "need of Repentance, . . . [the] need of Reduction"; it is the colonists' voluntary turning from "Inherent" and "Extrinsical" sin in his view that "make[s] up the sanative Plaister." In sum, both Danforth and Norton allow the forces of history to enter into their calculations, however circumspectly or gingerly. "Untill we are . . . awakened and convinced, there will be no hope of *Reformation*." The later jeremiads are at once more pessimistic and far more assured of the outcome. "*Nothing else is like to do us good*," they moan, "*unless God will pour out his Spirit on us. We have had experience of the inefficacy* of means upon us to bring us into order and to a good frame. . . . *Judgements* have not done it. . . . *Deliverances* do not do it. . . . *Renewal of stroaks hath not done it.*" A half century of scorned remonstration testifies that "all ordinary means . . . have been altogether ineffectual, unto . . . reformation."[74]

Unless God will pour out His spirit upon us: the qualification, repeated over and again, directly and indirectly, grows in volume as the jeremiads proceed into the eighteenth century: "*When God hath once set a People under* [his] *dispensation . . . their miseryes will be like to proceed, till there be the pouring out of the Spirit from on high upon them to their sound Conversion, and then there will be a restoration.*" The image of a helplessly degenerate saint awaiting conversion resembles those of the castigated or forsaken saint but goes well beyond them. It insists that New England's success will be unmerited, that "it is [solely] Gods prerogative to help in this case"—"untill infinite power set a work by free grace . . . it will not be done"—and that the settlers must therefore look to a sudden manna-like "dispensation of converting grace, unto an unconverted generation." The ministers compared their listeners to a destitute farmer with no prospect for survival unless (through no doing of his own) the rains would come. "The vine shall revive," they warned, only "when the Lord is pleased to pour out of his Spirit." And they reminded them in the same instant of that other vine to which they were ingrafted, and of the Conversion of the Jews. At the very time the Lord "had resolved to cast . . . off [Israel] . . . a very *Sinful, Backsliding People* . . . Yet God, in his Sovereign Grace, makes a sure Promise of Mercy and Salvation . . . and ingageth himself to perform it, by Saving of them, in a more immediate and extraordinary way of working by himself."[75]

The lesson for New England seemed inescapable. In general terms, it demonstrated *"that although Places that have been . . . Mountains of Holiness should become very degenerate . . . yet . . . God will again . . . bless them."* In immediate terms, it intimated that even "if it should come to pass that *New England* should yet be *more sinful & more miserable* than now it is . . . yet there is Scripture ground to hope, that after God had vindicated his Holiness by sore punishment on us, God would again *restore, reform* and *bless New England.*" More than hope, there was precedent and prefiguration. God once withdrew himself from Israel, "hid himself from them, carried himself as if he . . . took no care of them"; yet the Jews *would* "be delivered out of the depth of apostasy and calamity which they were fallen into . . . [as his] divine visit will turn us again to our God." In both cases, he would elicit their "stretched forth hands; and . . . suffer himself to be overcome at last, and *quasi,* commanded by [his people's] prayers, seeing they will not let him alone . . . yield to their importunity." And then, precisely when it seemed that "all the power of men and angels" could not turn that "degenerate plant into a noble vine," when it became evident that "the use of other means . . . [would] avail nothing . . . to save us from sins and judgments, . . . this great Physician heals . . . his people." Thus extending the rhetoric of Norton and Danforth to its imaginative conclusion, the jeremiads by their recourse to memory and anticipation rescued the present from the process of history. Recalling the fathers' "garden of pleasure," and mindful "of all the prophesies to be done in a way of Sovereign grace," they instructed the children to

Expect that God will . . . [save] *New-England* . . . by Sovereign Grace. . . . We have not only hope, but *a sure Foundation of Faith & Confidence in God for Salvation* (viz.) *His Covenant and all his promises* . . . [for] *the most full, perfect . . . and glorious Salvation that ever God worketh for this People in this world.* He will magnifie *New England* . . . before the World. . . . God will glorifie himself before all people in us, when he shall

thus Save us from our sins & apostasy, by the power of his Spirit, in a
general work of Conversion and Reformation . . . and when this comes
that great promise to the Church will be fulfilled.

That which we affirm is, that we ought not to be . . . believing they [the
promised "Restaurations"] shall come to pass, till we see Reformation in
good forwardness; but to hope and pray for the accomplishment of all
[things] prophesied to be done in a way of *Sovereign grace*. . . . If the
Restauration depended on the *Antecedency* of Reformation, and Reformation depended upon mans *free will*, it would be long enough before either
would come to pass. But God having foretold & promised both, our
dependence ought to be on his *Grace*. . . . The ruinous circumstances of
[the] *Jews* . . . are such . . . that there is little hope; either of Restauratior
or Reformation; were it not for the *Prophesy* and the *Promise*. . . . Therefore we should *hope for much* . . . though there be . . . little sign of *Reformation.*[76]*

The intensity of millenarianism at the turn of the eighteenth century
is best understood in terms of this attitude. While the expectations
of Christ's return pervade the whole period—though for the emigrant
clergy no less than for the author of the *Theopolis Americana* "the
millenium was not a metaphor for secular achievement . . . [but]
literally imminent," and destined moreover to begin in "the *American
Hemisphere*" (New Haven, perhaps, or Boston, or further inland
towards the West or South, but surely somewhere "upon that Earth
wherein Satan for many Ages, has peaceably possessed an entire . . .
empire")—nonetheless between 1675 and 1690 the expectations un-
dergo a perceptible change. First, they swell into a major chord of the

---

* The contrast I am suggesting appears clearly in Samuel Willard's work
*The Fountain Opened: Or, the Admirable Blessing plentifully to be Dispensed at
the National Conversion of the JEWS*, a treatise which went through three
editions by 1697, when it was appropriately appended to Samuel Sewall's
Phaenomena quaedam Apocalyptica (Boston, 1697) (with its millennial prognostications for New England). Like Norton, Willard takes as his main text
Jeremiah's "outcast healed of her wounds"—a passage that had been used since
Augustine with regard to the elect, since the Reformation with regard to the
Conversion of the Jews, and since 1630 by New England Puritans with regard to
their theocracy. Unlike Norton or Danforth (or better, far more clearly than
they) Willard implicitly draws all three levels together by openly dispensing with
the provisional elements in the promise. His rendering of the text submits all to
God and leaves nothing to man; it becomes virtually a prayer for divine aid.
The outlook thus articulated makes plausible (though from a different perspective than that which was originally intended) Perry Miller's apparently contradictory or confusing insight into the jeremiad "as a [chronometrical] cleansing
ritual unconnected with any real belief that New England was in fact decaying,
and as a factual declaration, deeply pessimistic" of any horological "means."

political sermons; secondly, they become more and more dissociated from the present. They carry with them an appeal for improvement and confidence, as they had formerly. "Shall we take *this season* then wherein to fail the Lord? . . . *Yet a little while and he that shall come will come.*" "Now there is a pale Horse come, . . . Stars are falling, our Heaven, and our Earth are shaking"—we see "certain Evidence" all about us that "God's ancient people [are about to be] brought home": "Is it now a time to . . . save an Estate" or should rather "his *New England* Churches and People *this day*" prepare themselves for "the most glorious Crown that can be worn upon Earth"? But their main concern, more pronouncedly after 1690 than ever before, lies with past and future. Their descriptions of the chiliad—itself a paradigmatic fusion of past and future (as well as of heaven and earth)— pointedly reflect those of the earlier theocracy. The New Jerusalem, write the ministers, "will . . . dispossess the *Divels* of our *Air*," "put a New, Joyful, Pleasant Face upon . . . all," and restore the country *"to its Paradise State."* In effect, it will only differ quantitatively from the earlier New World Eden. It will fulfill "that Blessing to his People . . . in a *more* Glorious manner," leave them "in a *more* Reformed State than ever," insure *"more wonderful . . . Deliverances,"* and make their church-state *"more* Glorious, *more* Heavenly, *more* Universal far away than what was in the former [times]."[77] As the theocracy had foreshadowed the New Jerusalem, so in turn the millennium appears as the Good Old Way writ large.

In sustaining this outlook, the Jeremiahs of the last decade considered it their constant duty to inquire into the exact time of Christ's descent. They took over the duty from their predecessors—among others, Thomas Parker had set the date for 1650, Cotton for 1655, William Aspinwall for 1673—but they dwell upon it with almost obsessive interest. It forms, for example, the background to "the most imposing of all jeremiads," Cotton Mather's *Magnalia Christi Americana; or, The Ecclesiastical History of New England*. Mather undertook the work shortly after he started "medling with" the prophesies, expressed confidence in their accuracy, and concluded that the "long line of *Inter-Sabbatical Time*"—the "*Six Dayes* [which] . . . were a *Type* of the *Six Thousand years*"—would expire in 1711, or else (his father opted for 1715) at the latest "M.DCC.XVI," when the calling of his "Immanuelian people" would lead to a universal " 'downpouring' of the Holy Spirit." "*O what has God wrought?*," he exclaimed in a thanksgiving sermon in 1689; "my Brethren, It looks as if God had begun the *Resurrection* of His *Dead* People . . . *O Lord God, Thou hast begun to shew thy Servants thy Greatness* . . . we shall . . . very quickly see those *glorious Things which are spoken of Thee, O thou City of God!*" Immediately before he began the work he learned by special providence (according to his diary) that he had been appointed "Herald of the Lord's Kingdome now approaching," and he rushed to the election stand to explain his calculations in detail. Through the "Figures variously *Embossed*" in the Bible's "*Prophetical* as well as . . . Historical *Calendar*," he had measured "the *Last Hours* of Time" and could assure the assembly that the "*Sabbatism* . . . seems just going to lay its Arrest *upon us*." In 1696, and again in 1698, the year he finished his church history, he took the election stand to announce "*Good Tidings of Great Joy*" (like the angel heralding the Incarnation) in "a Message from Heaven": "O People of God . . . *there is a* REVOLUTION *and a* REFORMATION *at the very Door* . . . [and] the bigger part of this Assembly, may in the course of Nature, live to see it: There stand those within these Walls this Day, That shall see . . . when the *Vail* that has been upon the Hearts of the *Jewish Nation,* shall be taken off. . . . *That Great Day . . . hasteth greatly!*" The time had come for those who were "acting upon such *Principles* as we have at last produced in the *American Desarts* . . . [to] *Lift up* [their] *heads . . . because Redemption draweth nigh. The Hundred and four-score* years are almost out." The phrases reappear throughout the History itself—"an history" the author tells us, "to anticipate the state of the New Jerusalem"—in which "the mighty deeds of Christ" elevate the pristine New England venture to its highest epic and mythical proportions, acclaiming it as the "last conflict with antichrist" in "*the utmost parts of the earth*," and linking it at the end, in a summary millenarian invocation, to the ever-imminent, world-transforming, sabbatical "THINGS TO COME."[78]*

---

* The attempts to force the *Magnalia* into the category of lamentation alone (into the common view, that is, of the jeremiad) invariably distort its content. Thus in a recent study Peter Gay claims that when Mather says "*De Tristibus . . .* may be a proper title for the book I am now writing" he is implicitly referring to the History as a whole (*Loss of Mastery*, p. 69). In fact, Mather here refers only to the seventh Book, whose purpose is to relate "the Afflictive Disturbances . . . Suffered From . . . Various Adversaries: And the Wonderful Methods and Mercies Whereby the Churches [of New England] have been Delivered out of their Difficulties" (II, 487). The significance of those deliverances are indicated by the title of the last section of this last Book, "Arma Virosque Cano," a title

In this respect, the *Magnalia* is indeed the *magnum opus* of the seventeenth-century jeremiad. Its seven-fold division not only images the Sabbatism—which through "the successes . . . of his chosen people in the Wilderness" was becoming "within the last few sevens of years nearer to accomplishment"—but, figuratively, holds aloft the *"seven golden candlesticks"* of the old-New Jerusalem and sounds the seven trumpet blasts that bring down the walls of Jericho, the final barrier to the consummation of the New World mission. The *Magnalia* stands at the acme of the jeremiad tradition in another respect as well: in the total isolation of the author from his audience. The sharpening alienation of the ministers, I have suggested, emerges through the very vehemency of their commitment; the more tenaciously they uphold the ideal, the more they seem to be talking to themselves (and for themselves). The process may also be traced in explicit terms, most directly through their changing views on their role as "watchmen." To the first generation, the word denoted the society's architect-guardians, men by whose "watch . . . you may be made conquerors." During the sixties the concept takes on the sterner implications of a *"watchfull shepherd"* warning his flock against temptations. Through the seventies the orthodoxy comes to see itself as a beleaguered watch-man for God, a "gap-man" holding back the floodwaters of apostasy and berated by those he sought to protect. Thereafter, they retreat further and further from the world around them. Like the prophets who foretold their errand, they raise the voice of one crying in the wilderness; wearing the philistines' "reproaches as our Crown," they set themselves to search out the future as exiled watchers for the Second Coming.[79]

This development forms the second major element in the *Magnalia*'s background, inextricably bound up with its imaginative intensity. Mather knew that in fact the colony had strayed beyond recall, that

---

that recalls the Vergilian invocation with which Mather explicitly opens the work as a whole (as well as the numerous echoes from the *Aeneid* thereafter), and so suggests the epic proportions of his narrative. For Mather, of course, New England's story not only parallels but supersedes that of the founding of Rome, as his literary "assistance" from Christ excels the inspiration of Vergil's muse, as the "exemplary heroes" he celebrates resemble but outshine the men of Aeneas' band—not only as Christians but as sea-farers and conquerors of hostile pagan tribes—and, most spectacularly, as the millennium toward which the Reformation is moving provides the far more glorious antitype of the Augustan *Pax Romana*. Undoubtedly, the proper title for Mather's work is the exultant one he gave it: *Magnalia Christi Americana, The Great Acts of Christ in America.*

by 1700 "hardly any but my Father, and myself . . . appear in Defence of our invaded *Churches*," and that the history itself would elicit widespread derision and abuse. He knew, too, that (in Samuel Willard's words) "to be *Watchmen* depends not upon the acceptance . . . of [our] Message, but is an absolute duty . . . whether they will hear or no." That absolute *was* New England, despite "their" invasion. Norton in 1661 acclaimed the great pattern "that sheweth what *New-England* is"; seven years later William Stoughton feared that "New England [is] in danger this day to be lost even in New England"; by 1683, the orthodoxy acknowledged "that *N-England* is not to be found in *N-England*." Mather accepts the legacy with embittered pride. In his General Introduction to the *Magnalia* (the most animated apologia on record for American Puritan historiography), he declares that with the "stones they throw at this book . . . I will build my self a monument. . . . Whether New-England may *live* [horologically] any where else or no, it must *live* [chronometrically] in our History!"[80]

Cotton Mather's defiant and solitary vision caps the last stage in the growth of the jeremiad. The century-long effort to unite two disparate levels of thought—the system which bent history, theology, and sociology to that single purpose—is ultimately forced back into the "monument" of the individual mind and will, and creates its most pronounced success out of *de facto* failure, through the individual's capacity at once to say No in thunder to reality and to internalize the mission of his society. This achievement lends special force to recent charges that the outlook of the colonial community at large differs substantially from that expounded by "the articulate few." The contrast may be traced by juxtaposing the orthodoxy's accounts of the colony's progress to those set out in the town and village annals—or, in the early eighteenth century, by juxtaposing Joseph Morgan's imaginary *History of the Kingdom of Basaruah* with the "naturalistic" study of the first settlers by Thomas Prince. Morgan's work has with some justice been compared to Bunyan's *Holy War*, but what makes it distinctive (rather than blandly "Puritan-allegorical") is its direct and obvious link to the political sermons: obvious in Morgan's account of the "poor barren Country" and its exemplary heroes, in his denunciations of schism and backsliding intermixed with prayers for the promise of the earthly Kingdom, and, summarily, in his eschatalogical description of the Land of Basaruah, whose name images the union of flesh and spirit, and whose history, founded on a divine past and a greater *"Chilia*

Ete" to come, holds out "as a final solution" to New England's problems the imminent descent of New Jerusalem. Prince's *Chronological
History of New England in the Form of Annals* breathes the contrary
spirit of the inarticulate or silent majority. Though it reflects the ideas
of the Enlightenment (and so is said to open "a new epoch in American historiography"), the work owes its interest for later readers
chiefly to the "precise Realities" it conveys in common with the early
records. "The *orderly Succession* of these Transactions and Events,"
Prince rightly remarks, had been far "too much neglected by our
[seventeenth-century] Historians," whose "artificial Ornaments and
Descriptions [were meant] to raise the Imagination." The "naked
REGISTER" he offers in their stead, "comprizing only *Facts* in a
Chronological Epitome," informs us of various *minutiae* in public and
domestic life, such as "*Number of . . . Offspring*" and "*Changes of
Government*"; "the meer Tables and Calculations I was forced to
make," boasts the author, "would compose a Folio." Amidst these
overwhelming tabular realities the old rhetoric dissolves, Cotton
Mather's chiliastic statistics vanish into thin air, and the spiritual
giants of the cloud-capp'd *Arbella* migration deflate to a prosaic,
dedicated, hard-working people concerned with "*Maintenance of
Trade*" and "Acres of Land to be allotted."[81]

On one level, of course, the majority report presents the more
dependable chart of colonial development. Nonetheless, the central
themes of American culture undeniably attest to the pervasive and
sustained mass impact of the minority myth. The impact is felt even
in Prince's writings: implicitly in the *Annals* themselves—where "*Seven*
Great *Periods* of Time" precede the climactic entry of New England
upon "the stage of History"—and explicitly in his forceful election
sermon of 1730. Turning for "verification" not to orderly transactions
but to a host of seventeenth-century jeremiads, *The People of New-
England* portrays the Bay planters as "the particular antitypes" of the
"ancient Israelites," a supernaturally "form'd" and "redeemed" remnant
for whom "the desert . . . blossoms as a rose" and upon whom "the
Spirit from on high is poured." "May we be Emmanuel's land," Prince
concludes, "and may the Lord make us an eternal excellency . . . [so
that] the nations see our righteousness and all kings our glory." His
conclusion (along with the parallel and proof texts he draws upon
throughout) give voice to America's defunct first elite, betoken a
system so clearly outdated thirty years before that "nothing—not even

Mather's monumental and most significant history—could save it."
Yet far from being artificial ornaments they clearly express for both
orator and audience a fundamental cultural aspiration. They suggest
further, in this context, that the Puritan Jeremiahs did *not* speak solely
for themselves, not even in the twilight of the orthodoxy when those
watchmen-prophets were compelled to define their dream entirely in
opposition to reality. Somehow, evidently, beyond their day-by-day
individualism and materialism, and despite the distinction they made
in practical affairs "between the sacred and the secular," the prosaic,
industrious New England colonists found a deep pride or solace in
contemplating the long-typed-out New Israel, and welcomed a sense
of collective identity in that ideal city, set upon a hill "to bridge the
gap between God and man," which in naked fact they forged into
modern secular society. In miniature, this duality may be discerned
as a leitmotif in the careers of a variety of representative American
Puritans (Samuel Sewall, for example, pragmatist and visionary, or,
in a more complicated way, Cotton Mather, self-declared failure and
"matinée idol" of the election-day desk, author of the *Diaries* and of
Bonifacius, "herald of the Enlightenment as well as of the Great Awakening").[82] More largely, the duality is set forth in the contribution of
the political sermons to the national mind: a contribution which,
proceeding through conflicting currents of thought, intellectual and
popular, highbrow and lowbrow, reflects the twofold, schizophrenic
thrust of the *Magnalia* and of the complex rhetorical tradition upon
which it builds.

THE LEGACY OF THE JEREMIAD (1): THE POPULAR MYTH

Come, Thou—and then the Wilderness
Shall Bloom a Paradise,
And heav'nly Plants t'adorn and bless
O'er this wild Waste shall rise:

Then Peace shall in large Rivers flow,
Where streams of blood have run;
Then universal Love shall glow
And all the world be one;

Then num'rous Colonies shall rise,
A People all Divine,
To fill the Mansions of the Skies,
And bright as Angels shine.
                    Samuel Davies, "Pious Breathings" (1751)

The popular aspect of the legacy consists in the exuberant national eschatology embodied in the American Dream. That it is a secular, purportedly anti-Puritan eschatology neither conceals nor substantially blurs its origins. The jeremiad could survive the disintegration of the theocracy because, founded as it was upon the convertibility of horological and chronometrical, it could assimilate new and alien ideologies, outwardly transforming itself in the guise of the age, applying heaven's time to the temporal progress of even such hostile concepts as democracy and toleration. In all its protean shapes, beneath the diverse influences and the enormous social and intellectual shifts it comes to absorb, the Dream retains intact the essential structure of the political sermon: the moral distinction between the Old and the New World (as between Egypt and Canaan), the equation of material and spiritual blessings, the identity of the exemplary individual and the nation at large, the concept of a new Promised Land or second Eden (with its special calling and special trials), the myth of the founding fathers and the distinctive historiographic view which, overleaping the present, extends the myth into the Apocalypse that stands "near, even at the door," requiring one last great act in order to realize itself. What more or less varies from one period to another is the exact meaning of the myth and promise. Much of this has received comment in recent years. An impressive number of historians and literary scholars have discussed "the notion of the millennium as the key to an understanding of our religious and social history," or detailed the other attributes just noted, each of them closely inwoven into the fabric of American millennial thought.[83] It remains here, on this popular level, merely to stress the continuity of the jeremiad's outlook by reviewing some chief characteristics of the national sense of mission.

Perhaps the first example presents itself in the continuities between Puritanism and the Enlightenment. It need scarcely be said that the two periods differ widely one from the other; it has also been demonstrated that in certain basic ways the Deistic-Liberal expectations for America did not so much replace those of the theocracy as change their emphases. If the provincial leaders now spoke of a "*reasonable paradise*," if they beheld "the wilderness blossoming like the rose, under the . . . hand of *industry*" if for them the nation's "great design" meant the advance "God intended" towards the "rational and benevolent" era of religious liberty, they nonetheless relied consistently upon the framework of corporate errand established a century before, and therefore in effect bolstered the framework, justified it by bringing it up to date. As several historians have observed, they revealed "not a new purpose . . . but only new instruments." The old instruments rendered the New World future as a heavenly version of the church-state, the new ones as "a mercantile version of the philosopher's heav-enly city." In both cases, the intention was to display for the colonists' encouragement and the world's admiration America's ordained destiny. "Look back," intoned the influential rationalist William Smith, "with reverance back . . . to the mighty purpose which your fathers had in view," and now, look about you and "Behold . . . the garden of the Lord!" Can any doubt that "the Genius of America will . . . rise triumphant . . . [as the] chosen seat of Freedom, Arts and Heavenly Knowledge[?]" The thematic similarities between such appeals and those of the preceding age become sharper still in terms of scriptural analogy. Thus the loyalist Thomas Frink, in his election sermons for 1757 and 1758 addressing *"the Tribes of the Lord* [in] . . . *Boston,* the *New-English Jerusalem* . . . of the *New-English Israel,"* adopts the earlier phrases *en bloc* to hail the country's "dawning age." Nehemiah's "Reformation," he cries, "does most graphically set forth in Figure this wonderful Reformation of the . . . World in the latter Days"; it stands as a central literal-prophetic "Type" of that "unfolding" uni-versal scheme in which America foreshadows "the Jerusalem coming down from Heaven," the *"blessed Millennium* . . . expressed by *new Heavens* and a *new Earth."* So, too, about a decade later, Philip Freneau and Hugh Brackenridge, fired "by the spirit of Jeremy," affirm that "all our labours" are fashioning "Paradise a new." In accordance with the ancient promises, God's new country (our "Canaan here") "shall excel the old": "the Rising Glory of America" is blissful prelude to Emanuel's reign," the "happy" setting for the "final stage" of time.[84]

The same images and hopes mold much of the literature of the Revolution. As Loren Baritz, Merrill Jensen, and others have noted, the parallel with the chosen people influenced such disparate theorists as Jefferson, John Adams, and Washington, and left its imprint even on Franklin and Tom Paine. And as before the parallel betokened above all the fusion of the possible and the promised: for most leaders of thought (urging the colonists towards "a victory . . . providentially predetermined") the war meant that "the millennium may actually commence in the territories of the United States." To be sure, theirs was now a "chiliad distinguished by . . . economic plenty" and the enlightened pursuit of happiness. But as they developed the specifics of the program which was thus "to bring heaven to earth"—their "secular mechanisms for forwarding the Work of Redemption"—they retraced the outline of Puritan historiography. In repeated appeals for purgation and prayer, the revolutionary pulpit called upon Americans to make themselves worthy of their approaching restoration to the "halcyon days of settlement" *and* "to those 'happy times' [to come] in which both church and state would achieve their perfection," the times when "the dragon will be destroyed . . . and the kingdom of our God . . . established to all the ends of the earth." The dragon in conflict with the "saving remnant" was George III rather than Philip; but the conflict itself followed the familiar pattern. "America," explained Washington's protégé, Colonel David Humphreys, "after having been concealed for so many centuries . . . was probably discovered in the maturity of time, to become the theatre for displaying the illustrious designs of Providence." Jacob Duché and Samuel Sherwood, examining those designs in sermons "delivered on public occasions" in 1774, 1775, and 1776, applied the images of *The American Vine* and *The Church's Flight into the Wilderness* to the time when God "conducted our Forefathers to this new world . . . CAST OUT THE HEATHEN . . . AND THE DESERT REJOICED AND BLOSSOMED LIKE THE ROSE." "What period or event is there in all history," asked Sherwood, "which these expressions more exactly describe . . . ?" The rhetorical question covered not only the 1630s but extended *ipso facto* to the present and beyond, illuminating the "immense prospect" of America's "growing greatness." "I see new kingdoms and empires," exclaimed Duché in the theopathic language of the Mathers, "rushing forward . . . eager to disclose their latent powers; whilst the old ones on the other side of the Atlantic, 'hide their diminished heads,' lost in a superior lustre. . . . I see the last efforts of a powerful Providence exerted, in order to reclaim our wandering race from the paths of ignorance and error." And to the partisans of an independent nationhood he cried: "Go on, ye chosen band of Christian Patriots!"[85]

Whatever the precise weight we assign to such appeals among the many other factors that led to revolution, it seems incontrovertible that they constitute an important definition of national purpose and that, like the Puritan myth upon which they feed, they reveal a distinctive biblical rhetoric imposed upon history. In this form, and with

this import, they recur in the speeches of eminent figures of the time
like John Adams, Samuel Cooper, Ezra Stiles, and Samuel Williams,
all of whom, with Humphries and Sherwood and Duché—and with
the long-dead theocrats—beheld in America the crowning wonder of
"the uniform plan of Divine proceedings": a new Canaan which was
also the vineyard of the elect, an "Eden *redivivus* and . . . prototype
of the millennium" destined to rise "high above all nations" as "the
asylum of liberty and true religion," and so "to promote *the perfection
. . . of mankind.*"

This great continent is soon to be filled with the praise, and piety, of the
Millennium . . . *here*, is the stem of that wonderful tree . . . whose topmost
boughs will reach the heavens. . . . Divine protection has been given both
to those who have gone before us, and to ourselves. . . . What has been done
here, therefore, we may safely conclude will terminate in something great and
glorious. . . . We may be cast down; but we shall not, I think, be destroyed.
*Thus saith the Lord that created thee, . . . O Israel, "Fear not, for I have
redeemed thee. . . ."*

The period is now on the wing in which "the knowledge of the LORD shall
fill the earth as waters fill the sea." . . . Another sun, rolling around the
great Centurial year will, not improbably, have scarcely finished his
progress, when he shall see the Jew . . . "reingrafted into the olive, from
which he was broken off." . . .
   Let us still "in patience possess our souls," "for yet a little while, and the
indignation shall be overpast." . . . In this situation [the soul] instinctively
asks, How shall these evils be averted from ourselves and ours? . . . Think,
if you are at a loss on this subject, of the manner in which GOD *bare*
your fathers in this land *on eagles wings.* . . . Recal their numerous deliverances. . . .
   A work, thus begun, and thus carried on, is its own proof, that it will not
be relinquished.

It should be reemphasized that this outlook is by no means confined to
the pulpit and the political platform. Indeed, in its fullest imaginative
power during these decades, it permeates Joel Barlow's *Columbiad*
and Timothy Dwight's *Conquest of Canaan*, those epic-jeremiads
which celebrate the spirit of '76 as a "second birth" in the "brightest,
broadest, happiest morn of man," and Washington as a second Joshua

> . . . whose arm to Israel's chosen band
> Gave the fair empire of the promised land,
> Ordain'd by Heaven to hold to sacred sway,

and in whose final "vision" the glories of the Holy Commonwealth
spread the Messiah's "sway to earth's remotest end."[86]

The vision extends powerfully into the nineteenth century. Ernest Tuveson has demonstrated the strength of millenarianism in the writings of prominent men throughout the period (one of whose "frequent themes" concomitantly concerns the struggle "to get back to what, theoretically, the people . . . had once been"). Equally impressive is the range of millenarianism. It feeds into reform movements and utopian experiments (such as Brook Farm), defenses of industrial capitalism which exalt the United States as a "Heavenly . . . epistle to other lands," evangelical tracts insisting that "the churches must live and act for the millennium, for nothing less," treatises on Christian Socialism and the Social Gospel (through the 1890s), and, climactically at mid-century, the Civil War. Historians have cited various factors linking the Irrepressible Conflict with the Revolution; nowhere is the continuity more transparent than in the national vision which links both events with the seventeenth century. In the chiliastic antebellum atmosphere the defeat of the slave system appeared (as had once the abolition of "foreign tyranny") to constitute "the next step [in] . . . the realization of the kingdom of God on earth." Cotton Mather had predicted that with that realization "the *Africans* [would be] no longer treated like meer *Beasts of Burden*, as they are in the Plantations of cruel *Americans*." Now Northern patriots saw a way to hasten the great event—to reconcile the "character of God and the condition of man" in "this land of . . . millennial glory"—and it was, accordingly, first and foremost the champions of "an ideal American destiny who rallied to the standard, believing that the war would be a short cut to national perfection." For many of them, in fact, it was less a short cut than a sacred duty, at once their affirmative response to trial-through-affliction (or as Lincoln put it, in proclaiming a national fast-day in 1863, to " 'punishment inflicted upon us for our presumptuous sins' to the end that the whole people might be redeemed") and their acquiescence to "America's fulfilling its God-given mission as model and forerunner" of things to come. The battle itself constituted his retribution for their backsliding and their aid in the progress toward the "apocalyptic union of God and human society." Its outcome would usher in the Holy City in accordance with the dictates of scriptural teleology.[87]

In light of these anticipations, the immediate philosophical underpinnings of the abolitionist cause may well be traced to the transcendentalists. Spokesmen for "a faith inherited from the Puritan past," they declared themselves, as George Hochfield remarks, to be "living on the threshold of profound and glorious change" and "wrote of America as though its destiny was to be a messiah among the nations." For men like Bronson Alcott and Orestes Brownson, the country had attained a "vantage ground to which no people have ever ascended before." It had been supernaturally appointed "to unite the infinite and finite . . . [and] bind together the past and the future"; after some two hundred years success at length seemed at hand: "that cause which landed our fathers on Plymouth Rock" was drawing to its close. "Verily it is near. . . . Humanity awaits the hour of its renewal . . . against which 'the gates of hell shall not prevail.' " "Our whole history," exulted Emerson in a famous essay, "appears like a last effort of the Divine Providence in behalf of the human race"; and in his journals, in an unconscious paraphrase of Cotton Mather's distinction between the New World and the chimerical paradises of More and Budaeus, he recorded his conviction that "the Utopian dreams which visionaries have pursued and sages exploded, will find their beautiful theories rivalled & outdone by the reality, which it has pleased God to bestow upon United America. . . . Here glory finds his final home."[88]

To be sure, the transcendentalist vision does not simply duplicate that of the "fathers." Rather, it translates its theological meaning into a modern (chronometrical) political equivalent: the errand into the wilderness becomes for them "the errand of genius and love," and the reign of the saints an ideal democracy, a "dream of the emancipation and unity of man" and of "human perfection." A similar process of secularization informs other, parallel aspects of the nineteenth-century sense of mission. It underlies the prophetic-eschatological paeans—"a nation born in a day!"—that hail the frontier movement, the widespread belief in the United States as the political-economic New Jerusalem, and the delight with which prominent thinkers greeted the rise of technology, convinced that the railroad and factory systems would instantly make "the whole land . . . a garden," a "paradise" where "mechanical power is to be matched by a new access of vitality . . . imaginative, utopian, transcendant," a "human-divine" society, according to Henry James, Sr., where the acquisitive spirit would come to "typify" the "perfect" citizen's obedience to "the infinite divinity he finds within his soul." Most broadly, of course, the secular metamorphosis of the Puritan vision appears in the rhetoric of Manifest Destiny. Drawing upon every progressivist rationale, the adherents of that "annexationist" ideology justified their shoddiest maneuvers by biblical precedents proving what John O'Sullivan termed our "destined" role, as the "Nation of Futurity," " to manifest to mankind the excellence of divine principles; to establish on earth . . . the Sacred and the True." O'Sullivan's cry was taken up with an alacrity that leaves no doubt of its deep roots in the culture. Within a decade the same phrases came to characterize not simply July Fourth oratory but the works of distinguished philosophers, historians, and social scientists. Nor did it "describe . . . merely a [temporary] national mood." When Representative Robert Winthrop of Massachusetts announced that "the right of a manifest destiny to spread will not be admitted to exist in any nation except the universal Yankee nation" he did no more than repeat in the language of 1846 what his renowned ancestor had expressed almost twice-four-score and twenty years earlier aboard the *Arbella*. His words echo through the Gilded Age and into the present era, in presidential addresses on "the leadership which Almighty God intended us to assume" and journalistic eulogies to "the American task: to make the New World a place where the ancient faith can flourish anew, and its eternal promise at last be redeemed."[89]

It has been generally asserted that the "watershed in American history" from which these many currents of national self-definition flow may be located in the revival movement of the 1740s. From this point scholars have marked the progress of millenarianism as "the common and vital possession of American Christians," and, more broadly, have explored the impact of conflicting intellectual and theological impulses upon the populace at large. A more detailed examination of the continuities between the Great Migration and the Great Awakening may therefore serve summarily to highlight the popular contribution of the jeremiad. Certain of these continuities have of course long been noted; lately Alan Heimert has called attention to still others, at least by implication. He observes, for example, that Jonathan Edwards differed from English revivalists, including Whitefield, by his concern with corporate mission (as opposed to their exclusive emphasis on personal regeneration); and he portrays the Calvinists' polemics as a restaging of the Puritan controversies against Brownism on the one hand and Roger Williams on the other. According to Edwards, the colonial Establishment sinned in its "lax Method of [church] Admission," whereas the Separates erred in their otherworldly, individualistic

"spiritual pride"; Edwards' Middle Way, and that of the Calvinists
with him, patently mirrored the stand taken by John Cotton. While
tending towards a "visible" polity as "pure" as that of the Separates—
indeed, one that set out "to be as close an approximation as possible
to the 'invisible church'"—he yet held that the congregation must
not remove itself from the world but function as a type of New
Jerusalem and hence as "an [earthly] instrument for bringing it into
being." The Spirit's work for him was "not the salvation of individuals
but of society [engaged in] . . . the forwarding of the Work of
Redemption."[90] Professor Heimert records some of the remarkable
affinities in this outlook with that of the early New England theocracy,
but he also argues that fundamentally Edwards broke with the past.
Undoubtedly in many ways he did. In others, however, particularly
in his view of America, he seems to me in essence to have carried
forward the message of the political sermon.

Probably the most common distinction in these terms between
Edwards and his predecessors lies in the conception of the end time.
We are told that the Puritans' premillenarianism differs drastically
from Edwards' postmillenarianism: the former, assuming that only a
cataclysmic Judgment would usher in the reign of the saints, excludes
human participation from the process, and so chains "men to the
wheels of the Juggernaut of history"; the latter, presupposing that an
aetas aurea within history will herald the Second Coming, posits a
gradualistic temporal development. This distinction labels the early
colonist as a "conservative," "disposed to see individual objects as
'special providences'" (or as the machinations of "providential
caprice" without pattern), expecting his little experiment to produce
no major alterations, and looking in the distant future for the unprecedented displays of God's wrath. It conforms to the image of him as
a rigid logician who "eschewed" typology, an anti-imaginative disci-
plinarian for whom New England "was not a 'place' . . . but a 'way,'"
the Parousia very "far off," and the whole business of prophetic specu-
lation a dangerous fantasy. And it makes of Jonathan Edwards a radically innovative historical theorist: the first New World spokesman for
a non-Augustinian "optimistic view" of progress in which "the Last
Judgment no longer remained dissociated from the present" and, more
"startlingly" still, in which despite his adamant anti-Arminianism
"salvation through works . . . [became] a possibility in the American
landscape" since he conceived of "American destiny . . . in American

terms as the millennium itself." I trust it is by now apparent that every major facet of this outlook resembles that of the seventeenth-century political sermons. Edwards differed from the orthodoxy in his imported postmillenarianism not as an innovator but as a traditionalist with a new angle. The writings in which he sets forth these theories—such as *Thoughts on the Revival of Religion, A Humble Attempt to Promote Prayer, Distinguishing Marks of a Work of God,* and most lucidly *A History of the Work of Redemption*—are from this perspective jeremiads in eighteenth-century dress, whose gradualistic apocalypticism simply provides a more effective vehicle for the old historiography.[91]

Edwards' approach, like that of the early colonists, begins in the juxtaposition of the two levels of time. "The work [of redemption] itself," he writes, "and all that pertained to it, was *virtually* done and finished [before Creation], but not *actually*." "Virtually," in the eye of eternity, every occurrence merges perforce with all others, all of them absorbed in and "subordinate to the great ends of redemption": the "events of providence are not so many distinct, independent works of providence, but they are rather so many different parts of the work of providence; it is all one work." "Actually," on the human level, the "grand design" opens into a series of distinct successive works, a pattern "not of mere repetition, but of recurrence and periodically increased momentum," of the harmonious unfolding of shadow and substance towards the ultimate fulfillment. Conditional and absolute, then, interpenetrate; as with the Puritans, providential history becomes a function of divine history. And with the Puritans, further, Edwards applies the correspondence especially to "these latter days" (as the Cambridge Platform put it) wherein we may "expect [to] . . . enjoy in this world a . . . *more* glorious condition." What distinguishes his application is primarily the greater consistency of its logic. His forebears' "well-developed theory . . . of a long, historical process, evolving according to divine ordinance," surely shows a strong internal coherence. The concept it relied on, however, of "partile accomplishments"—of quantitatively increasing glory from the Promised Land and Nehemiah's Jerusalem to the New Promised Land and the New Jerusalem—was marred (from the "actual" standpoint) by the final *qualitative* change, the "shattering of the order of nature" that would precede the Sabbatism. Edwards, simply by moving the Sabbatism this side of the Parousia, welded the whole temporal progression into an organic whole. That was his contribution. Seen in retrospect, it had

monumental import for the secularization of the millennial idea (aug-
menting as it did, albeit inadvertently, the shift from the eschatological
hope "of a chosen Elect to that of a broad electorate"). In its own
right it represents the logical extension of an inherited *Weltanschauung*. "Though there has been a glorious fulfillment of . . . prophecies already," writes Edwards, describing the chiliad in phrases that
make the legacy unmistakable, "other times are only forerunners and
preparatories to this," as the release of Israel from Babylon was "typified of old by the sounding of the silver trumpets" and as it shadowed
forth in turn the Reformation and the approaching "harvest-time,"
when Christ will have "the heathen for his inheritance, and the uttermost parts of the earth for his possession, . . . [when a] nation shall be
born in a day . . . [and] the Jews shall be called in. . . . [For] as surely
as the Jews were [and are again to be] delivered . . . even so surely
shall all these things be accomplished in their time"—and the New
World church-state, as the apex of that movement, become another
renovated Mountain of Holiness, "Beautiful as *Tirzah,* comely as
Jerusalem, and terrible as an Army with Banners": *"Put on thy beautiful garments,* O America, *the holy city!"*[92]

Edwards' conviction that this movement had come to a climax on
this continent seals his indebtedness to the Puritan outlook. The arguments of those who would read into his conviction "a radical departure
in the thinking of American Protestantism"—an integrated con-
ceptualization of the Connecticut apocalypse that diverged from
earlier "ingenuities" by its reliance upon "Divine declaration, imper-
vious to . . . arbitrary tampering" (or horological "jarrings")—seem
to me only to enforce the multifold parallels. Above all, the latter appear in the details of Edwards' version of American history: his review
of providences past, from the sublime purpose behind the New World's
discovery through the golden age of the first planters—whose miraculous "circumstances" and "uprightness" indicate that "the dawn of
that glorious day [will rise] . . . in New England"—to the Awakening
itself, which Edwards describes (in contrast to an utterly degenerate
Old World) as a sort of union of the Great Migration and the theo-
cratic garden of God:

a great and wonderful event . . . [was] suddenly brought to pass . . . such
as . . . has . . . scarce ever been heard of in any land. Who . . . would have
thought that in so little time there would be such a change? . . . The new
Jerusalem in this respect has begun to come down from heaven, and per-

haps never were more of the prelibations of heaven's glory given upon earth. . . . [Multitudes all at once] resort to him when he orders his banner to be displayed . . . [and like] an army . . . obey the sound of [his] trumpet. . . . Christ in an extraordinary manner . . . appears in his visible [American] church in . . . the prelude of that glorious work of God, so often foretold in Scripture, which in the progress and issue of it shall renew the world of mankind . . . [and of which] the great temporal deliverances that were wrought for Israel of old . . . were typical.[93]

The reverberations from another century in this passage—in its picture of a sudden change that emanates "prelibations" of future marvels, of the mass conversions that call forth what Edward Johnson dubbed a new Army of Christ—imply not only incidental correspondences but a basic structural affinity in the historiographic "model." The implication receives decisive support from other key elements in Edwards' outlook. His description of the chiliad, for example, as a permanent, more brilliant Great Awakening follows the Puritan rendering of the end-time as the former age writ large; and though the specifics of his forecast necessarily include the "wonderful discoveries" of the Enlightenment, the total impression they convey (conceptually and rhetorically) is not unlike the "state of more perfect harmony" anticipated by the seventeenth-century divines: "there will be an end of . . . Quakerism, and Arminianism" and other heresies; "the new heavens and the new earth," introduced by the discovery and settlement of New England, shall be "set up in a far more glorious manner than ever before"; in that "time of great light and knowledge . . . [established] agreeably to Jer. xxxi. 34 . . . difficulties in Scripture shall . . . be cleared up" (and even "the poor negroes," now treated like "beasts," shall "be enlightened"); in general, it will be "a time of great holiness . . . excellent order in the church . . . [and, as promised in Jer. 31, 33,] the greatest temporal prosperity . . . [with] health and long life."[94]

The jeremiad vision seems also to stand behind Edwards' view of the season of national probation that is to precede this time of light. In contrasting the two periods, scholars have set on one side the Puritans' "cosmic despair"—their "lamentation for departed spiritual glories" coupled with "doubts and fears" concerning the "apocalyptic mystery"—and, on the other side, the Revivalists' "high cosmic optimism" in "mankind moving in nearly linear progress toward felicity." Professor Heimert goes so far as to suggest that "Edwards' most impressive achievement was to purge Calvinist millenarianism of all those [pessimistic] seventeenth-century elements." We have seen that the political sermons amply refute the charge of cosmic despair; equally evident is the eighteenth-century Calvinists' emphasis on the cataclysms, the "ferment and struggle," the "mighty and violent opposition" which would prepare for the overthrow of Satan's visible Kingdom: darkness and evil, they explained, are "always to be expected in the beginning of something very extraordinary." In both cases, the ministers clearly expressed their progressivism by fusing threat and promise—"*Sinai's* dreadful Thunder" and "the Jubilee Trumpet of the Gospel"—in order to affirm the Great Line of Time that led "maugre Sathan's might" into the "Sabbatism of the world"; and in both cases they couched their affirmation in the metaphor of a "time of testing," as Edwards and Bellamy termed it, through which Christ's American soldiers "could prove their . . . sainthood" and as it were assert their right to "make New England a . . . heaven upon earth."[95]

Insofar as the Calvinists' concept of trial varies from the jeremiad's strategy of reassurance by threat it does so in being more direct: in discarding the horological alternative even as a purely rhetorical consideration. When he descries the "very dark time" to come, Edwards at once brings forward the "great reason we have assuredly to expect the fulfillment" of heaven's promise; as he delineates the "great outward calamities . . . [as well as] spiritual calamities . . . and the exceeding prevalence of . . . wickedness . . . in our land," he gathers hope that "a happy change is nigh." His view of probation, that is, largely eliminates the dialectical complexities of the early political sermons, with their Janus-faced Jehovah and their twofold image of Jeremiah. What remains is the God of National Salvation. Not he who cast off the chosen people is New England's judge, but he who would in due time restore them: a God pining "to be gracious to us, as though he chose to make us monuments of his grace, . . . and wait[ing] only to have us open our mouths wide, that he may fill them" (precisely as he was waiting at last to "melt and renew" the whole Jewish nation); a God who finds—this time it is Samuel Davies speaking—that *"Mans Extremity is the the Lord's Opportunity,"* and for whom "our day of great apostasy and provocation [is] . . . a day of . . . wonderful works." In such circumstances the options presented to the colonist no longer entailed the prospect of collective failure, as though the Lord might irrevocably abandon his own cause. Instead, as in the latter-day jeremiad, the substance of "trial" devolved upon acceptance

or acquiescence, upon the willingness "of his professing people [to]
. . . arise and acknowledge God in his work." That "GOD intended to
write upon these [American] Churches the Name of *New Jerusalem*"
(in Sewall's phrase) was "virtually" established; it now simply "be-
hooves us to encourage . . . this work." Like the preachers of half a
century before, Edwards underscores "how dangerous it will be [for
him who will] forbear to do so" (he shows "himself to be the son of
the bond woman"), and how blessed is the man who complies. And
appropriately he turns to the standard Puritan parallel to drive home
his point:

> When God redeemed his people from their Babylonish captivity, and they
> rebuilt Jerusalem, it was . . . a remarkable type of the great deliverance
> of the Christian church . . . in the latter days. . . . But we read of some
> that opposed the Jews in that affair, and ridiculed God's people . . . and
> despised their hope . . . [and so brought] Nehemiah's imprecation upon
> [them]. . . . But for persons to arise . . . in such a work . . . will be to put
> themselves very much in the way of divine blessing. . . . [All this, which]
> may be argued from . . . those that helped in rebuilding the wall of
> Jerusalem . . . [is eminently applicable to] such a time as this, when God
> is setting up his kingdom on his holy hill [in America].[96]

Despite the differences between seventeenth- and eighteenth-century
Calvinist eschatology, historiographically Edwards' terms of trial correspond strikingly to those developed in the political sermons. For him
as for the colonial Jeremiah, individual salvation was linked to corporate success and both flowed into the divine image of the work of
redemption. In part, perhaps, this development may be seen to have
influenced both the late Puritan and the revivalist emphasis upon doing
good: upon the precept set out in Cotton Mather's Franckian-Joachite-
chiliastic *Everlasting Gospel,* and subsequently echoed by Edwards
(from exactly the same perspective), that "*Faith* is not *within,* if *Good
Works* are not *without,*" since "*Justification* before *God*" is inseparable
from "*Justification* unto *Men.*" In any case, the concept of personal
accountability within a predetermined historical drama seems significantly to relate the covenant-renewal ceremony to the Concert of
Prayer (commonly ranked "among the most impressive institutions
introduced to western Protestantism by the Awakening"), especially
as these concern the efficacy of supplication in making manifest the
destiny of America. For the Calvinist dilemma, like the Puritan, was
that in the long run good works were not good enough. Inevitably, it
would seem, the form came to belie the content. When the revivalist

ministers looked about them, they had to admit that the visible saints
too often labored "to build up a *Shell*, to form a meer *Carcase of
Godliness* . . . void of *Internal Vital Principles*"; enquiring no more
than "*What strict Duty requires of them,*" their flocks displayed "but
little inward heart conformity to [Christ]." As before, they concluded
that "that kind of [true] religion that was professed and practised,
in the first, and . . . best times of New England, [had] grown . . .
out of credit!" And again they discovered a chronometrical consolation
in the principle of man's inadequacy. "The insufficiency of human
beings," said Edwards, "to bring to pass any such happy change in
the world as is foretold . . . does now remarkably appear." The one
"effectual remedy" for God's straying and afflicted people was to raise
"their cries . . . for a general outpouring of his Spirit," to unite "in
Extraordinary Prayer, for the . . . *Advancement of Christ's Kingdom
on Earth, Pursuant to Scripture Promises and Prophecies Concerning
the Last Time.*"[97]

The immediate historical conditions which induced such appeals
had little to do with the events of 1675 or 1690 (though all involved
national distress or at least "dissatisfaction"). But the distinctive rhetorical quality of mixed self-congratulation and self-abasement makes
plain the continuity of the historical vision. Edwards bases his assurance in prayer on the figural precedents of the Israelites pleading under
Joshua and under Nehemiah: then, in leading them through the wilderness to Canaan and from captivity to Jerusalem, now when the
"work of his grace has been begun . . . in New England," God was
calling upon his people "to a spirit of prayer . . . [in] solemn, public
renewing of their covenant." Had he not told his prophets that the
remnant would be restored by miracle rather than human strategem,
"Not by might, nor by power, but by my Spirit"? It was their duty
to be "seeking by earnest prayer, the promised restoration" because,
according to the old tautological saving device, the prophecies *foretold*
that very "spirit of prayer, as preceding and introducing that glorious
day . . . when heaven shall as it were be bowed, and come down to
earth." If any sense of temporal testing remains here, any possibility
of reversal in mankind's journey from Canaan through Northampton
to New Jerusalem, it is on the level of the "present miserable foresaken
condition of the Jews" (for whose "instruction and conversion" we
pray), or of the suffering saint: the imploring Job in the political sermons, emblem of the theocracy, or, in Edwards' *Humble Attempt,*

Samson the type of Christ who "received strength to pull down Dagon's temple, through prayer . . . [as] the people of God, in the latter days, will . . . [aid in] pulling down the kingdom of Satan." "With what confidence," Edwards concludes, "may we go before God, and pray for that, of which we have so many exceeding precious and glorious promises to plead!" According to the *Magnalia's* General Introduction, those promises had been "opened" in the ends of the earth by the Ark of Christ "victoriously sailing round the *globe*," changing geography into *"Christiano-graphy,"* the terrestrial into the divine. Exactly a century later David Austin, speaking in his "Advertisement" to the *History of Redemption* of the trial now underway in the United States, reiterated the promise and reaffirmed the confidence in prayer through his eulogy to Edwards:

> Though to the eye of unbelief, the Ark may seem, *now*, to be involved in tempestuous weather, and soon to be foundered through the probable failure of borrowed [horological] strength; yet, to the joy of the passengers there are those, who, looking through the mists of human or infernal jars, do hail the approach of MILLENNIAL DAY!
> On the Ocean of the Millennium [our] . . . Ark shall safely and uninterruptedly sail.[98]

Austin's rather belligerently visionary tone intimates (what was explicitly noted by contemporaneous and later commentators) that Edwards' *History*, like Mather's, seemed to many passengers aboard the American ship of state at best something of an anachronism. Indeed, through the eighteenth century the now-articulate opponents of the myth had developed a "conscious rejoinder" (deliberately expressed in the "flattest of expository and logical prose"), an approach to the meaning of America based on the total severance of "civil polity" from the "dictates of heaven," and in general upon the dichotomy of human and divine implicit in Jer. 31:32. The errand of the first settlers, they taught, consisted in making "money for themselves and for the British empire"; its consummation depended upon the furtherance of *"Useful* Knowledge." Those who linked the errand with heaven's plan were confusing business pragmatics with what was intended "in a *spiritual Sense only"*: they were "feeding on visions of a holiness and happiness," as Channing said of the revivalist Samuel Hopkins, which might bear fruit in some "region of imagination" but never in this world. As for Edwards' "long labour to prove the *Millennium* shall begin in AMERICA," they could only smile nonbenevolently at such "vain

Conceit," and hold it up as a lesson for "modest" men to turn from what "it *is not for us to know*." No doubt these forerunners of Plotinus Plinlimmon played their part in the shaping of the nation. That they failed to dissuade the people from the Calvinists' *"Vain Imaginings"* is attested to in the enormous impact of the Great Awakening, and in "the amazing rhetorical power" that impelled subsequent American movements through the nineteenth century and into the twentieth, fired them with the vision of a "chosen band," "removed from the depravations . . . of Europe," going forth to receive "the heathen . . . for an inheritance and these uttermost parts of the earth [for] a possession" as "a prelude to the commencement of the Millennium."[99] Behind such sentiments—and beneath their technological, moral, political, or geographical terminologies—lies the chauvinistic euphoria of the Revolution, and, further back, the long labor of Jonathan Edwards. Their first and fullest formulation appears in the political sermons of Puritan New England.

THE LEGACY OF THE JEREMIAD (2): THE IMAGINATIVE REMAINDER

> I heard a voice saying, Woe . . . for the time is at hand. . . . But what surprized me most of all there stood a man with his hands and eyes lifted up to Heaven, pleading with GOD, . . . Lord remember thy covenant with thy people!
>
> Samuel Clarke, *A Dream, or the American Wonder* (1776)

> When the substance is gone, men cling to the shadows. Places once set apart to lofty purposes, still retain the name of that loftiness, even when converted to the meanest uses . . . as if the people of the present would fain make a compromise by retaining some purely imaginative remainder.
>
> Melville, *Pierre*

The second, darker aspect of the jeremiads, the discrepancy they assert between the real and the ideal America, as between preacher and public, receives its finest expression in the leading creative works of the nineteenth century. If the popular imagination exalted the national purpose by imposing the Puritan myth upon the country's secular achievements—and upon its stereotypical secular heroes (visible saint become independent agrarian, pioneer-entrepreneur, or self-made captain of industry)—the major writers were driven, like Cotton Mather, to internalize the myth. Like him, they wrenched the ideal

out of time by relocating it within the exemplary, and necessarily isolated, individual. The cultural polarities implied in this relocation (or
dislocation) have been suggested in varying terms by a wide range
of modern critics, especially since Lionel Trilling in 1940 called attention to the "radical disunities" in American thought. Richard Chase,
for example, has defined the nineteenth-century "romance" through
the image of a broken circuit between the ideal and the real; Leo
Marx has found in the conflict between pastoral and technological
ideas a "recurrent metaphor of contradiction" that opposes an out-
moded green landscape to traditional institutions, thus reducing the
novelist's "inspiriting vision" to a token of individual survival; and
Roy Harvey Pearce has described the impulse toward antinomianism
in American poetry ("the paradox of a Puritan faith at once reborn
and transformed") as a decisive cleavage between author and audience:
a search for an authentic poetic identity, as "for an instrument which
is beyond doubting," which forces the writer into an "ideal world" that
"is not grounded in ours" but lies beyond history, in the mind and art
of the self-celebrating poet. For all these critics, the American hero is
ultimately a quixotic isolatoe, shut off from the public he would liberate
by his uncompromising and nostalgic demands; while the artist he
projects stands detached from the process of national development,
a kind of superfluous and unsought Philoctetes who tries to win his
way out of alienation by creating a mythic antihistory designed somehow "to halt, to stem the tide of the on-going process itself."[100]

In a sense, this judgment returns us once again (and with a vengeance) to Plinlimmon's diatribe against solipsistic absolutism. But if
so, the parallel recalls at the same time the "strange, unique triumph"
wrought from defeat by the Puritan orthodoxy. For the antinomian or
renunciatory role by no means signifies *merely* either an aesthetic
withdrawal into the realm of pure art or a romantic-nihilistic gesture
against social forms. Those reactions have characterized certain periods
in other national literatures; what distinguishes the American—and
what distinguished the colonial Jeremiah—is his *refusal* to abandon
the social mission. In Newton Arvin's words, his "polarized emotions"
include, in addition to a proud apartness from the culture, "a deep
identification with it and with its meaning for the . . . future." Moreover, the two extremes, it would seem, interact and reinforce one another. It is precisely his sense of national identification that impels the
American writer toward isolation. When he retreats into the self, it is

characteristically to an *American* self, one which may serve as an inviolable haven for what A. N. Kaul terms the "ideal community" against which the palpable horological "defeat of the promise," like the gates of hell, cannot prevail.[101] It serves, in short, like the rhetoric of the political sermons, as a wall to protect the New World garden of God from history.

In its most negative aspect, the technique is manifest in *The Education of Henry Adams.* At first glance, the autobiography conveys the opposite impression: it deals incisively with the historical forces that remolded the land and seems to berate the author, with an unrelenting masochistic tough-mindedness, for his inability to adjust. In fact, however, Adams makes it clear that the failure lies not with himself but with reality. Or to put it another way, his insistence on personal failure in virtually every attempt he makes to "master the facts"—as student and educator, diplomat and historian, scientist and art connoisseur—provides in sum a brilliant metaphor for denouncing a world that has abandoned "absolute standards" and "ultimate Unity." To have been unprepared for "the surge of a supersensual chaos"—to feel "altogether alone," "suddenly cut apart" from a universe in which "the moral law had expired"—attests to the heroic stature of his bewilderment. And, of course, what lends special poignancy and power to that heroism, what makes "the question . . . personal," is "the word *America.*" In this context, his impassioned lament for the country's desecrated hopes becomes in effect—like the *Magnalia*—a massive, defiant vindication of his forebears' "great and noble dream."[102]

Adams's strategy reverses Cotton Mather's, but the final import in both works is distinctly comparable. The *Magnalia* dwells almost obsessively, to the point of deliberate distortion, upon the "vigorous unanimity" between fathers and sons. Its brief excursions into the actual present (generally in epilogues or appendixes) have the effect of caustic theatrical asides which suggest the drama's superiority to, and independence of, its degenerate audience, and so tend to enhance the "Utopia that was"—and, within the *Magnalia* itself, still is—"NEW-ENGLAND." Henry Adams preserves the Utopia by placing all emphasis on an America rushing toward self-destruction in what might be called an entropic inversion of the work of redemption. ("God's purpose," according to Jonathan Edwards, promises "to be fulfilled with ever-doubling acceleration by geometric enlargement of the saintly host.") In any case, his picture of backsliding and confusion, of aimless, "godless materialism," of the chasm between generations, is as bleak and outraged as the most virulent colonial jeremiad: "the American people had no idea at all; they were wandering in a wilderness much more sandy than the Hebrews had ever trodden about Sinai. . . . [They] had lost sight of ideas; [and] the American priest had lost sight of faith." But he never allows his reader to lose sight of the old faith. On the contrary, his condemnation of the American Dynamo gains much of its substance from the counterforce he presents, albeit obliquely and wistfully: in the figure of his grandfather, for example, the remote, majestic symbol of the "moral principle" of an earlier age (and in this respect not unlike Mather's depiction of John Cotton); or in Clarence King, "the ideal American," a "type and model . . . of what the American, as he [Henry Adams] conceived, should have been and was not."[103]

Most movingly of all, Adams offers himself as counterforce to the tragic course of history, in a self-portrait which despite its many deferential and ironic touches evolves into something of a mythic representation. The protagonist of the *Education,* as he himself tells us in the Preface, is not an *"Ego"* but a *"manikin."* He is less an individual, that is, than a representative man, representative of the great "inheritance with which he took his name," of the "pure New England stock" which had nourished the Adams dynasty, of the whole configuration of "ideal values" which encompassed the Constitution, the beliefs of the Puritan emigrants, and "the revolution of . . . 310 when Constantine had set up the cross." That is why he must be, like his grandfather, "an estray," out of time and place, and, like King, must end a failure. The counterforce he projects in himself is meant to evoke our admiration *because* it holds out no practical alternative. One set of "real" clothes after another is discarded as useless, until we remain only with the manikin itself—a poor, bare, forked animal in some sense, but at the same time a *"model* [that] . . . *cannot be spared* [since] *it is the only measure of* . . . [the] *human condition; it must* [therefore] . . . *be taken for real; must be treated as though it had life."* The reversal implicit in Adams' qualifiers ("taken for," "as though") foreshadows the daring reversal of values that constitutes the full meaning of the *Education.* The model-manikin becomes the measure of humanity insofar as it teaches us to resist horologicals. By its very incapacity to adapt to reality, or to adapt reality to itself, it becomes a type of the ideal America, and, possibly, even of that improbable future when "sensitive and timid natures" would regard the world "without a shudder."[104]

The prospect is faint indeed, beset with irrefragable contrary forebodings. The *Education,* as I have said, is the darkest outgrowth, the *fleur du mal,* of the jeremiad tradition; its positive counterpart blossoms in the major writings of Whitman and Thoreau. Of course, both men also set themselves in the main against the "implacable advance of history." Like Mather before them and Adams after them, they often assumed the prophet's sackcloth—in Thoreau's words, the "halo of light" surrounding "one of the elect"—in order to denounce their "heathen" countrymen, through the now-familiar rhetorical opposition of the temporal and the absolute. The American, Thoreau writes in *Walden,* prefers "to have fashionable . . . clothes, than to have a sound conscience" and lives as though he could "kill time without injuring eternity"; he has contentedly "settled down on earth and forgotten heaven." So, too, in *Democratic Vistas,* Whitman contrasts the "fervid and tremendous IDEA," the "religious element" that informs "the true nationality of the States," with the country's actual "unprecedented materialistic advancement . . . canker'd, crude . . . saturated in corruption," one which threatens "to eat us up, like a cancer"—which has *already* made "our New World democracy . . . an almost complete failure in its social aspects," and surely "the most tremendous failure of time." "To work in . . . and justify God . . . is what America means," is the divine pattern, as Norton and other seventeenth-century ministers had expressed it, stamped on the forehead of the national mission. What America *is* stands "grotesquely" displayed all around us: in "all this tremendous and dominant play of solely materialistic bearings" that points toward "a destiny . . . equivalent in its real world to that of the fabled damned."[105]

Neither Thoreau nor Whitman, however, surrender to Adams' sense of futility, to the overwhelming, almost paralyzing bewilderment that seems to diminish the *Education's* manikin-hero. Instead, they resolve the dichotomy between "meaning" and fact through the visionary optimism that marks the theocracy's last solitary watchmen. With the beleaguered author of the *Magnalia,* they maintain that whether the "true America" may live historically anywhere else or no, it must live in their creations. Each became, as Alcott said of Thoreau, "the sole signer of the Declaration and a Revolution in himself"; each overcame his despair by finding in his soul the country's "convictions, aspirations, [and] . . . absolute faith"; each sang *en masse* by singing himself. In the case of Thoreau, this process has been amply demonstrated. His "Walden site," as a recent critic has noted, "cannot provide a refuge, in any literal sense, from the forces of change. . . . In the end Thoreau . . . removes [the national ideal] from history, where it is . . . unrecognizable, and relocates it in literature, which is to say, in his own consciousness, in his craft, in *Walden*." Most fully, perhaps, the process is illuminated by the influence upon Thoreau of the idea of the West, which he identified at once with America and with his own deepest aspirations:

> For Thoreau, there were two Wests: an ideal West . . . and a real West, which he hated and feared. . . . "The whole enterprise of this nation [he wrote] . . . is totally devoid of interest to me. . . . No, they may go their way to their manifest destiny which I trust is not mine." . . . The West was not [for him] a place or a direction, but an idea, a metaphor . . . [and] he knew he could make his case only . . . by making the West, and the Western pioneers, into metaphors more significant than the things themselves. . . . [He achieved this decisively in *Walden*, where the] Pond is his personal frontier between earth and Heaven, between natural and divine . . . [a frontier which] insists . . . on the identity of . . . physical and spiritual presence. . . . What the West stands for [as it is thus transformed in Thoreau's work] is . . . the future of the American continent, and then by analogous transfer . . . the [ideal] American, this new man . . . [and finally] the soul of the [true] American writer.[106]

Despite its very different phraseology, the process of this "analogous transfer" fundamentally reflects the outlook established two hundred years before. Thoreau's disgust at the whole corrupt enterprise leads him beyond Adams' despondency to a chronometrical historiography which supplants the nation's manifestly actual destiny with its platonic-metaphorical essence in the soul. The "glorious Edifice of Mount Sion," thundered Edward Johnson in 1654, and the world-rending earthquakes that are to herald the coming of the Son of Man, shall "rise from the West." Cotton Mather, believing the new age had already dawned, announced that "We have now seen the *Sun Rising in the West*"; twenty years later Edwards reiterated that "the sun of the new heavens and new earth . . . shall rise in the west, contrary to the course of this world," and in 1774 Jacob Duché saw "the *Sun of Righteousness* shining forth with seven-fold lustre to the utmost bourn of this western

Continent." Thoreau too accepts the prophecy—the sun "is the Great
Western Pioneer whom the nations follow. . . . Else to what end does
the world go on, and why was America discovered?"—but the movement for him serves to reject "the things themselves" by embracing the
things to come. "We go eastward to realize history . . . we go westward as into the future," a period which will prove "more imaginative
. . . clearer, fresher, and more ethereal" than any since "Adam in
paradise," and which will make real the "island of Atlantis, and the
islands and gardens of the Hesperides . . . [that] Great West of the
ancients, [hitherto] enveloped in mystery and poetry." Thoreau's
Matherian-Emersonian contrast between fable and realized history
on the one hand, and, on the other, reality and the ethereal future, is
palpably the democratic-Western translation of what the colonial
clergy had stated in Christian-apocalyptic language, that the promise
effectually expunged the material progress they "hated and feared."
And since the past-future promise rested with the country's self-exiled
spokesman, since the "realization of the Golden Age"[107] depended as
it were upon his natural-spiritual vision, it was in him that "the future
of the American continent" resided. Needless to say, his view incorporates a diversity of influences (many of them from Europe and the
Orient), but its chief source, I believe, and its overall direction, may
be found in the literature of early New England.

Whitman's view of America has a similar direction and source. If,
for all its concern with the country's bearings, *Democratic Vistas* has
proved disappointing as an investigation of "political realities . . . of
society or of history"—if, like *Walden*, it seems to have ignored all
concrete social means for reform—the reason, as in *Walden*, leads
back to the antihistorical myth developed from Puritanism. Indeed,
Whitman's great political sermon intensifies both main themes, the
futurism and the subjectivism, through which Thoreau formulates
his frontier dream. When he observes "the people's crudeness, vice,
caprices," Whitman acknowledges perforce that "the lowering darkness falls . . . as if to last forever." But when he turns to consider
God's promise to his people, "and it is as fire in his bones," his voice
and outlook alter altogether. Looking now towards the horizon from
the Pisgah heights of "immortal courage and prophecy," he sees "un-
parallel'd success" for the United States. "Amid opposing proofs and
precedents" below, he assures the nation, unconditionally, of a destiny
"outtoping [all] the past": "its possibility (nay certainty), underlies

these entire speculations." We recall Increase Mather's eschatological dialectic, whereby the "red and lowring clouds" of wrath come to signify the "glorious things coming to their birth." And though Whitman's speculations rely "almost entirely on the future," the end he predicts is no less certain than that of Increase for all its temporal indeterminacy:

[Perhaps] not ours the chance ever to see with our own eyes the peerless power and splendid *éclat* . . . arriv'd at meridian, filling the world [like the "illustrious Epithalamium" Samuel Sewall described] with effulgence and majesty. . . . [Notwithstanding,] there is yet, to whoever is eligible among us, the prophetic vision . . . [inspired by the] holy ghost, which others see not, hear not—with the proud consciousness that amid whatever clouds, seductions, or heart-wearying postponements, we have never deserted, never despair'd, never abandon'd the faith.[108]

What the never-abandoned, ever-elusive American future meant most deeply for Whitman reveals in exaggerated form both the "folly" and the achievement of the jeremiad tradition. Philosophically, his meaning is best stated in the doctrine of personalism which proposes to "resolve the contradictions of democracy by furnishing archetypal examples of perfect democratic persons" (like a procession of New England saints projected into the Sabbatism). The national purpose, in this view, consists in an evolution toward its exemplary "moral and religious character" and gathers strength from its capacity "unerringly [to] feed the highest mind" which will in turn embody the "final meaning of Democracy." Poetically, Whitman realizes this fusion of perfect individualism and the paradise to be regained through a pseudodialogue between self and community—a dialogue which really functions to *dissolve* society into the omnivorous first-person singular. "The United States themselves are essentially the greatest poem," according to the famous claim of the 1855 Preface; we are urged to read *Leaves of Grass* as drawing its "fullest poetical nature" from the inhabitants and geography of the nation it hymns. Modern critics from D. H. Lawrence to Charles Feidelson have shown that it works in precisely the opposite direction, constituting above all

an act of self-discovery, self-involvement, and self-creation carried through to completion. . . . [Whitman thus] gives the world a new meaning—transforming it by alienating it from itself and the crude, workaday, anti-poetic reality which characterizes it. Doing so, however, he intensifies his own alienation. . . . His conception of poetry not only made for his poems; it also protected him from the world to which he addressed them. For it

demanded that the anti-poetic world . . . have no claim to reality at all.
This is to a degree of mutilating concept of reality. Yet it is at the same
time . . . for Whitman perhaps *the* source of strength.[109]*

Whitman's mutilation of reality serves as a source of power because
it protects not only himself but, simultaneously, the "IDEA" of the
United States. Like Thoreau's, his social vision, transforming horologicals into "a sort of Hegelian Absolute," *necessitates* "belief only in the
self." Long before, the author of "the greatest Jeremiad of them all,"
considering "the provocation, which this our Church-History must
needs give," felt driven to cry out: " 'tis COTTON MATHER that has
written all these things; *Me, me, adsum qui scripsi.*" The outburst of
egocentrism, he tells us, stems from his foreknowledge of "a recom-
pense which will abundantly swallow up all discouragements"—that
of reconstructing in his "rhapsody" New England's "predestinate design," or as Austin Warren has put it, of preserving in his "Wonder
Book" "a Platonic Idea [of the colony] like that of the Prelapsarian
Adam." Whitman's egocentrism, though far more complex, expresses
a similar defiance and harbors a similar intimation of immortality.
Solitary, singing in a perfect West, his "self" merges, in his own words,
with the "subject" of his epic—"Adam, as central figure and type"—
and with that protean *"Person* . . . (myself . . . in America)" in
whom "America's busy, teeming, intricate swirl" shall be swept "to
the infinite future." And in *Democratic Vistas*, with an alienated-
millenarian fervor that rivals the *Magnalia's*, he hails the "self" as "the
divine literatus," the country's watchman-savior who shall "mediate to
. . . Democracy, interpret yet to them" the inter-Sabbatical Line of
Time. The "priest departs," he continues, along with his church history; in his place there comes the American Poet, "prophet and bard,"
whose "great original literature" will bridge the "vast gulf of difference
[that] separates the present accepted condition" from its "grandest
result": will "become [at once] the justification and [the] reliance"—
indeed, "the sole reliance"—of the national errand and its "infinite"
promise, "a new earth and a new man" in the New World.[110]

The polarity I have suggested between Whitman and Thoreau on

---

* "On the whole," Thoreau wrote concerning *Leaves of Grass*, "it seems to me
very brave and American"; then, commenting on his conversation with Whitman,
he added: "I remember that . . . in answer to him as representing America, [I
said] that I did not think much of America" ("Concerning Walt Whitman,"
in *Literature in America*, ed. Philip Rahv [New York, 1960], p. 149).

the one hand and Henry Adams on the other is not characteristic of their times. Most writers incorporate both aspects in a more or less uneasy balance. The nature of this contrapuntal view (already apparent in the late seventeenth-century orthodoxy) may be discerned in the leaders of the Great Awakening: first in Jonathan Edwards, driven by intellectual solitude to believe that he only of all Americans grasped the course of national history, and later in those of his followers who sensed that their program had failed and fled from a "confusing" present to the sanctuary of their myth, not as Separating purists but consciously as exiled seers tending the visionary flame that revealed "America a brighter type of heaven." In the nineteenth century this tension manifests itself in every area of thought, underlies the writings of numerous would-be patriots who, with Lincoln Steffens, tried unsuccessfully to make peace between the process of corruption they saw and "the holy commonwealth on earth" they envisioned. It rises to perhaps its most intense pitch in the historiography of the period. Advancing the concept of progress as a "divine law" or "timeless absolute," George Bancroft and subsequent major historians depicted the United States as the summit of human effort in terms of "a detailed, critical gloss upon the dream," a "scientifically composed" lamentation over the country's poisonous *de facto* materialism. They saw their role, David Noble observes, as "guardians" or "high priests" (Jerusalem's watchmen) chosen to "demonstrate that which is truly . . . American and that which is artificial and alien." In the latter category they placed "historical complexity," in the former "the organic unity of the real and the ideal . . . in the promised land"; and they attempted to gain the one by shutting out the other, to win back "the New World Eden" by recourse to what amounted to an antihistorical affirmation of the nation's "timeless harmony," or else (in the case of the active social reformers among them) by calling upon Americans to return to an outdated—often simply a utopian—way of life.[111] Their attempt appears almost to duplicate the Puritans'. It falls short because, being historians rather than poets or divines, they lacked the means with which adequately to overcome "complexity": they had neither the old millennial faith nor the new faith in the imagination. Like Adams, they could not bring themselves to impose a supernatural "solution" upon the future; unlike Whitman, they could not compensate by subsuming the historical within the absolute Self. Their writings constitute, certainly, a significant achievement in modern historiography and in "romantic art"; but in light of the great comprehensive pattern they (unwittingly) evoke, their vision seems incomplete, blighted for all its considerable power by the unresolved vacillation between exultation and gloom.

This tension takes its most debilitating form, I think, in Emerson's desperate and "dogmatic" optimism. Stephen Whicher has shown how the absolute hope that Emerson vaunted publicly was largely a makeshift cover for the void he felt in private, a too-much-protested (and therefore sometimes callous) faith thrust upon him by "the ghastly reality of things"; and his notion of the country, correspondingly (or consequently), tottered uncertainly between extremes: between misanthropy and chauvinism, nature worship and technology worship, the cult of the hero and total egalitarianism, shrill condemnation of a "corrupt populace perilously close to destroying . . . the ideal" and uncritical acclaim of an America radiating "the example of moral superiority to all nations." If the great nineteenth-century historians—partly because of their concept of the nature of their craft —had not enough conviction either in the actual or in the imaginary to sustain the jeremiad vision, Emerson had too much of both. Insecure in those inner spiritual recesses upon which his philosophy depended, he developed too cloistered or anarchic an individualism, too indiscriminate an attraction for practical affairs. It seems almost inevitable that he should eventually have turned to the more reliable alternative. By the time of the Civil War his doctrine of complete self-reliance, which had inspired Thoreau and brought Whitman's simmering confidence to a boil, had become at most a subsidiary function of his vehement espousal of the popular myth. The serenity of his last years glows with the self-satisfaction of a man who has rid himself of a lifelong irritant. "Now," writes George Frederickson, "there is no ambivalence; the practical man has won out completely." With an audible sigh of relief, Emerson turned with increasing admiration for Manifest Destiny to the actual America: the "social unities embodied in the state, . . . the sense of a social and historical whole which transcends the individual, . . . [and the] order shaped by history" as this expressed itself in the burgeoning civil institutions of God's Country.[112]

The same ambivalence, we know, could also generate a remarkable creative energy. It accounts for the strange eloquence of Cooper's Leatherstocking Saga, which builds upon the paradoxical dual commitment to class society and to the legendary frontiersman. Cooper's

own commitment to society seems at times to have led him wholly to
adopt the popular myth; it is in the latter terms that he discusses the
New World's "mysterious concealment" in *The Heidenmauer* as the
finale of the "grand movement of Providence" and in *The Crater* alle-
gorizes the United States as "an Eden of modern times," created "in
the twinkling of an eye" to lead humanity "towards the summit of . . .
perfection." But his ideal on this level stopped short at certain political-economic convictions; ultimately, it entailed a concept of aris-
tocracy, not of America, and these novels, accordingly, express little
more than angry social commentary. His fiction succeeded as art when
he discovered, as it were beyond horologicals, a modern correlative for
paradise which was at once specifically national and deliberately antihistorical. He elaborated it through "artificial ornament and descriptions meant to raise the imagination" in the image of a vanishing prairie
that becomes increasingly vital and realistic as it recedes further into
timelessness, and in the figure of an outsider who embodies the country's "beautiful myth"—its "visionary answer" to the ugly violence of
its history—and who is rendered useless by what Cooper proudly calls
"the march of the nation across the continent." A similar dual commitment appears (far more forcefully) in the best work of Mark Twain.
It characterizes, for example, his apocalyptic eulogy-lamentation over
industrial America in *A Connecticut Yankee,* and, with still clearer
reverberations from the Puritan past, the minority report he offers in
Huckleberry Finn, where the author's partial attachment to the "gen-
teel tradition" conflicts with but finally functions to highlight the
"subversive" imaginative meaning of the novel: functions by the very
discrepancy it creates between plot and content to enhance the tiny
"community of saints" whose "escape from society is but [its] way of
reaching what society ideally dreams of,"[113] and whose raft becomes
(with Natty's hill top and Thoreau's Walden) the terminus ad quem
of the city on a hill.

In the twentieth century, the tension between the twin traditions
of the political sermons has spiraled past ambivalence to something
like a state of conscious, self-denunciatory schizophrenia. The progression, if it is such, may be seen in the difference between Huck Finn
and the Beat or Hippie drifters, the self-proclaimed Children of
Whitman caustically "awaiting / a rebirth of wonder / . . . waiting
for the Second Coming / . . . waiting / for *them* to prove / that God

is really American"; or earlier, in the distance between Natty Bumppo
and Fitzgerald's Gatsby, bedazzled by the "green light" of the dollar
and the ideal, a carefully composite American standing at once for
the "valley of ashes" and for a "Platonic concept" that fuses "the last
and greatest of all human dreams" with "the orgiastic future that
year by year recedes before us." Most recently the process finds expression in the rhetoric of the New Left. Dissent in America has
leaned heavily as a rule upon the concept of collective destiny; the
student rebels of our day have followed the pattern, but often only to
invert it, to call into question both the fabled future and their own
vaunted idealism. In his confessional account of the Columbia Riots
(to cite a highly typical instance), Dotson Rader juxtaposes the two
streams of thought so as to reduce each to a self-aggrandizing illusion.
It goes without saying that he treats the illusions differently. The
majority belief—"that this land [is] . . . Holy Canaan Country" and
its inhabitants "the Remnant after the Captivity"—he condemns with
"redemptive hatred" through the text *Who is this who cometh from
Edom with his garments red with blood?*" The "purism" of the young
radicals, for whom "the desired was more actual . . . than reality,"
he portrays with pride and compassion. Yet his irony clearly cuts both
ways. It serves not only to renounce the popular myth but also, *and
for similar reasons,* to point up the "vain imaginings" of his "neo-Cal-
vinist" comrades: of the young suicide who had "acted in the name of
the promise of America," for instance, and the Negro homosexual who
demands (in an unintended parody of the Puritan chiliasts): "When's
America going to come true for us? How long we got to wait? . . .
How long, baby, how goddamn long?" In both cases the rationale
rests upon the same "national abstraction"; and in both cases the abstraction is belied by the same "barbarian" facts.[114] The title Rader
selects to sum up his own attitude, *I Ain't Marchin' Anymore,* recalls
not so much Thoreau's defiant self-assertion as the *vanitas vanitatis*
which marks Nick Carroway's farewell to the dreamworld of Gatsby.

This is not to deny the obvious: Rader's book abounds in the rhetoric
of the barricades. But the direction this takes would seem to lead him,
with his "compatriots," as far from Thoreau's solitary drummer as it
does from the American Army of Saints marching into the Apocalypse.
Having glimpsed at the end of those roads the mutually reflecting
lights, *come iri da iri,* of Walden and the *Theopolis Americana,* they
turn, or rather half-turn (their gaze lingering upon "the Foursquare

City with gates of pearl") toward the actual cities of the plain—"back to reality . . . engagement . . . social struggle"—with Nick Carroway part of that "immense metamorphosis" James Baldwin speaks of as characterizing our era, "a metamorphosis which will, it is devoutly to be hoped, rob us of our myths and give us back our history." The most vivid rendering of this transition comes in *The Armies of the Night*, Norman Mailer's "diary-essay-tract-sermon" about his "love affair with America." What he remembers and seeks, he tells us, in undertaking his march to the Pentagon, is "the land where a new kind of man was born . . . America, once a beauty of magnificence unparalleled"; what he finds is "a beauty with leprous skin," disfigured by an "irredeemable madness": "the America he saw in family television dramas" and "had always tried to believe . . . did not exist." His overt solution of the dilemma returns us by various routes back through Whitman and Adams to seventeenth-century New England: by its "romancing with Apocalypse" while raising a "mythic plaint" against "the disease that has betrayed the past," by detailing "the failure of American history" at the same time that it reveals in the author an unrepentant "lost leader" whose "fiction [is] to defend us in the face of a dark, disappointing [future]," and above all by its distinctive equation of self and society:

> Then he began writing his history of the Pentagon. It insisted on becoming a history of himself. . . . Yet in writing his personal history . . . [he sought] to elucidate the mysterious character of that quintessentially American event. . . . [And given this relationship, it was] fitting . . . that he should be an egotist of the most startling misproportions, outrageously and often unhappily self-assertive. . . . Once History inhabits a crazy house, egotism may be the last tool left to History.[115]

Mailer's assertive and unhappy egotism, however, resides only in part within the jeremiad tradition; it also mirrors what he calls the enervating "schizophrenia" at the country's "insane center." Earlier he had declared himself ready to discard the novel "in order to express political agony" and help remedy "America's cancer-breeding repressions." Earlier still, he had rejected history: "the American writer," he said in 1953, "works best in opposition" to "the American reality" (being "nourished" by "a sense of his enemy"), and, besides, has an obligation to replace the "triumph of fact" with "the prerogatives of metaphor." Here he attempts to incorporate fact and metaphor, to bestride both of "the two worlds of America [which had] drifted irretrievably apart." What results is alternately brilliant reportage and brilliant fiction, history as the novel or the novel as history, but not both simultaneously. Compared therefore to Whitman or even to Adams his vision of the nation, and of himself, seems indecisive, rent by an unresolved duality of purpose. As Alfred Kazin notes, the Pentagon demonstration taught Mailer once more (what Cotton Mather lamented in the solitude of his diary) that the country's leaders had betrayed "the political and moral sages who founded our culture. . . . 'They' [now] have all the power and 'we' have just imagination." He also learned what Cotton Mather (who would have substituted "the divine scheme" for "*just* imagination") adamantly denied, that power is ultimately far the more crucial of the two, not only in the "narrow" discrete view of events but as a definition of the meaning of America. And to the degree that he commits himself to this insight—as historian and reporter—Mailer explicitly revolts against the "need of Mission" with its "demand that the American Dream be realized" and "the City of God . . . be constructed on this unhappy planet," repudiates the aesthetic shelter of the "quintessentially American" self for the real if crazy house of history.[116]

The Armies of the Night, then, from this (partial) perspective, represents a last stage in the evolution from *God's Promise to His Plantations*. The apex of the tradition appears a century before, a product of the mixed exuberance and despair of the American Renaissance, in the sermon that frames the action of *Moby Dick*. Melville's changing views of national mission encompass the whole gamut of nineteenth-century responses, and he brings them all to bear upon the meanings of his epic. His "American apocalypse" on one level cries doom over the country's predatory "barbarism," like *Clarel's* Ungar. On another level, its vision looks toward the savage satire of *Pierre*, directed both against the illusion that the institutions of "this new Canaan" possess "divine virtue" and against the fatal self-deceit of those, like the novel's hero, who "in their clogged terrestrial humanities" sail blindly after "heaven's ideals" and "make a courageous wreck." On still another level, it celebrates the prophet-leader heralded in *White-Jacket*, "who ever marches at the head of his troop and beckons them forward," certain that "the van of the nations must, of right, belong to us . . . [since] our final haven was predestinated . . . at Creation." All of these strains coalesce in Father Mapple's discourse on the trials of

Jonah. Fortified from his congregation in his "lofty pulpit" and speaking with "heavenly enthusiasm" in the "form of Jeremiah's Babylonian prophecy," the minister extols the courage of the "annointed pilot-prophet" for proclaiming his "unwelcome truths in the ears of a wicked Nineveh." "Delight is to him," he concludes,

—a far, far upward, and inward delight—who against the proud gods and commodores of this earth, ever stands forth his own inexorable self. Delight is to him whose strong arms yet support him, when the ship of this base treacherous world has gone down beneath him. Delight is to him, who gives no quarter in the truth, and . . . who acknowledges no law or lord, but the Lord his God, and is only a patriot to heaven. Delight is to him, whom all the waves and billows of the seas of the boisterous mob can never shake from this sure Keel of the Ages.[117]

For all its manifold ironies, Mapple's image carries an immense significance for the novel (and for the culture which the novel expresses and defines), constituting "in itself a prophecy, of which the ensuing narrative is a fulfillment," and bespeaking simultaneously the ambiguous glory of the national quest and the tragic solitude of its watchman. In its immediate context, it looks forward to the hymn, "There is a Land of Pure Delight," which rings "full of hope and fruition" through the cold Christmas air when the *Pequod* sets out on her voyage—as it might have sounded, with equal appropriateness, at Southhampton pier in 1630 after John Cotton's farewell address:

> Sweet fields beyond the swelling flood,
>   Stand dressed in living green.
> So to the Jews old Canaan stood,
>   While Jordan rolled between.

In the context of this study, Mapple's sermon constitutes a final testament to the import and influence of the seventeenth-century political sermons. Its rhetorical forms serve summarily to demonstrate that their legacy lies neither in their "logical propositions" nor in the actual institutions they support but in their "suggestive, provocative, poetic speech": ultimately in their act of imagination.[118] And the ambivalent-heroic-tragic "spirit of prophecy" it conveys illuminates the long development which originates at the absolute Greenwich time of the Great Migration—with the chronometer carried from Babylon to the ends of the earth—and brings to their furthest reach the challenge and promise of that last and greatest of all human dreams which launched the *Arbella*:

I will appoint a place for my people Israel, and will plant them that they may dwell in a place of their own, and move no more. . . . I will [also] set up thy seed after thee. . . . I will be his father, and he shall be my son. If he commit iniquity, I will chasten him with the rod of men, and with the stripes of the children of men: but my mercy shall not depart from him, as I took it from Saul, whom I put away before thee. And thine house and thy kingdom shall be established for ever . . . according to all these words, and according to all this vision. . . . (2 Sam. 7:10–17)

Acknowledgments

Work on this monograph was aided by summer grants from the Huntington Library and the American Council of Learned Societies.

APPENDIX A

AMERICAN PURITAN RHETORIC

The intricacy of New England rhetoric—the dynamic tension between the spiritual, the temporal, and the developmental-typological points of view—may be illustrated by comparing the following five passages. Taken together, they suggest the basic continuity of American Puritan thought through the century. Taken separately, they suggest the diversity within that continuity: a diversity which (as I try to demonstrate) leads to shifting balances and various efforts at resolution. The first passage reveals how closely the purely spiritual or Augustinian mode—though characteristically restricted to the individual "journey"—relates to a collective experience. The second and third passages show how easily the jeremiad could shift from the historical to the atemporal mode, and, conversely, from the static parallel with Israel to gradualistic progression. The fourth passage is a clear demonstration of the linear-spiritual view of New England's mission, as distinct from (but not opposed to) both the providential and the Augustinian view of the parallel with Israel. The fifth passage combines a number of citations affirming the relation of individual and community through the figure of Job, a favorite "exemplary saint" in the treatises on grace, and, typologically, a foreshadowing of Christ not only in his *agon* but in his final triumph.

1. Michael Wigglesworth, *Diary*, in *Proceedings of the Colonial Society of Massachusetts*, XXXV (1946), 423–24: "Hezekiah's heart is lifted up, but wrath comes upon Judah and Jerusalem: all must go into captivity[;] so by my pride I bring downe judgements as with cart-ropes upon the people and place where I live and so become an Achan in the camp of Israel . . . [through the] grievous sin against myne owne soule . . . [which] provokes god to lead me through a howling wilderness of fiery temptations to humble and prove me and show me what is in my heart."

2. Samuel Danforth (son), *An Exhortation to All* (Boston, 1714), in *The Wall and the Garden: Selected Massachusetts Election Sermons, 1670–1775*, ed. A. William Plumstead (Minneapolis, 1968), pp. 152–53, 172, 176: "God's dispensations to his church were typical of the Messiah in many things; therefore also the same title of a vine comprehends both Christ and his church. . . . Those planted in this vineyard, tho' by nature

they are wild plants . . . yet are made noble vines . . . by effectual calling
and their implantation into Christ . . . so that as Israel were not the natives
of Canaan but God fetched this vine from afar off . . . so grace is . . . trans-
planted into us from . . . heaven [and we become] . . . vines planted into
Christ. . . . We have the promises and prophecies of the Scripture wherein
mercy is stored up for the people of God . . . and some pledges of it beforehand . . . [since] the churches of New England have been and are yet
the vineyard of the Lord of hosts . . . and from thence [we] should be
encouraged."

3. Urian Oakes, *New-England Pleaded With* (Cambridge, 1673), pp.
17, 20–23: "I may well parallel you with *Israel.* . . . [This] was a Land
which the Lord *espyed* out for . . . [and] decreed to make a *Canaan* to
you. . . . *You have had Moses . . . to lead and go before you* . . . [and]
men of Nehemiah's spirit. . . . This work of God set on foot and advanced
to a good Degree here, being spread over the face of the Earth, and perfected . . . will be . . . *the Kingdome of Jesus Christ.* . . . Happy art thou
oh *New-England-Israel!*"

4. Cotton Mather, *Magnalia Christi Americana; or, The Ecclesiastical
History of New England* (1702), ed. Thomas Robbins (Hartford, 1853),
II, 578–79, 653: "Og, the king of the woody Bashan, encountered by
Joshua, the Lord General of Israel, with his armies passing into Canaan,
was the . . . Python . . . destroyed by Apollo. . . . [Now,] 'twas . . . unto
a Shilo, that the planters of New-England have been making their progress,
and [the Indian] King Phillip is . . . the Python that has been giving them
obstruction in their passage and progress thereunto. But [under Governor
Phips, the Lord General of the New Israel] . . . all the *serpents* . . . have
found themselves engaged in a fatal enterprize . . . [and] 'tis our Lord
Jesus Christ . . . who is the great Phoebus [Apollo] who hath so saved
[us, thus] . . . foretelling of [millennial] *things to come.*"

5. Increase Mather, *Times of Man* (Boston, 1675), p. 5; John Higginson,
The Cause of God and his People in New-England (Cambridge, 1663),
p. 18; Samuel Sewall, *Phaenomena quaedem Apocalyptica* . . . (Boston,
1697), p. 60; Cotton Mather, *The Serviceable Man* (Boston, 1690), pp.
45–46; William Stoughton, *New-Englands True Interest* (Cambridge, 1670),
pp. 23–24: "As Satan said concerning Job, when God boasted as it were to
him of his integrity . . . Put forth thine hand and touch all that he hath,
and he will curse thee to thy face . . . [so now we find] Satan . . . tempting
and saying concerning us, Let that people of so much Profession in the
Wilderness be but thus and thus proved and tried." Accordingly, we may
turn to the "Holy counsell given to Job in . . . [his] distresses," and predict
"that the End of the Lord with *New England* will be such as was with
Job"—though at present evil events are "compassing and afflicting us on
every side," and "poor . . . New-England [is] stretching out her Trembling
Hands . . . and [pleading:] . . . *Have pity on me, O yee my Friends, for
the Hand of the Lord hath touched me!*"

APPENDIX B

BIBLIOGRAPHICAL AND EXPLANATORY

Because the themes and images traced in this study are common to the whole body of Puritan New England literature, any attempt to give full annotation would have made the references both cumbersome and redundant, and I have accordingly limited the endnotes to the works directly quoted in the text and (in several cases) immediately relevant studies. For a similar reason, I have avoided qualifying or enlarging adequately upon certain general statements and comparisons. This appendix is intended to compensate in some degree for these deficiencies.

The different effects upon Puritanism of the eschatological views of Luther and Calvin have often been discussed. For a variety of perspectives, see: Gordon S. Wakefield, *Puritan Devotion: Its Place in the Development of Christian Piety* (London, 1957), pp. 16–19 ff.; Le Roy Edwin Froom, *The Prophetic Faith of Our Fathers: The Historical Development of Prophetic Interpretations* (Washington, 1946–54), II, 241–307, 443–64, 554–97; Michael Fixler, *Milton and the Kingdoms of God* (Evanston, 1964), pp. 25–26 ff.; George W. Forell, "Justification and Eschatology in Luther's Thought," *Church History*, XXVIII (1969), 164–75; Heinrich Bornkamm, *Luther und das Alte Testament* (Tübingen, 1948), *passim* (valuable regarding typology and eschatology); Peter Y. De Jong, *The Covenant Idea in New England Theology, 1620–1847* (Grand Rapids, Mich., 1945), pp. 21–22; and Heinrich Quistorp, *Calvin's Doctrine of the Last Things*, trans. Harold Knight (London, 1955), p. 192. Regarding the importance, in these terms, of Jer. 50:5, see William Haller, *Liberty and Reformation in the Puritan Revolution* (New York, 1955), pp. 18, 298; Geoffrey F. Nuttall, *Visible Saints: The Congregational Way, 1640–1660* (Oxford, 1957), p. 75; John Cotton, *The True Constitvtion of a particular visible Church* (London, 1642), pp. 4 ff.; Thomas Hooker, *A Survey of the Summe of Church-Discipline* (London, 1648), pp. 37, 79. The standard Calvinist position on this text (as on Jer. 31:32) is that ever since the "naturall couenant made . . . in Paradise, was violated . . . the couenant which remaineth, is wholly to be ascribed vnto grace," and that God made the so-called "new covenant" only to bring to light "whatever had been shadowed forth under the Law" (Andrew Willet, *Hexapla* [London, 1620], p. 3). The concept of covenant-breaking and utter rejection, accordingly, becomes for Calvin no more than a metaphor (or a hyperbole), a stylistic device employed for certain didactic ends such as admonition (e.g., *Commentaries on . . . Jeremiah*, trans. and ed. John Owen [Grand Rapids, Mich., 1950], IV, 127). See further the glosses in the relevant sections of the Book of Jeremiah in *The Holy Bible, A Facsimile . . . of the Authorized Version . . . 1611*, ed. Alfred W. Pollard (Oxford, 1911), and cf. Johann Lindblom's discussion of the relation between "national" and "universal" eschatology in the prophetic writings, in *Prophecy in Ancient Israel* (Oxford, 1963), pp. 362 ff., 391–92 ff. On the vexing problem of the American Puritans' retention of these doctrines, see Everett H. Emerson, "Calvin and Covenant Theology," *Church History*, XXV (1956), 137–42, and Gerald J. Goodwin, "The Myth of 'Arminian Calvinism,'" *New England Quarterly*, XLI (1968), 213–37.

Many of the above scholars treat covenant theology. See also: William McKee, "The Idea of Covenant in Early English Puritanism (1558–1643)" (Yale University dissertation, 1948), Leonard J. Trinterud, "The Origins of Puritanism," *Church History*, XX (1951), 38–43, and William G. Wilcox, "New England Covenant Theology: Its English Precursors and Early American Exponents" (Duke University dissertation, 1959). The developmental view of the covenant "From *Adam* to *Noah*, from *Noah* to *Abraham* . . . to *Moses* . . . to *David* . . . to *CHRIST* . . . to the end of the world" (Peter Bulkeley, *The Gospel-Covenant* [London, 1651], p. 113) is a commonplace in the literature: see for example William Guild, *The Harmony of the Gospels* (London, 1626), pp. 40–41, and cf. Charles F. Kent, *The Origin and Permanent Value of the Old Testament* (New York, 1906), pp. 85–111, and Joseph A. Seiss, *Holy Types; or, The Gospel in Leviticus* (Philadelphia, 1866), p. 23. With regard to the concept of national covenant in particular, perhaps the most forceful single statement appears in Edmund Calamy's authoritative sermon of 1645 which argues its necessity on the grounds that "You shall find in our *English Chronicles*, that *England* was never destroyed, but when divided within it self." In this sermon, too, he explains that Jer. 50:5—as the basis for the "union" of Scotland, Ireland, and England—stands for "*a covenant of nature*," and that this natural or "*National Covenant* hath been a long time as it were dead and buried. . . . And therefore it is high time to raise it out of the grave" (*The Great Danger of Covenant-refusing* [London, 1646], title page, pp. 8, 18, 11, 1). Significantly, the royalist position on this issue is substantially in agreement with Calamy's: see Henry Leslie, *A Sermon preached at the Pvblique Fast* (Oxford, 1643), pp. 38–39 (and cf. Christopher Hill, *Puritanism and Liberty* [London, 1958], pp. 244–45 ff.).

In outlining the different uses of the national covenant and the covenant of grace, I have distinguished rather too sharply between Plymouth and Massachusetts. The contrast requires some modification. While it applies in the early decades, the Pilgrims come by and large to share the Bay settlers' historiography. In part, perhaps, the Bay clergy's influence was augmented by the ambiguities implicit in the position taken by Separatists like William Ainsworth and John Canne, who linked the Babylonian bondage typologically with the saint's state under the Church of England, and admitted at least the theoretical viability of a state-church modelled upon the Israelite theocracy: see Richard M. Reinitz, "Symbolism and Freedom: The Use of Biblical Typology as an Argument for Religious Toleration in Seventeenth-Century England and America" (University of Rochester dissertation, 1967), *passim*, and for the persistence of this ambiguity, see the assertion by the Anabaptist Hanserd Knollys—in his *Exposition of the Eleventh Chapter of the Revelation* ([London], 1679), p. 25—that "every one, who shall . . . consider the Type, and Antitype, will doubtless . . . say, *certainly . . . England* [is] like *Egypt* for Oppression, Exactions, and other Cruelties against the *Israel* of God." In part, too, the Plymouth leaders may have been driven in reaction against Roger Williams to identify more closely with their neighbours, an identification no doubt enforced by the "wilderness-condition" they shared with their nonseparating brethren and by various ideological pressures and cross-currents. For whatever reason, or configuration of reasons, it seems evident that the historiographic-doctrinal lines demarcating Boston from Plymouth became increasingly blurred after 1650: see William Bradford, *History of Plymouth Plantation*, ed. William T. Davis (New York, 1959), pp. 25–29, 45–46, 79–97, 137–56, 364, and the Plymouth election sermons by Thomas Walley, *Balm in Gilead* (Cambridge, 1669), and Samuel Arnold, *David Serving* (Cambridge, 1674).

My discussion of the theory of baptism in New England also requires modification. The emigrants were not of one mind on the subject; indeed, their treatises are sometimes contradictory, and now and then seem rather reticent about declaring a fixed opinion. Joy Gilsdorf has speculated that the leading emigrant divines "equivocated on the question of baptism" because they believed in the imminency of the "eschatological crisis": if the "new age" were at hand, "there was obviously no need to decide the worrisome question" ("The Puritan Apocalypse: New England Eschatology in the Seventeenth Century" [Yale University dissertation, 1964], p. 146). Furthermore, their views on the "line of election" clearly build upon the Reformers' developing concept of baptism through Tyndale and the Zurich theologians that the "unborn children are comprehended in God's covenant made with their fathers . . . [and] '*by keeping the covenants, we* [the children of the saints] *may be sure of the promises*' " (Jens G. Møller, "The Beginnings of Puritan Covenant Theology," *Journal of Ecclesiastical History*, XIII–XIV [1962–63], 57). But as C. J. Sommerville has shown, the European theologians also stressed that "Only God knew how the grace of covenant was applied. . . . Perkins [for example] decided that in baptism children were brought into the covenant 'by the meanes of their parents faith,' [yet] he could not help thinking that 'every person must have a faith of his owne' . . . since, as he noticed, few of any class or nation were

of the elect. He was afraid to ask too little of his readers by making
Christianity hereditary" ("Conversion Versus The Early Puritan Covenant
of Grace," *Journal of the Presbyterian Historical Society*, XLIV [1966],
185, 187). The same fear may also be found expressed by the New World
divines (e.g., Thomas Shepard, *The Sound Believer* [London, 1649], p.
209); nonetheless, there is ample evidence that by and large they consciously
linked baptismal doctrine to their historiography both before and after the
Half-Way Covenant. The concept of the later orthodoxy has been described
in some detail; for the views of the emigrant clergy, see: Charles Chauncy,
Gods Mercy Shewed to His People (Cambridge, 1655), p. 29; John Cotton,
The Covenant of Gods Free Grace (London, 1645), pp. 14–20, *The
Grounds and Ends of Baptisme of the Children of the Faithful* (London,
1647), pp. 40–46, and *A Treatise of the Covenant of Grace* (London,
1659), pp. 23–42; Thomas Hooker, *The Covenant of Grace Opened*
(London, 1649), *passim*, and *The Faithful Covenanter* (London, 1644),
pp. 10–22; John Eliot, quoted in Cotton Mather, *Magnalia Christi Ameri-
cana; or, The Ecclesiastical History of New England* (1702), ed. Thomas
Robbins (Hartford, 1853), I, 549.

The evolution of the concept of covenant renewal in New England,
though not so theologically involved as that of baptism, is equally important to colonial historiography. In discussing the significance of this ceremony, Perry Miller accurately notes that "Adumbration can be found even
before 1675, but the agony of King Philip's War made the practice general"
(*The New England Mind: From Colony to Province* [Boston, 1961], p.
116). These foreshadowings deserve attention in their own right since they
throw additional light upon the organic development of the jeremiad. A
full study of the subject would begin with the writings of the first emigrants
(e.g., Richard Mather, *A Farewel-Exhortation* [Cambridge, 1657], pp.
4–5). Later, the ministers claim that the "Converting Glory" which
appeared in the early days of settlement—when "multitudes were converted" beneath "the shine of mercy from the Throne"—proves that
although our sense of justification "is greatly beset . . . it will certainly . . .
recover it self out of all the dangers" by covenant renewal (James Fitch,
An Holy Connexion [Hartford, 1674], pp. 12–13; Thomas Shepard, *Eye-
Salve, Or A Watch-Word From our Lord* [Cambridge, 1673], p. 10; Urian
Oakes, *The Unconquerable . . . Soldier* [Cambridge, 1674], p. 1). So, too,
William Stoughton (*New-Englands True Interest* [Cambridge, 1670])
urging mass rededication to God, demands: "Why should we frustrate the
Lord of that *full vintage* which he justly expects from *our* Generation[?]
My Brethren, we are . . . the *Children of the Covenant* and of the *King-
dome* . . . that seed spoken of and promised Isa. 44. 3, 4, 5" ("Advertise-
ment," and pp. 5, 7, 27); and according to Samuel Torrey (*Exhortation
Unto Reformation, Amplified* [Cambridge, 1674]), "When God gives re-
forming grace, he alwayes renews his Covenant with his people, *Jer.* 31.
33 . . . that they might be a special people unto himself, above all people
. . . It is [therefore] the duty of all [of us] . . . *actually*, personally and

professedly to take hold upon [and] . . . thus to renew the Covenant"
(pp. 12–13, 41). Modern scholars have tended to view such statements
as an abandonment of Calvinist doctrine, especially perhaps with regard to
Cotton Mather's exhortations for covenant-renewal. Mather's theology does
raise complex questions, but his appeals in this case bespeak his link with
the past rather than his anticipation of "Franklinesque morality": e.g., see
his *Duty of Children* (Boston, 1703), p. 12, *et passim*.

I have not dealt at length with the colonists' belief that the Indians were
the ten lost tribes (potentially an important aspect of my study) because
I found that the idea was far less prevalent in New England than some
scholars have assumed (see Charles L. Sanford, *The Quest for Paradise:
Europe and the American Moral Imagination* [Urbana, 1961], pp. 90–93,
and Don Cameron Allen, *The Legend of Noah* [Urbana, 1949], pp. 125
ff.). First, it did not originate with the Protestant settlement but with the
Spaniard Joannes Frederico Lummius (1567) and various Jesuit mission-
aries (Lee E. Huddleston, *Origins of the American Indians* [Austin, 1967],
pp. 34 ff.). Secondly, it seems to have been taken up by the American
Puritans mainly in response to the enthusiasm it generated in England, by
way of Manasseh ben Israel's appeals for Jewish emigration to England
and John Eliot's numerous letters connecting his missionary work with the
advent of the millennium: see Ola E. Winslow, *John Eliot: "Apostle to the
Indians"* (Boston, 1968), p. 113, Thomas Thorowgood, *Jews in America*
(London, 1648), and John Dury, *Epistolical Discourse . . . that the
Indians are descended from the Israelites* (London, 1650). But Eliot's hope
never really took hold strongly in New England itself, in part because of
the limited (and always precarious) success of the Indian missions, and
in part because the idea obviously violated the Puritans' self-concept, their
fundamental rhetorical distinction (itself probably influenced in turn by
the Indians' intractability) between Christ's Army and its Satanic enemies.
"I cannot call it so much guess as *wish*," sighed Cotton Mather (*Magnalia*,
I, 560–61), commenting indulgently on Eliot's faith in "such possibilities."
His own view—that "the *Americans* are the Posterity of [the] Canaanites"
(*The Serviceable Man* [Boston, 1690], pp. 50–51)—reflects the dominant
metaphor of the period, implicit in John Winthrop's pre-migration *Conclusions for the Plantation in New England*, in *Old South Leaflets* [Boston,
1874–76], Vol. II, no. 50, pp. 6–7: the identification of the Indians with
the doomed "dark brothers" of the Bible (Cain, Ishmael, Esau, and above
all the heathen natives of the Promised Land); see further John Norton,
Discourse about Civil Government (Cambridge, 1663), p. 5, and Roy
Harvey Pearce, *The Savages of America* (Baltimore, 1953), pp. 19–35,
185–224. Indeed, the latter-day orthodoxy showed more millenarian enthusiasm about converting the "very considerable numbers" of emigrant Jews
(Samuel Sewall, *Phaenomena quaedam Apocalyptica* [Boston, 1697], p.
36), as Cotton Mather amply suggests in describing one such conversion,
in *Things to be More Thought Upon* (Boston, 1713), *passim*. Compare

Nuttall, *Visible Saints*, p. 143, on the English Puritan enthusiasm for such missionary work, following upon the doctrine of National Conversion.

Not all the English Puritans, of course, espoused the doctrine. Calvin himself sharply disagreed, and a number of influential divines sustained his opinion (e.g., John Calvin, *Commentaries on . . . Romans*, trans. and ed. John Owen [Grand Rapids, Mich., 1955], pp. 409–37, and William Prynne, *Israels Condition* [London, 1656]). Many others, like Hanserd Knollys, urged that the Jews' Conversion not only was clearly prophesied but was about to occur (*Mystical Babylon Unvailed* [London, 1679]). Still others, like Joseph Mede, wavered between the two possibilities, speculating that particular Jews might be redeemed but not all, while holding that "*S. Paul's Conversion* [was] . . . *The Type of the Calling of the Jews*," a "*Praeludia*" or "forerunner of the great and main Conversion . . . of the body of the Nation" (*Works*, ed. John Worthington [London, 1677], pp. 750, 891, 761). Closest to the colonists' position were S[amuel] H[utchinson], *A Declaration of a Future Glorious Estate . . . upon Earth* (London, 1667), p. 26, and Nicholas Byfield, *The Rule of Faith* (London, 1626). The latter work, positing the signs to be manifested before the Parousia, claims that all but the seventh are already fulfilled, "and that is the calling of the Nation of the *Iewes*" (pp. 513–15)—a view which is echoed in the declaration of the great Boston synod, *A Confession of Faith Owned and Consented Unto . . . in New England* (Boston, 1680), pp. 55, 111, 125, 152, as well as in John Cotton, *A Brief Exposition . . . of the Whole Book of Canticles* [London, 1655], p. 181.

Whether or not they believed in the Conversion of the Jews, most Puritan divines were influenced, directly or indirectly, by the rabbinical commentaries (e.g., see Herman Hailpern, *Rashi and the Christian Scholars* [Pittsburgh, 1963], pp. 103 ff., and my essay on "Milton's 'Haemony': Knowledge and Faith," *Huntington Library Quarterly*, XXXIII (1970), 351–59. The reverberations from the *Zohar* especially sound throughout seventeenth-century colonial writings, in numerous specific allusions. In general, the rabbis' concern with the prophesies of Daniel delighted the Reformers because of the parallels they discerned between these prophecies and those in Revelation. "We have a *Line of Time*, in the *Revelation* . . . [corresponding to] what has been said by *Daniel* about the *Fourth Monarchy* . . . [and to the] Studies upon the *Kingdom* of our Lord Jesus . . . [in which] Jeremiah had been deeply ingag'd"; when "in the last Century very many [Reformers] . . . looked into it, and made glorious discoveries, [it was] a blessed sign . . . that all the glorious things spoken of therein shall be fulfilled in this very Age . . . [for] inasmuch as the Book is unsealed, that is a sign the End is very near." And seeing this is so, "as the rabbins teach, . . . any man which hath not had communion with God in looking into these Mysteries . . . it is because he hath no grace in his soul" (Cotton Mather, *Things to be Look'd for* [Cambridge, 1691], pp. 35, 46, and *A Midnight Cry* [Boston, 1692], p. 29; Increase Mather, *Times of Man* [Boston, 1675], p. 13, *Mystery of Israel's Salvation* [London, 1669], p. 154, and *Morning Star*,

appended to *The Righteous Man A Blessing* . . . [Boston, 1702], p. 80).
On the Four Monarchies theory in its relation to rabbinical thought, see
Benjamin Keach's 1681 *Tropologia* (London, 1856), p. 229, and Lee M.
Friedman's discussion of Cotton Mather's *The Faith of the Fathers* (Boston,
1699; dedicated to the Jewish nation), in "Cotton Mather and the Jews,"
American Jewish Historical Society, Publications, XXV (1918), 204, *et
passim*. On the widespread Cabbalistic concept that the final period would
begin between 1648 and 1666, see Geoffrey F. Nuttall, *The Holy Spirit in
Puritan Faith and Experience* (Oxford, 1947), p. 109. As John Canne,
for one, declared in 1653, "the 1260 years of *Revelation* had expired in
1648 . . . and 1700 would mark the end of the [cosmic] War" (John F.
Wilson, "Another Look at John Canne," *Church History*, XXXIII [1964],
43). The apocalyptic militancy of Renaissance Jewry, implicit in such
notions, has been often disputed: e.g., by Norman Cohn (*The Pursuit of
the Millennium* [New York, 1957], p. 6; see also David Wasserzug, *The
Messianic Idea and its Influence in Jewish Ethos* [London, 1913], pp. 5 ff.,
and Heinrich Graetz, *The History of the Jews*, trans. Bella Löwy [Philadel-
phia, 1954], IV, 471–625). But the evidence clearly refutes this position,
as I attempt to demonstrate in my forthcoming Introduction to Increase
Mather's *Mystery*, for the American Studies Series.

A more crucial influence upon the New Englanders' apocalyptic outlook,
of course, were the Christian "progressivists," from the patristic period
through the Middle Ages and the Reformation. For general notes on this
theme see C. A. Patrides, *Milton and the Christian Tradition* (Oxford,
1966), p. 241, and Robert L. P. Milburn, *Early Christian Interpretations of
History* (New York, 1954), pp. 54–96. References to Thomas Brightman's
Apocalypsis Apocalypseos (1609), translated as *The Revelation of S. John
Illustrated* (3rd. ed., Leyden, 1616), and Joseph Mede's authoritative
The Key of the Revelation, trans. Richard More (London, 1650), pervade
American Puritan writings. John Owen's fame rested not only on his
orthodox doctrinal treatises but on such forceful apocalyptic sermons as
*The Advantage of the Kingdome of Christ in the Shaking of the Kingdoms
of the World* (Oxford, 1652) and *Predicted Events coming upon the
Nations of the Earth* (London, 1654). Eusebius' influence appears every-
where in the period, from John Foxe's 1563 Dedication to his *Book of
Martyrs* to William Caton's popular abridgment of the *Ecclesiastical History*
a century later, and, in New England literature, from John Cotton's *The
Pouring Out of the Seven Vials* (London, 1642) to Cotton Mather's
Magnalia. The precise impact of Joachim of Floris upon the Puritans is
difficult to determine (though occasional citations may be found in writings
on both sides of the Atlantic). Unquestionably, however, "the similarity of
tone" between Joachite ideas and those of seventeenth-century millenarians
"is sometimes striking," as Nuttall observes (*Holy Spirit*, pp. 104–5); and
it seems possible that certain early Reformers adapted to their own view
of history Joachim's theory of "stages"—a "conception of the progressive
development of revelation . . . diametrically opposed to the old Augustinian

concept"—whence it passed on to the movement at large (Froom, *Prophetic Faith*, I, 685, 695). Regarding the apparent presence of "the Joachite fanfare" in New England, see Kennerly M. Woody, "Cotton Mather's *Manuductio ad Theologiam*: The 'More Quiet and Hopeful Way,'" *EAL*, IV (1969), 18, *et passim*.

William Twisse was particularly popular in New England for his notion that America would be the seat of the New Jerusalem. In general, the ministers were fond of invoking Joseph Mede's contrary conjecture precisely in order to refute it by way of Twisse. Cotton Mather, for instance, speculates that God might "intend that the Divel shall keep *America* during the Happy *Chiliad*" so as more dramatically to announce the probability that "God will wrest *America* out of the Hands of . . . *Satan*, and give these *utmost ends of the Earth* to our Lord Jesus . . . and . . . *A Golden Age*, will arrive to this place" (*The Present State of New England* [Boston, 1690], p. 35); and in his *Way to Prosperity* (Boston, 1690), he toys with Mede's view before predicting that "our little New England may soon produce them that shall be commanders of the greatest glories that America can pretend unto" (p. 20). Nicholas Noyes (*New-Englands Duty and Interest* [Cambridge, 1698], pp. 44 ff.) and Samuel Sewall (*Phaenomena*, pp. 39–40) similarly note the "Antick Fancy of *America's* being Hell" to preface their "Demonstration" of how "it should be the New Jerusalem" (Sewall adding for the consolation of the English saints [p. 42] that Boston was no further from London than from Jerusalem).

It may be well to reiterate that these statements clearly contradict the idea that from "about 1650 on . . . every pious observer . . . traced the accelerating declension," expecting that God would "now wreak a terrible vengeance upon them" because of the colony's "universal depravity" (Perry Miller, "'Preparation for Salvation' in Seventeenth-Century New England," *Journal of the History of Ideas*, IV [1943], 250, 256)—that the "sense of impending doom became toward the latter part of the seventeenth century more ominous" (Edward K. Trefz, "The Puritans' View of History," *Boston Public Library Quarterly*, IX [1957], 118), and that "Increase Mather is the best example of many clergymen in the pulpits of 1660–1730 . . . trying to rub the strangeness from their eyes as if they had suddenly returned to a society which . . . was full of new ways and strange gods" (A. William Plumstead, ed., *The Wall and The Garden: Selected Massachusetts Election Sermons, 1670–1775* [Minneapolis, 1968], Introduction, p. 30). Equally inaccurate is Perry Miller's claim that the Mathers' obsessive millennialism was a kind of theological aberration, a notion at odds with the orthodoxy's view and diametrically opposed to that of the early emigrants, such as Anne Bradstreet who "wrote only of English streams and English birds" (*Colony to Province*, p. 189). Regarding Anne Bradstreet in particular, see for example her "Dialogue Between Old England and New" (1642), which proclaims "For sure" that "These are the dayes, the Churches foes to crush," and in which, significantly, it is *"New* England" that speaks summarily of the calling of the Jews and the imminent Resurrection Day (*Works*, ed. Adrienne Rich [Cambridge, Mass., 1967], pp. 185–87). For other representative primary works documenting the early Puritan's radical millenarianism, see: John Cotton's *An Exposition . . . of the Revelation* (London, 1655) preached in the late 1630s; Ephraim Huit's *Daniel Explained* (London, 1644), which sets the apocalyptic date at 1650; and John Eliot's *Tears of Repentance* (London, 1653), where the Apostle to the Indians connects his missionary work with the chiliasm. The parade of prominent names (Holyoke, Bulkeley, Hooke, Davenport, and others) proceeds into the "age of reason," in an unbroken line from Thomas Hooker's *Survey*—the major doctrinal treatise of the early theocracy which declares at the outset that "the times [are] drawing on wherein Prophecies are to attain their performances"—to Ezekiel Cheever's *Scripture Prophecies* (Boston, 1757), and Samuel Willard's *Compleat Body of Divinity* (Boston, 1727), the major doctrinal treatises of the early eighteenth-century clergy, which ring with similar hopes of "This being the season, when all the kingdomes of the world are becoming the Lords." Indeed, even Increase Mather's *Ichabod* (Boston, 1701) and *Discourse Concerning the Uncertainty of the Times of Men* (Boston, 1697), which seem at certain points to be exceptions to this pattern, contain many positive notes (quoted above), and in any case the pessimism they voice should be read alongside that author's numerous references—before and after the turn of the century—to an American millennium (including those in *The Glorious Throne*, which he had bound with *Ichabod*).

Intrinsic to the orthodoxy's millenarianism, I have suggested, is the growing sense of its alienation. The four-fold pattern I have traced in this connection is somewhat over-schematic (it neglects a number of foreshadowings and overlappings), but the overall impression it conveys is, I believe, an accurate one. Following are representative testimonies in the clergy's developing definition of its role: (1) *to 1660*: our ministers "are neerest unto God . . . and they bring others also neerer. . . . The Lord gives us to conclude that the future harvest is great, when he sends forth already so many labourers" (Chauncy, *Gods Mercy*, pp. 11–12; see also Winthrop, *Conclusions*, p. 6, and John Norton, *The Heart of N-England rent* [Cambridge, 1659], p. 45); (2) *1660–1670*: "the Word of God is likened to *fire*, and to a *hammer*, Jer. 23.29. in its efficacy" and the minister himself to the prophet urging the people of Israel "to consider their wayes [so as] . . . to stir them up to remove the Cause, that the Effect might cease" (John Davenport, *Gods Call to His People* [Cambridge, 1669], pp. 6–8; see also J[ohn] S[herman], Preface to Jonathan Mitchel, *Nehemiah on the Wall in Troublesom Times* [1667; Cambridge, 1671], sigs. A2ʳ–A2ᵛ); (3) *1670–1680*: "Time was, when the Messengers of Christ . . . were precious and welcome (even when they *came with a* Rod . . .) and their . . . *words* . . . were as *Goads* and *Nayls* that made great *Impression*. . . . But now they are become the Enemies . . . because *they tell* . . . the *Truth*" (Urian Oakes, *New-England Pleaded With* [Cambridge, 1673], p. 26; see also Samuel Willard, *Useful Instructions for a professing People* [Cambridge,

1673], pp. 46, 56, and John Oxenbridge, *New-England Freemen, Warned and Warmed* [Cambridge, 1673], p. 2); (4) *1680–1700*: "It's the quarter of the night wherein the world is to have that Midnight Cry sounded in its heavy Ears, *Behold, the Bridegroom comes*," and our ministers are accordingly proclaiming that "the Day is at hand," after "the example of the Baptist, *who was the voice of one crying in the wilderness*" (C. Mather, *Midnight Cry*, p. 7, Preface to *Things to be Look'd for*, and *Diary, Massachusetts Historical Society, Collections*, 7th ser., VII [1912], 147 [Apr. 29, 1692]; see also Samuel Whiting, *The Way of Israel's Welfare* [Boston, 1686], p. 30, and Increase Mather, *A Sermon . . . [Concerning] Persecution* [Boston, 1682], p. 22).

This last stage in a sense returns us to the first, for in both the minister stands as harbinger of a new era. The difference, however, in the image of the "labourers" preparing the community for the harvest and that of the Baptist in the wilderness suggests the imaginative development I have been describing and its increasing divergence from, and defiance of, social realities. The question of the popular impact of this imaginative or mythical view upon the colony at large has been treated incisively by Kenneth B. Murdock, "Clio in the Wilderness: History and Biography in Puritan New England," *New England Quarterly*, XXIV (1955), 221–38. Compare David Donald's similar conclusions about the Lincoln legends, in *Lincoln Reconsidered* (New York, 1959), p. 164.

The transition from mythical to "enlightened" historiography—from the theocracy to the Age of Reason—involves a number of more or less transitional works. For example, Professor Plumstead contends (*Wall and Garden*, pp. 179–82) that Thomas Prince's *The People of New England* (Boston, 1730) is "the most complete" as well as "the purest and freshest" of all election sermons. But Prince shows here a considerable rationalistic distance from the seventeenth-century Jeremiahs he cites—Higginson, Hubbard, Mitchel, Stoughton—as Plumstead himself indicates when he discusses the author's "interesting tactical move" in meeting objections from both the "literalists" and the "unbelievers" in his audience. Conversely, Plumstead's claim (*Wall and Garden*, pp. 4, 223) that the Massachusetts election sermon for 1734 "dramatizes" the shift away from "Puritan epic mythology" neglects the influence upon it (however diluted) of the former *Weltanschauung*, as in the peroration comparing the colonists to "his people of old," and promising that "the awful commination of God" will issue in the revelation of New England as the lasting "'. . . habitation of justice and mountain of holiness' (Jer. 31.23)" (John Barnard, *The Throne Established by Righteousness*, in *Wall and Garden*, p. 280). The same continuity holds true for Jonathan Mayhew's sermon twenty years later, which Plumstead selects (p. 284) to show that period's "new, anti-Calvinistic views." Mayhew denies that "civil polity . . . [can be] molded . . . by the immediate dictates of heaven," and admits that "Our ancestors [were] . . . not perfect and infallible." Yet he, too, is swayed by the myth; he, too, applies the Apocalypse to "the smiles of a gracious providence" upon the New Englanders, depicts what was "once desert . . . [to be now] blossoming as the rose, the glory of Lebanon . . . the excellency of Carmel and Sharon," and concludes therefore that "God will . . . give us to see the good of his chosen" (*A Sermon Preach'd*, in *Wall and Garden*, pp. 291, 301, 299, 302). See also in this respect Ebenezer Pemberton's *Brief Account of the . . . Province of Massachusetts Bay* (Boston, 1717), pp. 2–3 ff., Thomas Buckingham, *Moses and Aaron* (New London, 1729), esp. p. 15, and John Lathrop, *A Sermon Preached to the . . . Artillery Company* (Boston, 1774), pp. 27–29 ff.; and cf. Henry B. Parkes, *The American Experience: An Interpretation of the History and the Civilization of the American People* (New York, 1955), pp. 76 ff., and Claude M. Newlin, "The Dawn of the Enlightenment in New England," *Philosophy and Religion in Colonial America* (New York, 1962), pp. 23–71.

The parallels between the outlook of the jeremiads and that of the revivalist writings are more numerous than space allowed for in the text. Since the subject is both important to my argument and widely controversial, it may be well to elaborate upon the various areas of continuity. First, regarding the historiographic view—especially the gradualistic process of prophetic fulfillment and the place of the Reformation in this process (entailing Jeremiahs' dicta on Babylon)—see David Austin, *The Downfall of Mystical Babylon* (Elizabethtown, N. J., 1794), Aaron Burr, *The Watchman's Answer* (New York, 1757), and John J. Zubly, *The Law of Liberty* (Philadelphia, 1775); cf. Cotton's *Brief Exposition of Canticles*, pp. 47, 49. With respect to Jonathan Edwards in particular, see his *Humble Attempt to Promote . . . Extraordinary Prayer*, in *The Works of President Edwards*, ed. John Erskine (New York, 1849), III, 430, 473–74, and (on the parallel between the Sabbatism and the order of Creation) *The Distinguishing Marks of a Work of the Spirit of God*, in *Works*, I, 558, and *Miscellaneous Observations on Important Doctrines*, in *Works*, I, 565, 573. Further indirect testimony may be found in Alan Heimert's comments on the importance for Edwards and the Calvinists of Nehemiah as "an exemplary political leader," and on their view that the "course of history . . . largely respected the manner in which God came to 'the help of his people'" (*Religion and the American Mind, from the Great Awakening to the Revolution* [Cambridge, Mass., 1966], pp. 60, 499, 295).

Direct parallels between Edwards' view of trial and that of the Puritans may be found in Increase Mather's *The Day of Trouble is near* (Cambridge, 1674), esp. p. 12, and in his son's exhortation beginning "the Blacker you see the *Troubles* of the Age to grow, the sooner and the surer may be the *Peace* which we are hoping for" (Cotton Mather, *Things to be Look'd for*, p. 25). Heimert distinguishes between the Puritan fear of the apocalyptic earthquakes and the optimistic-symbolic Calvinist view which "interpreted the tremors [wholly] as . . . a harbinger of the millennium" (*Religion*, p. 75; see also p. 60). While the contrast has validity, it should be noted that the Calvinists also saw in the tremors fearful physical ramifications, and that, on their part, Puritans throughout the century spoke hopefully of earthquakes as symbolic events "which shall shake yet . . . the *Papal Empire* to pieces" (C. Mather, *Serviceable Man*, pp. 52–53). Finally, it should be pointed out that the differences I have noted between the view of trial in the early jeremiads and that held by the revivalists is not *consistently* true; on some occasions Edwards does invoke the early rhetoric concerning "life or death." In *Thoughts on the Revival*, for example, he states (*Works*, III, 333–34) that "God, according to his wonderful patience, seems to be still waiting, to give us opportunity . . . [to] acknowledge him. But if we finally refuse . . . the pourings out of his wrath will be proportionable to the despised out-pourings of his Spirit and grace. . . . The work that is now begun . . . would make New England a kind of heaven upon earth: is it not therefore a thousand pities, that it should be overthrown . . . ?" Even here, however, the ambiguity in God's waiting to *give* the opportunity suggests Edwards' optimism; and three pages later he confirms this (precisely as the later orthodoxy did) through the dialectic between the conditional and the absolute in the salvation of souls: "some ministers [of the Awakening] have been greatly blamed for . . . speaking terror to [their congregations. But] . . . they terrify them only . . . [to] convert them. . . . The more . . . the light is terrible to them, the more likely it is, that, by and by, the light will be more joyful to them."

For parallels between the covenant-renewal ceremonies and the revivalist Concerts of Prayer, compare Samuel Davies, *The Crisis* (London, 1757), pp. 26–27, 35, with John Oxenbridge, *A Quickening Word* (Cambridge, 1670), pp. 16 ff. See further: Babette M. Levy, *Preaching in the First Half Century of New England* (New York, 1969), p. 41; Perry Miller's discussion of how, "in 1740, when the commotion started . . . all parties began with the ancient assumption that this was a recognizable 'pouring out of the grace of God upon the land'" ("The Great Awakening from 1740 to 1750," *Nature's Nation* [Cambridge, Mass., 1967], pp. 82 ff.); Heimert's paraphrase of Bellamy on prayer (*Religion*, p. 345), Miller's comments ("Covenant to Renewal," *Nature's Nation*, pp. 110, 117) on the revivalist "coalescence of abnegation and assertion" (which lasted through the nineteenth century, with men like Beecher and Finney seeming at times to believe that the "harvests were wrought by supernatural grace" alone), and Cotton Mather's ceremonial exhortation beginning "Parents, I will show you the *Hand-writing of God*, which you shall carry and argue before Him" (*Duty of Children*, p. 61).

Of the many minor correspondences, two or three might be mentioned as representative. One of these lies in the way the Calvinist notions of the millennium sometimes carry forward the earlier expectations in more or less similar terms: e.g., the furtherance of learning, and the increase in temporal blessings which are in turn "a type and forerunner of what is approaching in spiritual things, when the world shall be supplied with spiritual treasures from America" (Jonathan Edwards, *Images or Shadows of Divine Things*, ed. Perry Miller [New Haven, 1948], p. 102). Another is the use of what might be called types of evil; like Edwards, the New England Puritans define the kingdom of God and the historic process leading up to it, in opposition to a variety of *figurae diabolis*: "the Moabites [as] . . . Types of the present Antichristian generation" (I. Mather, *Day of Trouble*, p. 19), for example, or Antiochus Epiphanes as a "most lively . . . Type" of Rome (William Hooke, *New-Englands Sence* [London, 1650], pp. 13–14). See further Anne Bradstreet's "Four Monarchies," in *Works*, ed. Rich, p. 72, and Richard Mather on the types of Judas, Cain, and Joseph's brothers, in *The svmme of certain sermons vpon Genes: 15.6* (Cambridge, 1652), p. 32; and cf. Roger Williams, *Complete Writings* (New York, 1963), I, 68; IV, 36–37, 59–60, 117, 142, 172, 216, 241, 325, 402.

Still another minor but telling instance of this correspondence is the emphasis of both the orthodoxy and the revivalists upon the figure of John the Baptist. It is well known that the "Calvinist ministers from William Tennent to David Austin considered themselves the successors of John Baptist (and dressed accordingly)" (Heimert, *Religion*, pp. 62, 64, 7n.). The Puritan ministers were not histrionic in the same way; that they shared the view behind the gesture, however, is attested to throughout the literature. For instance, in his famous reference to Matt. 11:7 (also Luke 7:24)— "What went ye into the wilderness to see?"—Samuel Danforth describes John the Baptist as a "*Harbinger* and *Forerunner*" who not only "applied the Types" to Christ but himself typified further unveilings of divine meanings, specifically comparing John's "Ministry . . . in the Wilderness" with that of the theocracy, and, at the same time, with the millennial revelation of "Christ on the Throne" (*A Brief Recognition of New-Englands Errand into the Wilderness* [Cambridge, 1671], pp. 14, 1, 4). As Increase Mather wrote the year before, concerning the chiliasm, "there was a partial and typical fulfillment of this . . . in the Ministry of John Baptist. . . . That great and notable day wherein the Jewish heaven and earth was utterly dissolved . . . may be looked upon as a Type" of our latter days and ultimately "of the last and great day" (*Mystery*, p. 102). Other sermons render this progression even more explicit. When "John the Baptist arose like a bright and shining light," Jesus appeared to him "at the end of the Jewish world . . . *in the end of the world* [i.e., the wilderness]"; another bright light shone forth more clearly to reveal Christ "when the *Reformation* began . . . [after the] long night [of] the Antichrist," with "the Reformed Churches comming out of Popery"; to bring that light to its full brilliancy was "the end of our coming hither" to America—and now, looking back on our accomplishments, "you may conclude that the Sun will quickly arise upon the world" in that "glorious day approaching" when God's chosen people shall "be Triumphant not only in Heaven to all Eternity, but here on Earth too, when New Jerusalem shall come down from Heaven" (Danforth, *Brief Recognition*, p. 6; I. Mather, *Morning Star*, pp. 71, 75–76; John Higginson, *The Cause of God* [Cambridge, 1663], p. 11).

The connections I have noted between Puritan and nineteenth-century

thought are implicit in many studies other than those cited in the text:
e.g., Ephraim D. Adams, *The Power of Ideals in American History* (New
Haven, 1926), pp. 70, 80; Hans Kohn, *American Nationalism: An Inter-
pretive Essay* (New York, 1957), pp. 57 ff.; Frederick Merk, *Manifest
Destiny and Mission in American History: A Reinterpretation* (New York,
1963), pp. 3, 24, 263; and cf. Bernard W. Sheehan, "Paradise and the
Noble Savage in Jeffersonian Thought," *William and Mary Quarterly*,
XXVI (1969), 327–59. Regarding the specific relationship between Cotton
Mather and Henry Adams, see J. C. Levenson, *The Mind and Art of Henry
Adams* (Cambridge, Mass., 1957), pp. 165–67, 376–79, and Ernest Samuels, *Henry Adams: The Major Phase* (Cambridge, Mass., 1964), pp. 341–
56 (on Adams' nationalism versus his sense of failure and isolation), and
Robert F. Sayre, *The Examined Self: Benjamin Franklin, Henry Adams,
Henry James* (Princeton, 1964), p. 200, on the *Education* and the *Magnalia*
as "autobiography become epic." A full comparison between the two men
in the terms that I have suggested would take account of Mather's *Diary*—
which asserts over and again (like the *Education*) that all efforts at a
renascence of the Good Old Way were futile—and Adams' *History of the
United States of America* which (like the *Magnalia*) is a long defence of
the author's forebears, a filiopietistic exoneration of his forebears' contribution to the American Idea (see Peter Shaw, "Blood is Thicker Than Irony:
Henry Adams's History," *New England Quarterly*, XL [1967], 165–87).
Such a comparison might further describe the various personal resemblances
between Adams and Mather: as the dispossessed heirs of New England
dynasties; as intellectuals of enormously wide-ranging interests and with
profound instincts for the trends of the future who were yet imaginatively
and emotionally bound to a former age (both of them caught up in an
archaic ideal and in apocalyptic expectations); as men whose "education"
failed them at every turn and who thus found themselves cast adrift—beyond even their progressive contemporaries—into the "chaos" of a new
century.

The interaction between idealism and realism, optimism and despair,
has long been noted in Whitman (e.g., D. H. Lawrence, *Studies in Classic
American Literature* [Garden City, N. Y., 1951], pp. 182–83). In
Thoreau, too, a muzzled desperation often lies close beneath the surface
bravado. In the draft version of *Walden* (Boston, 1854), he writes: "I could
tell a pitiful story respecting myself . . . with a sufficient list of failures, and
flow as humbly as the very gutters" (xerox 1120 of Huntington MS. 924);
his famous emendation, which became the motto of the first edition, reads:
"I do not propose to write an ode to dejection, but to brag as lustily as
chanticleer in the morning, standing on his roost, if only to wake my
neighbours up" (title page and p. 92). From a different but parallel perspective, several critics have shown that in Henry James' novels the tragic
"cult of experience" clashes and interacts with an "American dream of
Eden," a "vision of the New Jerusalem . . . founded on a [democratic-
theological] concept of personal freedom": see Sanford, *Quest*, pp. 208–10;

Frederic I. Carpenter, " 'The American Myth': Paradise (To Be) Regained,"
PMLA, LXXIV (1959), 601–3; Philip Rahv, "The Cult of Experience in
American Writing," in *Literature in America*, ed. Rahv, pp. 358–60; and
cf. Quentin Anderson, *The American Henry James* (New Brunswick, N. J.,
1957), pp. 207–81.

Significantly, it is precisely the absence of such conflict that blights
Cooper's anti-democratic novels. For example, the choice presented in
The Crater (democracy or squirearchy) never rises above horologicals—
as the hero, Mark Woolston (unlike Natty), never attains to any stature
larger than his class provides—and though in his introduction Cooper hints
"that the mercy of a divine Creator may still preserve that which he has
hitherto cherished and protected," the novel itself concludes in a scene of
total disaster: "paradise had sunk beneath the ocean" (*The Crater*, vol.
XV of *Works* [New York; 1901], pp. iv, 478). In short, reality overcomes
the ideal and the allegory of the American Utopia reduces to a Plinlim-
monian case-history. On the other hand, the intensity of the conflict adds
considerable power to Hawthorne's major work: e.g., in the scene where
the Reverend Arthur Dimmesdale delivers his election sermon on the
"relation between the Deity and . . . New England"; and as he draws
"towards the close a spirit as of prophecy" comes upon him, as once it had
upon "the old prophets of Israel . . . to foretell a high and glorious destiny
of the newly gathered people of the Lord." His message here unmistakably
sums up the author's hope for his country—"But," adds Hawthorne,
"throughout it all, and throughout the whole discourse, there had been a
certain deep, sad undertone of pathos" (*The Scarlet Letter*, ed. Larzer
Ziff [New York, 1963], p. 234). The pathos rises to surface, with much
greater emotional force than Hawthorne would allow himself, in the sermon
that adumbrates the action of *Moby-Dick*.

Many parallel popular American attitudes suggest themselves in this
context: the tendency, for example, "to regard America as having greater
obligations than other nations and therefore to consider her sins more
heinous than those of other nations" (Sanford, *Quest*, p. 134); or the
nostalgia of "sentimental American art" (Wright Morris, *The Territory
Ahead* [New York, 1963], *passim*) that presupposes a powerful if vague
hunger for the mythic world of the Good Old Days (and by extension a
profound disappointment with American reality); or once again, the fusion
of both of these views (as in the jeremiad) with the radiant vistas ahead:
"We are forever feeling our pulses, because we feel, we *know*, that a little
while ago it was in our power, new men in a new world (and even yet
there is hope) to make all perfect" (Leslie Fiedler, Symposium on "Our
Country and Our Culture," *Partisan Review*, XIX [1952], 296). As Frederic
I. Carpenter observes, "there have been two American myths—that of a
paradise lost, and that of a paradise ultimately to be regained. The two
have often been superimposed—the one upon the other—until they have
. . . in a sense become one" (" 'The American Myth,' " p. 606).

Finally, regarding the "metamorphosis" which seems to have marked the demise of the American Puritan vision, see Matthew Josephson, "Historians and Mythmakers," *Virginia Quarterly Review*, XVI (1940), 108, on the need for "less myth and more history"; Leslie Fiedler on the "disenchantment" of American novelists since 1940, in "Adolescence and Maturity in the American Novel," *An End to Innocence: Essays on Culture and Politics* (Boston, 1955), p. 191; Roy Harvey Pearce on the demand of "the younger poets" for "a poetry of *men* . . . conceived as in their history," in *The Continuity of American Poetry* (Princeton, 1962), pp. 432–33; and Leland Baldwin on America in world affairs, in *The Meaning of America: Essays Toward an Understanding of the American Spirit* (Pittsburgh, 1955), pp. 291–319.

UPROAR IN THE ECHO:
THE EXISTENTIAL AESTHETIC OF
BROWNING'S *THE RING AND THE BOOK*

Paul F. Mattheisen

SOME ASPECTS OF BROWNING'S POETIC THEORY

$\mathbf{M}$uch recent criticism of Browning's dramatic monologues tends to reinforce the view that these are more or less "objective" poetic explorations of the human psyche under the stress of extraordinary circumstances. In *The Ring and the Book,* however, a strong insistence on the absolute nature of Truth seems to obscure the sense of relativity which Browning is thought to have attempted in the separate monologues. To explain this apparent contradiction, critics have asserted either that Browning failed to carry out his intention fully, or that he did not clearly understand it himself. Thus, Robert Langbaum says that Browning's "aim . . . was to replace the objective view of events . . . with points of view," although he has to admit that the poet "does not entirely succeed."[1] Wylie Sypher thought that Browning's admiration for his "immoral" characters suffered from limited perception: "Browning does not reach [a] mature philosophy of perspectivism chiefly because he is not able to conceive a full modern relativity. . . . Guido is, by absolute moral standards, 'bad,' and Pompilia and Caponsacchi are 'good.'" The result is "a strangely intermediate kind of moral judgment which appreciates the fact that all truth is personal and therefore relative, but also, seen from a distance, fixed, unchanging, and divinely ordained. Browning's admiration for the immoralist is compromised by his belief that truth is an accurately balanced judgment of the facts."[2]

I

The tendency to read this poem with an assumption about auctorial intention is inescapable, since the persona of the two framing books is so intensely identified with the poet himself that the normal distinction between author and persona tends to break down. The British

Public, twice addressed directly as readers who "like me not" but who "may like me yet," is clearly Browning's own public, and the author appears to be stepping outside of his poem in addressing them; and it is Browning himself who is so concerned that he wants to save their souls as well as his own (XII, 863–64).* That a mere persona may have a soul is at best improbable; that it should busy itself saving the souls of others may be regarded as an impertinence. And when the persona, in Book XII, associates himself with Christ, coming "in the fulness of the days" (827), we are to think that the poet himself is intimately related to the "truth" he means to convey. Such a relationship, it will be seen, is essential to Browning's theory of existential communication. *The Ring and the Book* seems to reflect the poet's own personality more directly than is usually the case in poetry; when we speak of the poet's intention, we rightly seek the persona for an expression of it within the poem.

When Wylie Sypher speaks of Browning's characters as illustrating his admiration for the "immoralist," he seems to be reading into the poem some modern manifestations of existentialism which were alien to Browning's outlook. He pays lip service to Kierkegaard as the ultimate source of such notions, without any recognition of the significant changes they have undergone in our time. In *Fear and Trembling* there is a "suspension of the ethical," but it is a teleological suspension in which the "absurd" arises from the introduction of the infinite into the finite[3]—an idea which, being repugnant to the rational intellect, is therefore an object of passion and of belief. Admittedly, says Kierkegaard elsewhere, two kinds of passionate individual may understand him: "Those who with an infinite passionate interest in an eternal happiness base their happiness upon their believing relationship to Christianity, and those who with an opposite passion, but in passion, reject it—the happy and the unhappy lovers."† Like Browning, how-

---

* Citations to *The Ring and the Book* in my text are to the first edition (London, 1868–1869). Quoted lines are from Book I unless otherwise indicated. Quotations from Browning's other poems are taken from the Centenary Edition of 1912, edited by Sir Frederick Kenyon.

† Søren Kierkegaard, *Concluding Unscientific Postscript to the Philosophical Fragments*, trans. David F. Swenson and Walter Lowrie (Princeton, 1944), p. 51; hereafter referred to in my text as *PS*. I do not in this paper propose a new interpretation of Kierkegaard; my interest here is literary, and I employ his ideas only as they seem to me to bear on Browning's poetry. Such a procedure must necessarily leave Kierkegaard's philosophy imperfectly reflected. In treating of Book I of *The Ring and the Book,* for example, I have ignored altogether the aesthetic category of existence, a category which is directly related to such

ever (and the Pope, who in many ways has been regarded as Browning's spokesman within the ten monologues considered apart from the framing ones), Kierkegaard specifically addresses himself to the "problem" of the inauthentic Christian within Christendom. To him, the teleological suspension of the ethical involves an absolute dependence upon God, and constitutes a removal to a higher order of existence, not a movement towards "immoralism." Abraham's willingness to sacrifice his son is not "absurd" if that is taken to mean a simple and absolute meaninglessness or a mere assertion of the self above any moral framework. The normal ethic retains its rational integrity as an expression of the finite, but the temporal order to which it belongs is superseded by Abraham when he attaches himself to the infinite order. Such a view as this may serve partly to explain the role of the persona in the framing monologues of *The Ring and the Book*, who sometimes seems to regard himself as a sort of *Scriba Dei*, introducing his perception of the infinite as a way of sorting out the human situation.[4] The belief expressed in the poem that God is operative in the world and may be found there by the poet enables us to reconcile the apparent discrepancy in the poem between the absolute and the relative. The characters are certainly "objective" in that they represent "points of view." But they may also be seen as reflecting degrees of acceptance, rejection, or indifference to the absolute which underlies them all and which accommodates the poet's moral intention.

Robert Langbaum's persuasive and seminal theory of the dramatic monologue yields by far the most successful reading of *The Ring and the Book* to date;[5] yet exactly insofar as it leads to an assertion of Browning's failure to achieve his own poetic aim, we must wonder whether it perfectly explains the poet's actual intention. Since my own reading of the poem is based on an interpretation of Browning's aesthetic theory, it must necessarily conflict with Langbaum's on several particular points. It does not, however, altogether resist his general theory of the dramatic monologue, nor many of his fine insights into

characters as Guido and the young Caponsacchi. A full comparative study of the two writers, furthermore, would require an encounter with the literary and philosophical ideas exactly in the form they are presented in all of Kierkegaard's major works, where the matter of form is decisive. Since I mean only to clarify Browning's poem, I draw exclusively on the *Postscript*, where Kierkegaard explains his previous volumes in a discursive way more suitable to my purpose. It is significant, however, that an excessive concern for personae, and for communication through personae, is common to both writers.

the poem. For example, Langbaum says that "the dramatic monologue offers certain advantages to the poet who is not committed to a religious position, or who is addressing readers not committed and not wanting to be."[6] To this I would add that, in assessing the poet's intention, we must know how he stands on the matter of conviction, whether we agree with him or not, whenever the poem makes such knowledge relevant. In *The Ring and the Book*, Browning did assume a religious position, and I think he tried to convince others to accept it; but certainly the poem is best read as the work of a poet who is highly conscious of addressing some readers not so committed and perhaps not wanting to be. Since Browning's aesthetic theory is intimately related to his religious belief, and since that conviction is stressed so distinctly in the poem itself, it seems best to discover his intention in those terms rather than to assume that Browning simply failed in his own aim. Langbaum returns to this criticism near the end of his chapter on the poem:

It is certainly a valid criticism of *The Ring and the Book* that good and evil are not sufficiently interfused. Our judgment is forced from the beginning, whereas it would seem to be peculiarly the genius of a poem treating differing points of view toward the same story to treat each point of view impartially, allowing judgment to arise out of the utmost ambiguity.[7]

Yet if the poet does not really expect our mere judgment of guilty or not guilty to arise from strictly impartial evidence, then such a criticism cannot be altogether valid, even though a reading of the poem according to the author's aesthetic theory may seem to have a partly reductive effect. Since the somewhat Chaucerian catalogue of dramatis personae at the end of Book I clearly locates each character in the scale of right and wrong, we must be prepared to admit as a possibility that the particular genius of these "point of view" monologues may be the revelation of a total "truth" which, while it may be "in" the characters themselves, is nevertheless independent of them, and may be fully discerned and communicated only by the seer. As we shall see, Browning held that only the "whole poet" may know the "whole truth." Langbaum points out that a good deal of the "truth" in the poem is psychologized; yet it is also externalized insofar as it refers to a basic form of Christianity, even though we may come to it chiefly through the poet's personality and his analysis of character. What is necessarily psychologized is the "truth" of human motive—the assessment, not of actions, but of moral guilt. This has nothing to do with ethical relativity, however. The moral judgments are clear from the beginning of the poem; to them, the poet added the complexity and ambiguity of real life, always retaining his full control over the meaning. If he failed in his intention, it was in misleading us to assume that he intended to present the story with complete impartiality.

II

Readers interested both in existentialism and in Browning's poetry will find that the reflection of certain Kierkegaardian ideas in *The Ring and the Book* has an interest of its own, validated merely by the fact of the parallel.[8] But some attention to the details of Kierkegaard's theory of artistic communication may also serve to liberate Browning's ideas from the particular expression he gave to them, placing them within a larger context of which he may have been aware; and it may also draw out implications which he may have seen obscurely or not at all. For this it is not necessary to prove that Browning had read the works of his Danish contemporary. Kierkegaard gave philosophic focus and articulation to a good many notions which were "in the air," and he therefore often dealt with ideas accessible in some form to Victorians of Browning's generation. Since Kierkegaard was also deeply original and developed a unique philosophical language, there are naturally points of difference between the poet and the philosopher. But insofar as such general ideas may be said to lie partly implicit in literary works, a genuine use of Kierkegaard is to provide us with a technique for discovering and a language for expressing them critically. Without such aid it is easy to misread Browning's intention (or even individual lines of his poetry). Unhappily, for example, we are still occasionally reminded of Browning's old reputation as a simpleton in the realm of ideas; and occasionally some of his central ideas are viewed too strictly in terms of their psychological origin.

It is a little depressing, for example, to find the legend of Browning as a mediocre thinker perpetuated in so recent a treatment as Altick and Loucks' *Browning's Roman Murder Story*. There the authors take great pains to dissociate themselves from the apparently quixotic notion that Browning might have been capable of an original thought: "As we begin to describe the leading ideas of the poem, it may be well to emphasize that they are, almost without exception, intellectual com-

monplaces. Browning's originality resides in the fresh expression he
gives to these familiar metaphysical, ethical, and religious attitudes,
not in the ideas themselves."[9] I think nothing would advance the cause
of Browning criticism more than a general recognition that the impression of him conveyed in such a passage is unsatisfactory and largely
untrue. It must, of course, be admitted that any poet works within a
certain framework of language and ideas which are to a large extent
commonplace, and which form a matrix of communication: to be
absolutely "original" in these matters is to be unintelligible. Furthermore, any poet who writes within the Christian tradition may be said
to employ commonplaces in a very precise sense of that term. The
Divine Comedy and the *Canterbury Tales,* for example, draw heavily
on ideas which are now more frequently recognized as commonplaces
of the age in which they were written, though it often takes a good
deal of scholarship to discover them today. But are we left with no
more than tired ideas dressed up in fresh expressions? Any "truth" in
a commonplace depends on the sense of complexity required to bring
the idea into relationship with real life, and if the writer of a dramatic
poem undertakes to convey that sense of complexity (as Browning
does in *The Ring and the Book*), then the idea in the mind of the
reader is hardly the same as it was: the complexity gives content to
the commonplace, not the other way around. Insofar as a poem thus
contributes to the mental response to an idea, it may be said to contribute to the idea itself. The trouble with commonplaces is that they
tend to become meaningless abstractions; surely a poet can be original
not only by restoring their power in poetic language but also by giving
them substance as ideas. "Men must endure / Their going hence, even
as their coming hither; / Ripeness is all." Is anything really gained by
emphasizing that this idea is an intellectual commonplace?

Perhaps a word should also be said about the separability of form
and content implied by Altick and Loucks. The somewhat Arnoldian
notion that ideas must be established intellectually first and then the
poetic expression added for those who cannot find themselves moved
by the naked truth is foreign to Browning's sensibilities. One may even
speculate that Browning urged Arnold to restore *Empedocles on Etna*
to his poetic corpus because the poem illustrated for him the suicidal
despair that comes when the intellect is regarded as the sole arbiter of
truth. For Browning, I think, the myth comes first and the intellect
invests it with idea. The mind here has three equally important func-

tions: it provides an intellectual expression for the belief, it destroys a
merely ridiculous belief, and it introduces the significant element of
doubt into any belief. But the doubt is genuine because it is predicated
on belief, not on the investment of an idea with poetic sentiment. In
my view, Browning's ideas on these matters are anything but commonplace; certainly they are not the commonplaces of his own era.

Part of the problem is that the lines which Altick and Loucks cite
as the occasion for their observation are described as "a passage which
sums up the metaphysical burden of the poem":

> learn one lesson hence
> Of many which whatever lives should teach:
> This lesson, that our human speech is naught,
> Our human testimony false, our fame
> And human estimation words and wind.

(XII, 831–36)

It seems to me that for such a "lesson" we do not need 21,000 lines of
poetry. Furthermore, at the end of the poetic paragraph from which
the passage is taken, Browning speaks of his intention to "save the
soul"; if a recognition of the platitude in lines 831–36 may be regarded
as tantamount to salvation, then surely the Second Coming is at hand.
We must, I think, accept Browning's claim in those lines that this is
just "one" of the "many" lessons which "whatever lives should teach."

The long paragraph in which the quoted passage occurs is one of the
most difficult and mysterious in the poem; it is given an emphatic
location, and it is surrounded by curious biblical allusions, such as the
reference to the Star Wormwood. It is not unreasonable to expect that
the full burden, if expressed there at all, will be expressed in the paragraph taken as a whole, and that to an analysis of it we must bring
our whole knowledge of the poem. If the poem does reflect the ob-
jective/subjective ambiguity which is the subject of this paper, then
that part of the burden which may be expressed as directly as it is in
lines 831–36 is only a facet of the objective meaning, as is the apparent
conviction a few lines later (845–57) that art exists solely in order to
call a man a fool without offending him. I hope to show later that, in
Browning's theory, the subjective burden cannot be expressed in such
a direct fashion, but its nature may be suggested in many ways: by
speaking of saving a soul, by linking it with Beethoven's "Andante," by
the allusion to the poet as Christ, or by the high honor given to art as
the only way of speaking essential truths, not commonplaces. When

Browning, therefore, just after the quoted lines, asks the question "Why take the artistic way to prove so much?" we must be prepared to take the irony: that isn't really very much to say, and it hardly requires art to say it at all.

Like Kierkegaard, Browning has also been accused of being deliberately anti-intellectual. It seems to me that he can be called so only if the phrase is taken to mean that he discredited the discursive intellect as the sole arbiter of ethical and religious truth. I think he would probably have regarded an absolute trust in man's rational powers as yet another myth of man's making, but it is important to note that even in ethical and religious matters he does not deny all value to the intellect, once its nature and its limitations are recognized. In addition to testing the myth and bringing forward the possibilities which make ethical choice possible, the intellect in Browning's scheme has the important function of rendering the belief intelligible enough for a man to act with the conviction that he has not been merely irrational, and that he has employed his power of judgment. Not all beliefs are equally good, and for Browning the success or failure of the mind in seeing them through depend on whether love is the motive and the direction. The process itself is explored in the poetry. For that reason, it is a little misleading to say that Browning, in claiming that his poems were "so many utterances of so many imaginary persons, not mine,"[10] was merely trying to render them more "objective" and therefore less "personal."[11] Certainly Browning is not to be identified with the views of his characters, but the poems are nonetheless personal; they are always informed by his own point of view, so that the subjective element of "meaning" is in his control. Some of the more discursive monologues, such as *Christmas-Eve* and *Easter-Day*, where Browning is thought to express his own ideas more directly, serve to demonstrate the role of abstract thought. But they reveal the process of thought in an individual at a specific moment in time; their effect is to show that speculative thought is endless, that it is subject to renewal under different circumstances, and that it is the circumstances which give rise to the thought.

Some of these ideas can be clarified by noting a line twice repeated (with slight variation) in "One Word More." It expresses an idea which is not only of major importance in much of Browning's poetry, but which is especially central to the meaning of *The Ring and the Book*: "Where my heart lies, let my brain lie also!" (4;142). Browning's apparent conviction here that the heart is "superior" to the brain has sometimes appeared to support the charge of anti-intellectualism. I take the line to mean that in the pursuit of ethical "truth" man's abstract intellect is not the absolute sole lord, but is fulfilled and rendered effective by his prior disposition towards love. It is altogether appropriate that such an idea should urge itself through experience rather than in a more purely abstract manner, since it acquires its peculiar force only in a philosophy directed towards the charting of experience. But in addition to its being a fact in Browning's psychological development, as Mrs. Miller views it in her psychological study of Browning,[12] it also has the status of an idea. Stated abstractly, the idea may seem to be little more than a platitude: the mind may be diverted to good or to evil, and there needs no ghost come from the grave to tell us that. But the simple statement is not the idea; that receives real content only in the poem, where we experience directly the complex relationship between the operations of intellect and love. Here the notion that abstract thought, though unavoidable, is not in itself decisive in the pursuit of ethical "truth" (which is Caponsacchi's formulation of the idea) in some ways anticipates the "modern" notion that man acts not so much according to what he "knows" as according to the "myth" he believes.[13] Browning is unusually aware of the role of the mind in testing the myth and in rendering it intelligible (as Kierkegaard puts it, "Nonsense therefore he cannot believe against the understanding, for precisely the understanding will discern that it is nonsense and will prevent him from believing it. . . ." [PS, 504]), but clearly that process need not involve abstract thought alone. It may require another kind of thought, in which the mind is directed towards existence, rather than abstracting from it.[14] *The Ring and the Book* embodies Browning's fullest encounter with such ideas; for him they absolutely require artistic expression and resist any other kind. In such matters Browning is in distinguished philosophic company, and in our search for his meaning we may legitimately enlist the aid of such thinkers as Kierkegaard in order to see more clearly what the poetry itself says.

III

At the same time, it is important to see *The Ring and the Book* as Browning's most mature fulfillment (and amplification) of the poetic theory worked out in his 1851 *Essay on Shelley*. The most successful study of that difficult work is by Thomas J. Collins, who interprets it according to the moral-aesthetic development he traces so ably in Browning's early poems.[15] Collins develops DeVane's assertion that Browning regarded himself as an objective/subjective poet, and substantiates more fully and accurately Philip Drew's contention that Shelley is also regarded as having combined the functions of both kinds of poet.[16] In doing so, however, he is obliged to admit not only that Browning in the *Essay* is "as inconsistent and ambiguous as he frequently is in his poetry,"[17] but also that he was capable of the most obvious contradiction. Browning, in a crucial passage, claims that all poets possess a degree of both the subjective and the objective faculties, and then continues as follows:

A mere running in of the one faculty upon the other is, of course, the ordinary circumstance. Far more rarely it happens that either is found so decidedly prominent and superior as to be pronounced comparatively pure; while of the perfect shield, with the gold and the silver side set up for all comers to challenge, there has yet been no instance.°

If, as Collins claims, Browning means here that "English literature has not produced an artist who is capable of brandishing a 'perfect shield,'"[18] meaning that he does not possess both faculties equally, then it is simply a contradiction for Browning to claim (as he does later) that Shelley possessed both faculties. But it is best to explore all possible interpretations of the passage before resting an argument on the assumption that Browning simply forgot on one page what he had written on another. Collins' argument does not, I think, sufficiently encounter the distinction Browning maintains between the personality of the "whole poet," Shelley, and the poems which reflect it. It is one thing to claim that Shelley, in his personality as a poet, possessed equally the subjective and the objective faculties, but another to say that in his poetry itself he perfectly employed these capabilities.

Collins explains Browning's apparent notion that in Shelley's case biography is helpful only because of the poet's unique personal circumstance:

Browning writes that while it is necessary to know the biography of the subjective poet in order to fully understand his work, it is only because Shelley died in his youth, and because his life has since been misunderstood

° The text of the *Essay on Shelley* is in the Cambridge edition of Browning's poetry (Boston, 1895), pp. 1008–14. Citations from it are hereafter identified as *ES*. Since the essay is short and the pages long, I give page numbers only for long quotations.

and falsified, that biography is helpful in his case. Like the objective poet, Shelley's personality shines forth from his poetry.[19]

But for Browning it is precisely because the objective poet's personality does *not* "shine forth" from his poetry that in his case biography is irrelevant:

Still, fraught with instruction and interest as such details [of biography] are, we can, if needs be, dispense with them. The man passes, the work remains. The work speaks for itself, as we say; and the biography of the worker [the objective poet] is no more necessary to an understanding or enjoyment of it than is a model or anatomy of some tropical tree to the right tasting of the fruit we are familiar with on the market-stall. . . . (*ES*, 1008–9)

On the other hand, says Browning, since the personality of the subjective poet is always in a sense the subject matter of his poetry, we *always* stand in need of biography: "as readers of his poetry, [we] must be readers of his biography also." Shelley's position is unique in two ways. We are, first of all, thrown "back on the evidence of biography" because "the misconstruction of his moral nature prepar[ed] the way for the misappreciation of his intellectual labors." Were it not for that situation (accidental to the value of his poetry), we would see that Shelley was superior to other subjective poets because he revealed himself almost perfectly through his poetry: "the unmistakable quality of the verse would be evidence enough, under usual circumstances [the absence of prejudice], not only of the kind and degree of the intellectual but of the moral constitution of Shelley: the whole personality shining forward from the poems, without much need of going further to seek it" (*ES*, 1010). From this point on in the *Essay*, it is clear that Browning is taken up with the poet himself, and with the poetry only as it reflects the personality. Shelley certainly possessed the subjective and the objective faculties, having the "function" and the "virtue" of the "whole poet" even when his poetry failed as art. He elevated himself to his own conception of the ideal man, and he aspired to elevate the human to the "actual Divine"; he also possessed the "subordinate power of delivering these attained results to the world in an embodiment of verse more closely answering to the indicative of the process of the informing spirit, (failing, as it occasionally does, in art, only to succeed in the highest art) . . . than can be attributed to any other writer whose record is among us" (*ES*, 1011). It is only near the end of the essay that Browning returns to comment specifically on "Shelley as a poet." There he explains his view that, although Shelley failed to realize perfectly his vast potential, yet the brilliant revelation of personality renders his poetry more valuable than art. Calling Shelley's poetry "a sublime fragmentary essay," he continues:

It would be easy to take my stand on successful instances of objectivity in Shelley: there is the unrivalled *Cenci*;[20] there is the *Julian and Maddalo* too; there is the magnificent *Ode to Naples*; why not regard, it may be said, the less organized matter as the radiant elemental foam and solution, out of which would have been evolved, eventually, creations as perfect even as those? But I prefer to look for the highest attainment, not simply the high,—and, seeing, I hold by it. There is surely enough of the work "Shelley" to be known enduringly among men, and, I believe, to be accepted of God, as human work may; and around the imperfect proportions of such, the most elaborated productions of ordinary art must arrange themselves as inferior illustrations. (*ES*, 1014)

Shelley's greatest achievement was himself; he may eventually have created subjective, or even subjective/objective, poems as perfect as his objective ones, but to the degree that his "imperfect fragments" reveal himself they are superior to all art.

In thus holding to a distinction between Shelley's poetic faculties and his imperfect realization of an objective/subjective poetry, Browning was not merely, as Collins says, "projecting into the name and person of Shelley the ideals and aspirations which he himself had assimilated by 1851,"[21] he was also defining the extent of Shelley's failure to achieve them poetically. Shelley was, according to Browning, the "whole poet," having both objective and subjective faculties, but he "died before his youth ended," and before his art had fully matured. He *"would have* finally ranged himself with the Christians," but he did not. His final vision was more akin to that of Browning's David; prophetic, indeed, but nonetheless a vision of things yet to come.

Collins shows clearly that Browning, when he wrote the *Essay,* had not yet fulfilled his own aspirations in poetry. But by 1851 he had recognized himself as possessing both poetic faculties, he had resolved his moral-aesthetic speculations, and he had come into full possession of his poetic powers. Significantly, in discussing the "perfect shield" of which there had "yet" been no example, he has moved from poets to poetry. In the past, he says, English poets have produced examples of either subjective or objective poems, but there is no reason "why these two modes of poetic *faculty* may not issue hereafter from the same poet in successive perfect *works*, examples of which . . . we have hitherto possessed in distinct individuals only." But, as we see later in the *Essay,* we have now had an example of at least one "whole *poet,*" who, possessed of an equal balance of poetic *powers,* could produce both "successful instances of objectivity" and purely subjective "effluences." It remains for Browning, in the future, to produce the first examples of the subjective and the objective elements fused together in the same poem—to produce "the perfect shield, with the gold and the silver side set up for all comers to challenge."[22]

IV

There is no doubt, as Collins says, that *"Men and Women* represents the culmination of Robert Browning's moral-aesthetic development,"[23] and that in it he tried to illustrate the theory established in the *Essay on Shelley.* The dramatic monologue, which Browning now recognized as his true medium, was in fact perfectly designed to combine the objective and the subjective, since the poet's own vision of "truth" might be embodied in a series of "objective" representations taken from the manifold of existence surrounding him. Presumably, the two elements are so fused together that the skillful reader sees at once each character's psychology and its relation to the poet's truth. But that requires a total view of the poems taken as a whole. The inherent limitation of such a collection as *Men and Women* is that which Collins notes when he observes that readers have "tended to treat [Browning's] mature poems as isolated units."[24] Furthermore, the "objective" *form* of the poetry prevents the poet from telling the reader of his (the poet's) own relationship to it, and the real problem is to keep the objective and the subjective elements clear and distinct. Actually, Browning saw the problem, and in such poems as "One Word More" he attempted to give the collection a unity, claiming that it is the poet himself who could "enter" into each of the men and women, "use their service, / Speak from every mouth,—the speech, a poem" (131-32). But without an explicit statement of his aesthetic theory, the subjective element tends to be lost through no fault of the reader. The variety of interpretations given to such poems as "Bishop Blougram's Apology" illustrates the difficulty. Browning must speak only through a series of personae; since none of them as independent characters can perfectly reflect the poet's total view, it is difficult to find a touchstone to determine which ideas belong to Browning, which to the personae. With

few exceptions, futhermore, each poem reflects only a facet of "truth."
The three basic themes of religion, love, and art are taken up variously
by the several personae and given the particular coloration of personality and circumstance characteristic of real life; in none are they
unified and placed in relation to the poet himself. Even in such poems
as "Fra Lippo Lippi," where all three themes are found together,
Browning must have his painter speak "objectively" for him, but often
in terms that seem more appropriate to the persona's own experiences
than to the poet's, unless we care to speculate on Browning's admiration for the bordello as well as the immoralist. In such a collection
there is no "external" reference to function as a determinant of meaning
in such a way as, for example, the allegorical strata do in the *Canterbury Tales* or in the *Divine Comedy*.

Some corroborative evidence that Browning himself felt the weakness of his plan lies in the extensive alterations to which he subjected
Men and Women for the revised version in the collected edition of his
poems in 1863, the year before he actually began writing *The Ring and
the Book*. In place of the fifty poems in the first edition, the selection
of 1863 opens with a prefatory poem, "Transcendentalism: A Poem in
Twelve Books," and contains only twelve others, not all of them drawn
from the original fifty, but each obviously intended to be taken as one
of the "twelve books." It seems likely to me that by 1863 Browning
had already conceived the formal plan of the *Ring*, and that he tried
to impose upon *Men and Women* an order and structure similar to
that of the poem he recognized was to be his greatest achievement.
At any rate, while there may be only the most general thematic similarities between these poems and the twelve monologues of the *Ring*,
the first and last poems after the "prologue" do have functions quite
similar to those of Books I and XII. "Transcendentalism," in a comic
and partly ironic manner, introduces the distinction between lyric
poetry and the poetry of ideas, a distinction which may be considered
a rough analogue to that between objective and subjective poetry.
No resolution is provided here except by implication, but when the
speaker tells the poet (presumably Browning) "You are a poem,
though your poem's naught," we are ironically reminded of Browning's
characterization of Shelley as one who failed to give perfect poetic
expression to his subjective powers, but whose own being was above
all art. The resolution comes in "How it Strikes a Contemporary," the
poem which, in my opinion, parallels Book I of the *Ring*. This piece is

also based on an ironic situation: the speaker, who is obviously a man
of limited knowledge and experience, nevertheless manages to describe
a poet who combines the objective and subjective faculties. From the
very beginning, he invests inanimate things with significance, as if to
follow the advice in "Transcendentalism," to "tell us what they [ob-
jects] mean." The poet's suit, for example, is "conscientious still, / And
many might have worn it, though none did." The "ruff" has "significance"; the "hat" is "scrutinizing." Having established the meaningful-
ness of objects, the speaker prepares us to accept this poet's actions as
symbolic of the concerns of the objective poet; in fact, when he
remarks that this poet "took such cognizance of men and things," he
echoes Browning's description of the objective poet's interest in the
Essay on Shelley. Such a poet takes for his materials "the doings of
men," and his endeavor is to "reproduce things external," things which
he, as seer, is able to understand more fully than the rest of mankind
and to render intelligible. However, when the speaker suggests that
this poet perhaps "took account / Of all thought, said and acted, then
went home, / And wrote it fully to our Lord the King," he not only
reflects Browning's view that "The Poet's concern is with God," but
he is also describing the work of the subjective poet, whose concern is
with "absolute truth" as that is reflected in his own soul.

   It is clear that the speaker in "How it Strikes a Contemporary" is
often groping for meaning, and that he cannot really understand many
of the implications of his own comments. Part of the success of the
poem, in fact, is that the speaker manages to communicate on Browning's behalf what he himself is not quite able to grasp. Perhaps this is a
way of suggesting that the ordinary reader need not understand with
his critical intelligence the impact a poem (here, a poet) may have
upon him; but at any rate, through an ironic reversal, the speaker
presents a perfect image of the station belonging to the objective/
subjective poet:

> Did the man love his office? Frowned our Lord,
> Exhorting when none heard—'Beseech Me not!
> 'Too far above My people,—beneath Me!
> 'I set the watch,—how should the people know?
> 'Forget them, keep Me all the more in mind!'
> Was some such understanding 'twixt the Two?
>
>   (66–71)

In the syntax of the poem, these questions are rhetorical only to the

speaker; the implied answers place the poet as an intermediary between God and man. As objective poet, he is not "too far above"
mankind, he is sufficiently on top of his materials to make them
intelligible. As subjective poet, he is indeed "beneath" God, but his
personality reflects the absolute and tries to make it accessible to the
lower portions of mankind. In this way, the poem serves to introduce
the poetic theory illustrated in the succeeding ones.

We shall see that Book I of the *Ring* introduces the same theory in a
far more elaborate manner. Of particular interest now, however, is the
symbolic image of the poet's station which parallels that in "How it
Strikes a Contemporary." It occurs after Browning has somewhat
prosily described the contents of the Old Yellow Book. Preparing now
to summarize the murder story itself through an act of creative imagination, he first describes the process as a mixing of "Something of
mine" with the "gold" of the Old Yellow Book. Before turning to the
narrative, however, he speaks of his rapt absorption in the Old Yellow
Book, and then describes the scene carefully:

> . . . the while I read and read
> I turned, to free myself and find the world,
> And stepped out on the narrow terrace, built
> Over the street and opposite the church,
> And paced its lozenge brickwork sprinkled cool;
> Because Felice-church-side-stretched, a-glow
> Through each square window fringed for festival,
> Whence came the clear voice of the cloistered ones
> Chanting a chant made for midsummer nights—
> I know not what particular praise of God,
> It always came and went with June. Beneath
> I' the street, quick shown by openings of the sky
> When flame fell silently from cloud to cloud,
> Richer than that gold snow Jove rained on Rhodes,
> The townsmen walked by twos and threes, and talked,
> Drinking the blackness in default of air—
> A busy human sense beneath my feet. . . .

(477–93)

Clearly, this allusive passage is not merely a "realistic" description of
the setting; it is a symbolic placement in his proper situation of the
poet who is about to imitate God's creative act in man's limited
manner. He is placed somewhat above the ordinary actions of mortals
in order to observe them from a higher vantage point, but at the same
time he is subject to an influence from the heavens, symbolized by
Jove's golden rain.

V

The parallels between "One Word More" and the corresponding Book XII of the *Ring* are not, of course, exact. Just as Book XII briefly summarizes the theory elaborated in Book I, however, so "One Word More" provides a statement in the poet's own voice of the poetic theory suggested in "How it Strikes a Contemporary." As we have seen, perhaps the most important aspect of this statement is his claim that he has provided not merely an "objective" portrait of his various "men and women," but that he has employed them in order to convey something of his own; his practice has been to "Enter each and all, and use their service, / Speak from every mouth,—the speech, a poem." The suggestion that such a fusion of the subjective and the objective involves also a combination of personal and public utterances is taken up in Browning's treatment of "Rafael's sonnets" and "Dante's picture." Each artist, he says, yearns to find, for an expression of his private love, an art other than the one he employs for his public and prophetic expressions, one which will be seen only by the beloved. "Heaven's gift," he says, "takes earth's abatement"; apparently, the great artist must fear that the revelation of his private emotions may destroy the effectiveness of his public art: "Never dares the man put off the prophet." In Section XII of the poem, however, Browning makes it clear that he is untouched by such a problem in expressing his love to his wife:

> I shall never, in the years remaining,
> Paint you pictures, no, nor carve you statues,
> Make you music that should all-express me;
> So it seems; I stand on my attainment.
> This of verse alone, one life allows me;
> Verse and nothing else have I to give you.
> Other heights in other lives, God willing;
> All the gifts from all the heights, your own, Love!

Clearly, this is no admission of inadequacy, but a boast that he has done in his single art what others require two arts to accomplish. He tells Elizabeth to "Take these lines, *look lovingly and nearly,* / Lines I write the first time and the last time" (italics mine). Other artists may do as they like; as for the poet, "He who writes, may write *for once* as I do." The implication, of course, is that he has put into his poems everything that can be said at all. Even when he claims that the poems belong to "all men," and that now he wants to "speak this once in my true person," all he can say is "look on these my men and women, / Take and keep my fifty poems finished." In so dedicating his art to his wife, he is making his love complete: "Where my heart lies, let my brain lie also." Apart from that, he can only "bless myself with silence." But this return to his wife at the end of *Men and Women* introduces a subject which, as we will see later, is also of crucial importance in *The Ring and the Book.*

VI

The aesthetic theory I have been discussing is, at best, vaguely suggested in the poems of *Men and Women;* it is most fully described in the *Essay on Shelley.* In recognizing that *The Ring and the Book* was to be his masterpiece, however, Browning must have felt the enormous advantage, provided so miraculously by his discovery of the Old Yellow Book, in producing a group of monologues all held together by the same series of events. Since the individual characters in the poem see the events only from their own points of view, they may be located morally in relation to the larger truth of the whole, which is appropriately expressed in the poem by the objective/subjective poet in his own person, because only such a "whole poet" may see the "whole truth" (117) of the book. In that way he can combine the effects of an *Essay on Shelley* and a *Men and Women.* Browning was probably using no mere figure of speech in claiming that his discovery of the Old Yellow Book was "predestined" (40). God's absolute truth as reflected in the poet's personality is the direct concern of the subjective faculty as described in the *Essay.* Divine intervention in the discovery and in the understanding of the poem's materials is part of the creation itself, and Browning is obliged to include it in the poem, a procedure he could effect only by introducing himself in the context of his whole poetic theory. He can thus explain his own relationship to the poem and free his characters to illustrate his theory, giving body to his subjective truth in a re-creating of real existence, and providing a framework for interpreting that reality. We may therefore view *The Ring and the Book* as Browning's "perfect shield," reflecting the fullest development of the ideas expounded in the *Essay on Shelley,* and providing a model for interpreting such collections as *Men and Women.*

THE EXISTENTIAL AESTHETIC

At the beginning of this paper, I objected that many critics read Browning's monologues merely as objective psychological portraits. It should be remembered, however, that in these poems Browning does supply all the materials for such readings. In his continuing attempts after *Sordello* to write in a more popular vein, and in his claim that the poems are utterances of "so many imaginary persons, not mine," I think Browning saw that he must strengthen that aspect of his poetry which would, as he said, be apprehensible and acceptable to the "aggregate human mind." The subjective meaning, of course, may also be seen in the portraits; it may be got at partially by noting certain images and allusions, and by carefully reading lines that have meaning on both levels. But since the subjective ultimately requires that the poet engage the moral energies of certain readers as specific individuals, I think he expected that the subjective would be taken up only by a few readers. Such a view may help to explain his apprehension, expressed in a letter to Ruskin, lest "the public, critics and all, begin to understand and approve me,"[25] and his assertion there and elsewhere that "a poet's affair is with God."

The objective aspect may come from the poet's invention, which in a realistic poem has an obvious reference to observable reality; to this the subjective/objective poet adds the subjective element as he perceives that also to lie in the reality surrounding him. The subjective, in other words, is not merely the gratuitous contribution of the poet acting according to his own peculiar theory, it is also grounded in a reality outside of himself, though he can express it only as he views it. In *The Ring and the Book*, the objective materials are called "fact" also because they refer to events that actually happened apart from the poet's power of invention. In this case, the subjective meaning was put into real existence by God, and the poet simply employs his subjective faculty to find it there.[26]

I

The terms in which Browning describes the objective poet in the *Essay on Shelley* have clear relevance to *The Ring and the Book*. His brief definition of dramatic poetry describes the ten interior books of the poem and introduces an important emphasis on action; the objective poet, he says, "chooses to deal with the doings of men, (the result of which, in its pure form, when even description, as suggesting a describer, is dispensed with, is what we call dramatic poetry)" (*ES*, 1009). Such a poet "endeavors to reproduce things external (whether

the phenomena of the scenic universe, or the manifested action of the
human heart and brain)"; just so, in *The Ring and the Book*, Browning
will reproduce the "facts" of the Old Yellow Book, twice described as
having been "Secreted from man's life when hearts beat hard, / And
brains, high-blooded, ticked two centuries since" (36–37; 87–88). And
just as in *The Ring and the Book* the poet removed himself (the alloy)
from the poem by means of the acid, disappearing under question so
that the Old Yellow Book itself "grew all in all" (687), so in the *Essay*
Browning says that the work of the objective poet "will of necessity be
substantive, projected from himself and distinct." An objective poem—
Shakespeare's *Othello*, for example—becomes a "fact itself"; and in
The Ring we are asked the rhetorical question whether "fiction which
makes fact alive" is "fact too" (705). In short, what the subjective
poet eschews, the objective poet takes for his materials: "the noisy,
complex, yet imperfect exhibitions of nature in the manifold experience
of man around him."

In stressing so urgently the objective poet's concern with the external, the "manifested *actions*" of men (italics mine), it is clear that
Browning means to emphasize the poet's attention to the actual realities
of existence, so that the poetry is partly governed by observable truth.
"The spiritual comprehension may be infinitely subtilized, but the raw
material it operates upon must remain." This is a kind of basic, bed-
rock poetry which must never be disregarded, since it grounds thought
in real life: "There may be no end of the poets who communicate to us
what they see in an object with reference to their own individuality:
what it was before they saw it, in reference to the aggregate human
mind, will be desirable to know as ever" (*ES*, 1009). For this reason,
in *The Ring and the Book* Browning insists that the basic materials out
of which his poem was made are "fact"—"pure crude fact," a record
of actions that really happened, at a certain time in a certain place.
Whatever else he does, the objective poet begins with observation of
external actions which can be viewed by all men.

Since the objective poet also aims to probe the psychological and
moral nature of the events,[27] it is important to note that in this theory
action acquires a peculiar status as the locus of meaning. The subjective poet, indeed, avoids dealing with human actions because these
"imperfect exhibitions of nature in the manifold experience of men"
serve only to "distract and suppress the working of his brain," as they
did to Shelley when he became involved in practical matters.[28] When

such a poet draws his materials from nature, he selects only those "external scenic appearances which strike out most abundantly and uninterruptedly his inner light and power," the aspects which most immediately reflect his own personality. His endeavor may seem to border dangerously on the merely personal and the abstract: he is given to "drawing out" and "lifting up" an "ideal of a future man" which he has "described as possible"; he may return to the concrete only if he assimilates this ideal "to the present reality of the poet's soul already arrived at the higher state of development," and embodies it in verse "closely answering to the indicative of the process of the informing spirit." He thereby becomes less abstract, but not less personal. The objective poet, however, is not confused by human actions.[29] He begins with them, not only as giving priority to the actual over the possible, but also as the primary evidence of the informing idea which he infers from them, and as a test of truth in that idea. In thus locating an idea in action, he guarantees that the truth of it is independent of his own personality.

Browning's known distrust of abstract reason divorced from actuality may be seen as a form of Kierkegaard's view that ethical truths find their only appropriate expression in action, not in language nor in thought. Kierkegaard held that speculative thought abstracts precisely from temporal being, where the ethical finds its only possible function; it therefore expresses only the category of possibility, not that of an existence involving change. Thought cannot really accommodate movement at all, and from that point of view it has little to do with ethical reality. It cannot even impel a man into action, since it is by nature endless. Termination of thought in the interest of action is thus regarded as an operation of the will, a faculty more closely related to belief and to existence than thought, which in turn requires circumstances to evoke it and action to translate it into existence. In other words, ethics removed from actual, temporal existence ceases to be ethics at all. Since the ethical is in this sense always at the mercy of the real, action provides a crucial test of truth in the idea, and in the individual the only real evidence of his own quality of will. The moral life is occasioned only by circumstances outside the personality; though guilt or innocence is established according to the internal intention, the effect of intention on the personality is incomplete until it is located in action, which alone may provide the sense of continuity necessary in encountering moral crises as they present themselves in time.

Kierkegaard does not, of course, deny the role of mind. He simply insists on its necessary relationship to action, which gives it content and ultimately governs its direction, so that the ethical is not merely the problem of *knowing* right from wrong: "the ethical is not merely a knowing, it is also a doing that is related to a knowing . . ." (*PS*, 143). Again: "if the content of thought were reality, the most perfect possible anticipation of an action in thought before I had yet acted, would be the action. In that manner no action would ever take place, and the intellectual would swallow the ethical" (*PS*, 362). The point therefore is not that thought has no validity (provided its real nature is recognized), nor that it is necessarily empty of meaningful content. It is simply that speculative thought, helpful as it may be in increasing one's awareness and the range of possibilities available to action, is unreal in terms of ethical existence; it does not come into real being until it acquires decisive expression (one involving choice) in action. "Between the action as represented in thought on the one hand, and the real action on the other, between the possibility and the reality, there may in respect of content be no difference at all. But in respect of form, the difference is essential. Reality is the interest in action, in existence" (*PS*, 304). Since Browning's ultimate aim is a moral one, a theory such as this points up the significance in his use of the dramatic monologue; it is to represent ethical truth *in its proper form* that he, as objective poet, reproduces the external actions of men. In his dramatic monologues, thought is focused upon action as the basic materials of existence.

II

The ethical must here be regarded first in the Greek sense, as an obligation to conform to an external and universal ideal of conduct; consequently, ethical striving is a constant attempt to reveal the self in terms apprehensible to the aggregate of humanity. Visible action, not language, is the indispensible condition of that self-revelation: "Even another human being with whom [a person] lives can reveal himself to his observation only through the external . . ." (*PS*, 127). In the assessment of motive, however, the external cannot define its own significance: "It would be stupid for anyone to suppose that I mean . . . to make the external the test of action" (*PS*, 127). The Greeks tended to make ethics too purely a matter of knowledge alone, assuming that whoever knows the good will do it. Such a view tends to minimize the moral struggle, an area of human experience so central in Browning's ethical thought. For Kierkegaard (and, I think, for Browning), the ethical really tends towards the religious for its fulfillment. The real ethical meaning of an act lies in the will, the inwardness of the idea it expresses, and for this reason the inward movement of the man is decisive: "the real action is not the external act, but an internal decision in which the individual puts an end to the mere possibility and identifies himself with the content of his thought in order to exist in it. This is the action" (PS, 302–3). Similarly, in *The Ring and the Book*, while we are reminded that action is the necessary element in bringing thought into decisive existence so that the idea may be articulated, we are not allowed to forget that it is the inward idea which informs the action. The Pope, for example, speaks of the Convertite Monastery as "A thing existent only while it acts, / Does as designed, else a nonentity, / For what is an idea unrealized?" (X, 1500–1502). On the other hand, in judging the actions, he is aware that the merely external is not the test of action. Although he sees in Guido's marriage an "act" which he can "sever from his life as sample" (X, 525–26), his purpose in analyzing it is to discern Guido's "habitual creed exemplified / Most in the last deliberate act" (X, 520–21). And when he imagines himself standing before God to receive final judgment, commanded to "Show me thy fruit, the latest act of thine!" (X, 341), he is at the same time aware that "it is the seed of act, / God holds appraising in His hollow palm, / Not act grown great thence on the world below" (X, 271–73). Finally, as if to confirm again the relationship between the thought and the act as the necessary revelation of it, he recognizes that his own decision in the case, which was determined before he begins to speak, is nevertheless incomplete until it is realized in act: it is his business "The thought, to clothe in deed, and give [to] the world" (X, 280).

This stress on the relationship between action and meaning has important consequences in Browning's poetic theory. It should be noted that the Pope has made his decision before he speaks, and has therefore, in Kierkegaard's phrase, employed his will in identifying himself with his thought. In line 280, the inward action is given existence in the visible world, a process necessary for revealment. The monologue itself, however, is an examination of judgment, which is only one element in making a choice. The poet must begin with the external as the only evidence of the other two processes which preceded it, and which may be said in that sense to be "in" the external action. For that reason,

Browning did not, as has been suggested,[30] try to "justify stamping an interpretation upon the facts"; his claim, at least, is that his analysis of mental and ethical process is rooted in an actual reality which in some sense governs it, so that he infers the unseen on the evidence of the things that are seen. In analyzing the process of judgment, the poet draws upon his own understanding, which corresponds to the objective faculty; but since the will is required to bring the decision into existence, identifying the man with his thought, the poet must re-create the moral aspect of the action as a condition of knowledge. The moral aspect thus has an epistemological import, and for it the poet draws upon his own moral nature, which corresponds to the subjective faculty. In such a view, no actions are without moral content, though of course one may consider them in that way. For Browning, I think, we do not fully understand the experience unless at the same time we receive it in terms of our own moral nature. Like Kierkegaard, he may have thought that ultimately there is no such thing as experience "for its own sake," since an action always, whether we are aware of it or not, contributes something to ethical character—which, like time, cannot be suspended for a moment. At any rate, in revitalizing the events recorded in the Old Yellow Book, Browning is restoring their moral character as he understands it to be implied by the events themselves.

III

Both Kierkegaard and Browning concern themselves with the basic problem that emerges in this kind of theory: how the poet (and ultimately the reader) may pass from the external acts to the internal idea they express. Visible action may be essential to ethical revelation, but the interpretation of it by an observer is always ambiguous. In the *Essay on Shelley*, Browning holds that the objective poet may move beyond a mere description of external events and probe the idea behind them, but the process by which he does so remains obscure; one wonders whether he is not partly employing the faculty of the subjective poet, since the two faculties are rarely found in their pure state, but merge into each other much as the ethical runs into the religious. To the extent that he deals simply with moral and psychological fact, of course, his aim falls short of the subjective poet's, whose "loftier vision" is conveyed by "intensifying the import of details and rounding the universal meaning" (*ES*, 1009). The objective poet is simply above ordinary mortals because he understands more and can select the details which convey meaning: he sees an external event "more clearly, wisely, and deeply than is possible to the average mind, at the same time that he is so acquainted and in sympathy with its narrower comprehension as to be careful to supply it with no other materials than it can combine into an intelligible whole,"[31] a whole which will convey meaning as that is apprehended in terms of the "aggregate mind" rather than just that of the poet. Concerning himself with the manifested actions of real men in the manifold of existence, and leaving out the more subjective elements of his personality in the interest of probing reality as it was before he saw it, he may describe the action and even its moral nature, although he is prevented from "placing" the act in the universal scheme of things which subjective poets see "with reference to their own personality."

Kierkegaard introduces the problem in a way that may be seen to have a clear bearing on *The Ring and the Book:*

[A human being] can reveal himself to . . . observation only through the external; and in so far the interpretation is necessarily affected with ambiguities. But the more complicated the externality in which the ethical inwardness is reflected, the more difficult becomes the problem of observation. . . . It becomes more and more difficult even for a judge to find a clear way through the mazes of his case, the more significant the parties involved. And yet the judge does not have the responsibility of passing an ethical judgment, but merely a legal one. . . . (*PS,* 127)

In the poem, of course, we do not view the judges directly, but Browning insists four times in a paragraph of 102 lines (141–252) that their judgment was based exclusively on written documents, "the trial / Itself, to all intents, being then as now / Here in the book and nowise out of it" (152–54). Browning himself, then, assumes the role of the judges; the same materials are available to him, and except for the mere passage of time his situation in no way differs from the contemporary one. It is clear, however, that he is not making merely a legal judgment, but a moral one. All of the characters in the poem who represent a degree of "truth" recognize that at some point the legal and moral issues are as inseparable as the ethical and the religious ones. Caponsacchi, for example, when he attacks the judges most fiercely, repeatedly links law and gospel, as if to suggest that the law is ultimately dependent on religion for its truth, or that the judges can reach truth only to the extent that their natures are grounded in the

Christian virtue of Love: "Better late than never, law!" he says; "You understand of a sudden, gospel too / Has a claim here . . ." (VI, 136–37). But the section of Book I mentioned above (141–252) deals only with the legal aspect, and in it Browning is simply describing the nature of the Old Yellow Book—the nature of the materials out of which the poem is made. He is re-creating the trial, not the events leading to the murder. The record of the trial thus becomes primary fact, out of which the secondary facts (the events themselves, which contain meaning) must be inferred. While the objective poet concerns himself with both, he is governed by the primary facts to the extent that he must accept such matters as the innocence of Pompilia and the guilt of Guido, as established by the court's judgment and confirmed by the Pope. Such a poet may proceed to investigate the psychology of the speakers as that is suggested in the documents, but as he moves from a merely descriptive statement of the ethical nature of the actions to a judgment of their significance, his role ultimately becomes that of the subjective poet who sees the ethical significance within a larger scheme of things. It is the latter who gives us the sense that he has "resuscitated" the very act itself of Guido and the rest,[32] employing the action to convey the ethical significance.

IV

This process necessarily involves the poet's own personality. Later we will pursue this idea in the poem itself, where Browning says that it is out of his own "live soul" that he can restore to life the materials which lay inert in the Old Yellow Book. In the *Essay on Shelley*, where he ascribes this power to the subjective poet, he uses terms which echo the Pope's concern with "the seed of act / God holds appraising in His hollow palm":

[The subjective poet] is impelled to embody the thing he perceives, not so much with reference to the many below as to the one above him, the supreme Intelligence which apprehends all things in their absolute truth. . . . Not what man sees, but what God sees,—the *Ideas* of Plato, seeds of Creation lying burningly on the Divine Hand,—it is toward these that he struggles . . . preferring to seek them in his own soul as the nearest reflex of that absolute Mind. . . . [His poems] cannot be easily considered in abstraction from his personality,—being indeed the very radiance and aroma of his personality, projected from it but not separated. (*ES*, 1009)

The subjective poet, then, communicates the real ethical meaning which lies beyond the psychological and moral facts. His own personality is involved because, as Kierkegaard points out, man only understands the ethical by understanding himself: "For the study of the ethical, every man is assigned to himself. His own self is as material for this study more than sufficient; aye, this is the only place where *he* can study it with any assurance of certainty" (*PS*, 127). And it is therefore only through that knowledge that he can understand the ethical nature of historical personalities:

Only by closely attending to myself, can I arrive at an understanding of how an historical personality must have conducted himself while he lived; and only so do I understand him, when in my understanding I preserve him alive, not in the fashion of children, who smash the watch to pieces in order to find out what makes it run, or in the fashion of speculative philosophy, which transforms the historical personality into something different in order to understand him. But I cannot, by apprehending him as dead, learn from him what it means to live; that I must experience by myself. And therefore I must first understand myself, and not conversely. . . . (*PS*, 131)

In *The Ring and the Book*, Browning introduces the problem directly at two points. In the first, he describes his task as the re-creation (in theatrical fashion) of historical acts, but he warns the reader (and himself) of the difficulty in interpreting them:

> Let this old woe step on the stage again!
> Act itself o'er anew for men to judge,
> Not by the very sense and sight indeed—
> (Which take at best imperfect cognisance,
> Since, how heart moves brain, and how both move hand,
> What mortal ever in entirety saw?)
>
> (824–29)

The poet is indeed re-creating the very actions, the secondary facts inferred from the trial record, but a merely objective description of them is inadequate to the real truth the poet means to convey. In a line which reveals in little the basic psychological and moral concern of *The Ring and the Book*, Browning spells out his theory that man's ethical and emotional character really determines the direction of his thought, and that both achieve reality only in action: mere action, he says, cannot adequately reveal "how heart moves brain, and how both move hand." When he returns to this problem again towards the end of Book I, it is after the poet himself has intervened between the events and the reader's "observation" of them in the poem. As intermediary, he suggests that, in restoring the "old woe" to life again, he has also conveyed it with the complexity and elusiveness of real life, so that the reader confronts the poem much as the poet has confronted the Old Yellow Book:

> See it for yourselves,
> This man's act, *changeable because alive!*
> *Action now shrouds, now shows the informing thought;*
> Man, like a glass ball with a spark a-top,
> Out of the magic fire that lurks inside,
> Shows one tint at a time to take the eye:
> Which, let a finger touch the silent sleep,
> Shifted a hair's-breadth shoots you dark for bright,
> Suffuses bright with dark, and baffles so
> Your sentence absolute for shine or shade.
>
> (1364–73; italics mine)

The poet has created a subjective/objective world, in which the actions themselves are imperfect reflections of inwardness. In creating such a world, Browning has, as he claims, imitated "in man's due degree" (717) God's initial creative act. But in asking the reader to make a moral judgment, the poet must "intensify the import of details" and "round the universal meaning." Like God in the first instance, the poet must in his world provide the means of interpretation: he must find a kind of language and a form of art which may communicate the ethically inward meaning, which nevertheless lies in the action, not in language about the action. The problem is now not one of observation, but of communication.

V

At the basis of Kierkegaard's treatment of existential communication is the crucial principle that no ethical truth which depends for its value and meaning on real existence within an individual can ever become the content of communication: "existential reality is incommunicable, and the subjective thinker finds his reality in his own ethical existence. When reality is apprehended by an outsider it can be understood only as possibility" (*PS,* 320). One aspect of such reality is ideational, of course, and hence communicable; yet that aspect must not be isolated from those of passionate involvement and temporal striving which define its actuality. When the experience has been translated merely into an idea and is expressed in the form of abstract philosophical

propositions, it becomes quite different from the ethical. Even if
another person could manage to "appropriate inwardly" the idea, still
that is entirely due to his own ethical self-activity, and there remains a
question as to whether anything ethically significant has been communicated. Real communication is rooted in the method of the So-
cratic dialectic.

The difference between the idea and the ethical expression of it can
be seen in several ways. One raises the question of involvement;
objective thought, says Kierkegaard, "is indifferent to the thinking
subject and his existence," but the "subjective thinker is an existing
individual essentially interested in his own thinking, existing as he
does in his thought" (*PS*, 67). Again, ethics is a striving, but objective
thought abstracts from the motion which is characteristic of time:
"movement [is] the inexplicable presupposition and common factor
of thinking and being, and [is] their continued reciprocity" (*PS*, 100).
Or again, objective thought reflects only the result of a process, not
the process itself, and thus has characteristics of finality and certitude
inappropriate to a living human being:

> [Subjective thought] has therefore a different type of reflection, namely the
> reflection of inwardness, of possession, by virtue of which it belongs to the
> thinking subject and to no one else. While objective thought translates
> everything into results, and helps all mankind to cheat, by copying these
> off and reciting them by rote, subjective thought puts everything in process
> and omits the result; partly because this belongs to him who has the way,
> and partly because as an existing individual he is constantly in process of
> coming to be, which holds true of every human being. . . .
> The reflection of inwardness gives to the subjective thinker a double
> reflection. In thinking, he thinks the universal; but as existing in this
> thought and as assimilating it in his inwardness, be becomes more and
> more subjectively isolated. (*PS*, 67–68)

For these reasons, the linguistic form of propositional philosophy,
since it is *immediate* and *direct,** cannot communicate an existential

---

* These two terms may cause confusion, since in some modern criticism they
have come to take on meanings quite different from that of Kierkegaard. An objective communication may be said to be immediate because it is exactly
equivalent to the idea it expresses in reference both to the communicator and to
the recipient; abstracting from the real personality, it acquires no particularity
by its intellectual reception in an individual. Subjective communication, however,
involves more than the abstract idea; since it is indirect, it is a way of mediating
between two individuals. Note in this connection Browning's phrase in Book XII
(855–57), where he says that in communicating truth "Obliquely," art will not
"wrong the thought," by "missing the mediate word."

reality, but only possibility. According to Kierkegaard, poetry also expresses mere possibility, and thus shares with philosophy the inability to communicate ethical truth, although it may convey aesthetic mood and attitude. But Kierkegaard had in mind, I think, a particular kind of romantic poetry;[33] contradictory as it may seem, he did hold that some form of dialectical "communication" is possible, and that it involves a highly developed artistic form. He could not forbid this form of art to kinds of poetry of which he was unaware, and I see no reason why his theory of artistic communication may not apply specifically to the kind of poetry we find in *The Ring and the Book,* in the same sense that it applied to Kierkegaard's own works.

VI

While the artist may seem limited to the conveying of possibility, there yet appears to be a sense in which possibility grounded in existence may retain a distinct *reference* to the actual:

Everyone who makes a communication . . . will therefore be careful to give his existential communication the form of possibility,* precisely in order that it may have a relationship to existence. A communication in the form of a possibility compels the recipient to face the problem of existing in it, so far as this is possible between man and man. . . . Whatever is great in the sphere of the universally human must therefore not be communicated as a subject for admiration, but as an ethical *requirement.* In the form of a possibility it becomes a requirement. Instead of presenting an account of the good in the form of actuality, as is usually done, instead of insisting that such and such a person has actually lived, and has really done this or that, by which the reader is transformed into an admiring spectator, a critical connoisseur, the good should be presented in the form of a possibility. This will bring home to the reader, as closely as is possible, whether he will resolve to exist in it. A communication in the form of the possible, operates in terms of the ideal man (not the differential ideal, but the universal ideal), whose relationship to every individual man is that of a requirement. In the same degree as it is urged that it was this particular man who did the deed, it becomes easier for others to make him out an exceptional case. (*PS,* 320–21)

---

* It should be carefully noted that Kierkegaard here views the term from a different aspect. In discussing aesthetic mood and abstract ideas as possibilities, he means that they do not reflect ethical actuality in an individual; the individual does not live in them, but escapes into them by forgetting his actual self. In the present context, however, the possible is viewed as that which presents itself to the individual as an ideal, inviting him to realize it within himself as a necessity. In both cases, possibility is opposed to impossibility, but that is more important in the second usage.

This long passage expresses precisely the situation of Browning as the intermediary between one reality and another, though it is complicated by his own theory of employing the double function of the "whole" poet. As objective poet, he pays attention indeed to what has actually happened in these particular characters who really existed, in order that the ethical idea, so grounded in actuality, may have the character of a possibility (as opposed to impossibility); in the "realistic" portraits of such figures as Guido, Pompilia, and Caponsacchi, however, he introduces himself as the subjective poet, "intensifying the import of details," heightening the portrayals to those of ideal types[34] of their respective virtues and vices, depicting the ideal within the real in order to communicate the ethical as the kind of possibility which urges internal appropriation as a requirement for the recipient, who must in turn "resolve" whether "to exist in it" or not. Browning, in other words, will "write a book shall mean, beyond the facts, / *Suffice the eye* and *save the soul* beside" (XII, 862–83; italics mine), combining the objective and the subjective. It may be added that in Kierkegaard's "ideal" characters such a "resolve to exist" in the ethical is described as occurring in moments of crisis. He thereby stresses the need of passion as opposed to mere reflection, and emphasizes the communication as a possibility *requiring* the volition of the recipient for its actuality.[35] It is evident that this crisis technique is important in the monologues of *The Ring and the Book*. Without the appropriation and the interested self-activity of the reader, of course, the poem returns to the status of "objective" communication. The real communication requires the help of the reader.

Because direct and immediate expression of such matters is a contradiction, even ordinary language is disabled in the communication of them. Kierkegaard describes the situation in terms that will remind us later of the Pope's treatment of language:

When one man sets forth something and another acknowledges the same, word for word, it is taken for granted that they are in agreement, and that they have understood one another. . . . [The speaker] does not suspect that an agreement of this nature may be the grossest kind of misunderstanding. Nor does he suspect that, just as the subjective existing thinker has made himself free through the reduplication given his reflection, so the secret of all communication consists precisely in emancipating the recipient, and that for this reason he must not communicate himself directly. . . . (*PS*, 69)

The greatest artistic attention is therefore given not only to the language but also to the form of the communication. Since it must be an indirect form, expressing a relationship to existence rather than merely an idea, it must avoid any direct and objective relationship between the author and the reader which would unite them only in idea and therefore only impersonally:[36]

> Wherever the subjective is of importance to knowledge, and where appropriation thus constitutes the crux of the matter, the process of communiction is a work of art, doubly reflected. Its very first form is precisely the subtle principle that the personalities must be held devoutly apart from one another, and not permitted to fuse or coagulate into objectivity. It is at this point that objectivity and subjectivity part from one another. (PS, 73)

At the same time, the communication must be informed by a reflection of the subjective relationship between the author and the idea. One cannot ignore the ideational aspect, but its relationship to existence can be conveyed only by a reflection of the relationship between it and the ethical reality of the artist, so that the reader apprehends as a necessity the principle of appropriation through self-activity. The communication thus requires the "double reflection" mentioned above:

> The form of a communication must be distinguished from its expression. When the thought has found its suitable expression in the word, which is realized by means of a first reflection, there follows a second reflection, concerned with the relation between the communication and the author of it, and reflecting the author's own existential relationship to the Idea. (PS, 71)

The art is therefore grounded in the author's own reality, and it is this reference to existence which gives the work the sense of possibility as a requirement. The existential reality cannot itself be communicated, nor can the artist properly be said to "motivate" the reader;[37] but he can reflect his own involvement, providing that is not merely stated but expressed indirectly in the form:

> The difference between subjective and objective thinking must express itself also in the form of communication suitable to each. That is to say, the subjective thinker will from the beginning have his attention called to the requirement that this form should embody artistically as much of reflection as he himself has when existing in his thought. In an artistic manner, please note; for the secret does not lie in a direct assertion of the double reflection; such a direct expression of it is precisely a contradiction. (PS, 68–69)

VII

Such a theory as this underlies the Pope's well-known attack on language, and explains to a considerable extent the form and function of Book I. Kierkegaard points out, as we have seen, that "what is in itself true may in the mouth of such and such a person become untrue" (*PS*, 181). So the Pope, in his analysis of language, says:

> Why, can [a man] tell you what a rose is like,
> Or how the birds fly, and not slip to false
> Though truth serve better? Man must tell his mate
> Of you, me and himself, knowing he lies,
> Knowing his fellow knows the same,—will think
> "He lies, it is the method of a man!"
> And yet will speak for answer "It is truth"
> To him who shall rejoin "Again a lie!"
> Therefore this filthy rags of speech, this coil
> Of statement, comment, query and response,
> Tatters all too contaminate for use,
> Have no renewing. . . .
>
> (X, 364–75)

This is not merely an assessment of human motives and intentions, it is a reflection of the incommensurability between language and man's inner disposition. In this context, to tell "what a rose is like" is to communicate the full experience, sensory and emotional as well as ideational: presumably language cannot do that any more than it could convey anything significant about the flying birds, even if Browning knew the laws of aerodynamics. This kind of absolute inadequacy is then transferred to the ordinary objective statements man employs in trying to reveal himself through language: all attempts at communication are baffled simply because language as a vehicle involves untruth: man *must* tell a lie, for it is inherent in language. And yet the Pope sees that language in some form is nonetheless man's only instrument for communication, and he resigns himself to the use of it: "be man's method for man's life at least" (X, 381). This is essentially the view taken by Browning in his own voice in Book I. Although he is perfectly aware that through language man can expect nothing more than "truth mixed with falsehood," we must nonetheless listen, not merely for an echo from out of the past, but for the "Uproar *in* the echo" (834; italics mine): we are dependent on language as "helping us to all we seem to hear: / For how else know we save by worth of word?" (836–37).

In the Pope's monologue, the more positive justification of language acquires a religious formulation: "He, the Truth, is, too, / The Word" (375–76). Ultimately, Browning's own solution to the problem is also a religious one, since in this poem he is enlisting art in the service of religion. The objective poet explores the "lower moral point of view, under the mere conditions of art," but the subjective poet recognizes, like Kierkegaard, that the ethical always tends towards the religious for its fulfillment. Browning's justification of language in terms of art, then, gradually passes into the more subjective element, the formal involvement of the poet's personality in the poem. In Book XII, speaking of the "lesson" which "whatever lives should teach," he says: "Art remains the one way possible / Of speaking truth, to mouths like mine, at least" (839–40). A merely objective confrontation, of course, involves the difficulty that truth, "by when it reaches him [the recipient], looks false" (850). Art therefore seeks to prevent any such immediate and objective connection between the two personalities, attempting in some way to "mediate" between them: "Art may tell a truth / Obliquely, do the thing shall breed the thought, / Nor wrong the thought, missing the mediate word" (855–57). Art, that is, may work so indirectly that there is no real "communication" in the usual sense of the word: in providing the means for the "thought" to arise existentially in the recipient himself, it engages him in an essential manner, drawing him into ethical self-activity, by presenting the ideal as the possible. Such an artist transcends the objective poet's portrayal of events as they appear to the aggregate mind; in eliciting from the reader's mind a music that is "deeper than ever the Andante dived," he attempts to "Suffice the eye and save the soul beside" (863)—his own soul, as well as the reader's.[38] We may see more clearly how this intense involvement of the poet is accomplished in our later discussion of the ring figure. For the moment, it is instructive to remind ourselves of the terms Browning uses in describing Shelley at his most "subjective." Shelley, he says, succeeded in "drawing out, lifting up, and assimilating [his] ideal of a future man, thus descried as possible, to the present reality of the poet's soul already arrived at the higher state of development." Since the ideal thereby is shown as possible, the process by which it is accomplished is of utmost importance: Shelley has therefore the "power of delivering these attained results to the world in an embodiment of verse . . . closely answering to the indicative of the process of the informing spirit." For that reason, Browning is less interested in the "successful instances of objectivity in Shelley" than he is in the man himself—"the work Shelley."

I would rather consider Shelley's poetry as a sublime fragmentary essay towards a presentment of the correspondency of the universe to Deity, of the natural to the spiritual, and of the actual to the ideal, than I would isolate and separately appraise the worth of many detachable portions which might be acknowledged as utterly perfect in a lower moral point of view, under the mere conditions of art. (*ES*, 1014)

An objective poet may perfectly satisfy all the requirements of art while dealing merely with the "lower moral point of view." Poetry in the hands of a seer may serve the interest of the "higher vision," placing the lower within the context of a more universal insight which includes the divine as well as the human. An objective/subjective poem may combine these two functions, the author removing himself as the obvious subject of the poem (just as acid removes the surface alloy from the ring) by locating his visions in the actions of men, apprehending the ideal in the real. When the full scope of *The Ring and the Book* is taken into view, it would be difficult to find for the poem a more appropriate description than "an essay towards a presentment of the correspondency of the universe to Deity, of the natural to the spiritual, and of the actual to the ideal." The impersonal record of the Old Yellow Book becomes a kind of objective "truth" independent of the poet; using his own personality, the seer-poet can then discern the "whole truth" which, since it is an ethico-religious one, may be related through himself to that analogous Book containing the revelation of Love which Browning uses throughout the poem as a touchstone of ethical sincerity. By re-creating the moral life of the characters (the materials for which are from the poet himself as well as the Old Yellow Book) in a series of monologues which can thus be measured against both the "truth" and the "whole truth," Browning could represent the whole moral reality of his poetic "world" more successfully than he could do in a series of monologues not bound together by the central event.

VIII

The most direct literary expression of this double objective/subjective structure in the poem is in the seasonal imagery towards the end of Book I. We have seen that, in the *Essay on Shelley*, while both types of poet may draw upon "nature" for their materials, yet nature as it occurs in the actions of men serves only to confuse the subjective poet. Usually, therefore, such a poet leaves the doings of men to the objective poet; "appealing through himself to the absolute Divine mind," the subjective poet "prefers to dwell upon these external scenic appearances which strike out most abundantly and uninterruptedly his inner light and power. . . ." To do that alone was not Browning's intention. In summing up his achievement, he claims to have created for us

> A novel country: I might make it mine
> By choosing which one aspect of the year
> Suited mood best, and putting solely that
> On panel somewhere in the House of Fame,
> Landscaping *what I saved, not what I saw*:
> —Might fix you, whether frost in goblin-time
> Startled the mood with his abrupt bright laugh,
> Or, August's hair afloat in filmy fire,
> She fell, arms wide, face foremost on the world,
> Swooned there and so singed out the strength of things.
>
> (1348–57; italics mine)

He might, that is, have preferred to dwell only upon "those external scenic appearances which strike out most abundantly" his inner light. But that would be necessarily to limit the canvas, to leave incomplete the total picture of his newly created country:

> Thus were abolished Spring and Autumn both,
> The land dwarfed to one likeness of the land,
> Life cramped corpse-fashion.
>
> (1358–60)

Browning is a man for all seasons, and his business is to revive corpses. He has restored the "old woe" in its full psychological depth, and then surrounded it (as in real life) with the universal significance, reflecting the whole pattern of existence. His choice is to "abolish" neither spring and autumn on the one hand, nor summer and winter on the other:

> Rather learn and love
> Each facet-flash of the revolving year!—
> Red, green and blue that whirl into a white,
> The variance now, the eventual unity,
> Which makes the miracle. See it for yourselves,
> This man's act, changeable because alive!
>
> (1360–65)

Unlike Shelley, Browning is not confused by human imperfection. The seasonal imagery here is perfectly apt, treating as it does the world of human action under the figure of natural scenery, thus combining in a single metaphor the functions of the objective and the subjective poet.

The suggestion of seasonal progression is again reflected in Browning's metaphoric description of the poem's structure, which from one point of view is a model of the alteration in the course of history between the eras of subjective and objective poetry as those are described in the *Essay on Shelley*. Truly subjective poets will be followed by "a tribe of successors (Homerides)" who will successively water down the achievement until "the world is found to be subsisting wholly on the shadow of a reality." Then is the turn of the objective poet to restore reality "by a supply of fresh and living swathe," and to replace the Homerides "by the right of life over death." When the objective era has run its full course, then "its very sufficiency to itself shall require at length an exposition of its affinity to something higher, when the positive yet conflicting facts shall again precipitate themselves under a harmonizing law, and one more degree will be apparent for a poet to climb in that mighty ladder, of which, however cloud-involved and undefined may glimmer the topmost step, the world dares no longer doubt that its gradations ascend" (*ES*, 1010). The language here reflects Browning's description, in *The Ring and the Book*, of his progress from the level of "to-day" up to the "summit of so long ago," and then, step by step, back down again. In the context, "to-day" takes on the meaning of truth visible to aggregate humanity, and the "summit" that of the poet's higher vision, or the more universal meaning as seen in the poet:

> Finally, even as thus by step and step
> I led you from the level of to-day
> Up to the summit of so long ago,
> Here, whence I point you the wide prospect round—
> Let me, by like steps, slope you back to smooth,
> Land you on mother-earth, no whit the worse. . . .
>
> (1330–35)
>
> Shall not my friends go feast again on sward,
> Though cognizant of country in the clouds
> Higher than wistful eagle's horny eye
> Ever unclosed for. . . ?
>
> (1340–43)

Yet heaven my fancy lifts to, ladder-like—
As Jack reached, holpen of his beanstalk-rungs!

(1346–47)

IX

In discussing Kierkegaard's view on the communication of existential truth, we noted his insistence on art, first as a means of preventing false objectivity, and then as a way of ethically engaging the reader through an indirect reflection of the poet's own soul. The communication, he says, requires

art enough to vary inexhaustibly the doubly reflected form of the communication, just as the inwardness itself is inexhaustible. The greater the artistry, the greater the inwardness. If the author of the communication had much art, he could even afford to say that he was using art, certain of being able in the next moment to insure the inwardness of his communication, because he was infinitely concerned for the preservation of his own inwardness; it is this concern which saves the individual from every form of slovenly positivity. (PS, 72)

The passage perfectly describes the function of the framing monologues in *The Ring and the Book*. In the ten remaining poems, the poet's personality, while it necessarily informs and controls the revelation of character, is held below the surface, just as the alloy, in the metaphor which opens the poem, is submerged under the repristinated gold surface of the ring. In Book I, however, Browning says that he is using art, and he describes his own relationship to the communication. He points out that the truth therein reflects, to a considerable extent, the poet's own soul. Since the soul got into the poem chiefly through the alloy which is its analogue, it will be sufficient now to discuss as fully as possible the implications of the ring metaphor, which may be seen as the basic structural instrument of Book I.

A READING OF BOOK I

The meaning and the appropriateness of the ring figure have been the subject of much dispute.[39] Few critics seem to think it is entirely successful, and those who accept it as appropriate often suggest that the metaphor should not be scrutinized too closely or pushed too far. Such confusion arises first, I think, from the difficulties Browning introduces before he clearly makes the comparison between the process of ring making and the creation of his poem. But most critics have also assumed that there are only three constituents in this process: the gold of the Old Yellow Book, the alloy of "fancy," and—whatever is meant by the "spirt of acid." The problems can be solved, I think, by reference to Browning's theory of the objective/subjective poet. The poem must be read with both aspects in mind.

We should note first that there are three levels of reality in the poem. The poem itself provides the most important level, of course, since that is all the reader encounters directly. For the poet, however, the ultimate materials of the poem are the actions taken by the various characters at a moment in time before they were recorded in any fashion. For Browning, God is the artist-creator and sustainer of that "real" world in which the poem is grounded, and Browning explains that the human artist can merely imitate God's creative act to the degree of man's capability; that is, he can revivify, not create out of nothing. But the poet's only access to those actions of "real life" is the Old Yellow Book, the third level of reality in the poem's creation. As a record of the manifestations of "heart" and "brain," it is said to contain the "whole truth" (117), though partly by inference alone. The original "alloy" of the "gold" which this book represents was the souls of the characters themselves; in digging out the "truth" from the Old Yellow Book, the poet substitutes his own soul for the original alloy.[40]

I

Readers have been so accustomed to expect the ring-poem comparison which is worked out later in the poem that it is perhaps difficult now to feel the confusion introduced in the first two paragraphs. In the first, Browning simply mentions the four elements in the manufacture of the ring: the gold, the alloy, the hammering-embossing process which he later calls "craftsmanship," and the repristination by means of the "spirt of acid." But only later do we look for analogues to these four; at the end of the paragraph, we are seeking to identify two things, not two processes. Meanwhile we note that the ring was made in imitation of some rare and ancient "Etrurian circlets" which were found in rather strange circumstances:

> 'Tis Rome-work, made to match
> (By Castellani's imitative craft)
> Etrurian circlets found, some happy morn,
> After a dropping April; found alive

> Spark-like 'mid unearthed slope-side figtree-roots
> That roof old tombs at Chiusi: soft, you see,
> Yet crisp as jewel-cutting.
>
> (2–8)

The passage is too allusive to be regarded simply as a piece of realism, describing the accidental discovery of a prized object. The ring is, first of all, found "alive" amid the "death" implied by the "old tombs at Chiusi," an image linking together the two extremes of human existence, and stressing the importance of the place of discovery as the burial place of a lost civilization casting up live remains. Nor can we ignore the significance of such words as "alive" and "spark-like," especially in a poem where the author describes his act of resuscitation in terms of finding an "ember yet unquenched," blowing "the spark of flame" in order to create a poem which "lives" by embodying lessons which "whatever lives should teach" (XII, 828–33). The Etruscan circlets, in fact, are invested with a good deal of mysterious life; we are prepared to accept them as a symbol.

When Browning gives us the name of Castellani, the family most successful in duplicating old Etruscan jewelry, he invites us to investigate the process employed in these reproductions, the process which he apparently describes in the rest of the paragraph. Curiously enough, the method used by Castellani was quite different from Browning's description, however. There was, for example, no "spirt" of acid; and the Etruscans produced their surface patterns not by filing or embossing but by soldering to the surface globules of gold so tiny as to be nearly invisible to the naked eye. The elder Castellani solved the difficult soldering problem for the first time, but he could not successfully reproduce the tiny workmanship on the finest Etruscan pieces. In Browning's time, little was known about the highly refined Etruscan civilization; Augusto Castellani's own comments on their jewelry increase the sense of awe with which Browning invests the circlets:

It must . . . with humility be confessed that we see at present, arising as if by enchantment from the forgotten cemeteries of Etruria and of Greece, objects in gold of a workmanship so perfect that not only all the refinements of our civilisation cannot imitate it, but cannot even explain theoretically the process of its execution.[41]

Since Browning presumably has in mind his later characterization of the poem as a revivification of something which once had an independent life, it seems clear that he intended the Etruscan circlets to be a symbol of that second level of reality I have described above, the world of God's creation, in which the "process" of "execution" is equally inexplicable and inimitable. If this is so, then by implication, in the first metaphor of the poem, Browning's own work imitates God's creation just as Castellani's ring imitates the Etruscan circlets which are "soft, you see, / Yet crisp as jewel-cutting."

Since there is obviously no parallel between Castellani's technique and the process of Browning's poem, we must suppose that Browning deliberately substituted a description of the modern process of ring making in order to provide an apt metaphor for his "modern" poem making. However, the figure linking the poem to the ring has yet to be worked out in the poem. At the end of the first paragraph, he tells us directly that the ring itself is to be taken as a symbol; and in the final line he suggests that he will now speak of "the thing signified." Here we are suddenly surprised to find that the Old Yellow Book, not the poem, is apparently to be compared to the ring. The title of the poem, of course, gives us that metaphor from the start. Now attention is drawn to it more strongly by the similarity of the questions which begin the poem and the second paragraph of it. "Do you see this ring?" he asks at the start; then, turning to "the thing signified" by it, he opens the second paragraph with the question "Do you see this square old yellow book[?]" If this comparison were to hold, then the Old Yellow Book would stand to reality as the ring does to the Etruscan circlets; just as the ring has undergone a process of which the evidence is apparently wiped out by the acid, so has the book undergone a process by which it has "secreted" certain facts "from man's life."

The first hint of an immediate breakdown of that false metaphor, however, occurs in the third line of the paragraph, where the book is called "pure crude fact," a phrase looking ahead to the later identification of the book with pure gold. The real breakdown, however, becomes evident when, in the same paragraph, the book is treated as if it were the equivalent of the Etruscan circlets. These are described as having been found "alive / Spark-like 'mid unearthed slope-side figtree-roots," just as the Old Yellow Book was found amid "odds and ends of ravage." During the rest of this section, until lines 141–44, the poetry is heightened in tone, just as it was during the brief description of the circlets, and the book is surrounded by events so mysterious and allusions so suggestive that we feel it too must have been "found alive," even though its facts are later described as dead. The discovery of the book was, first of all, an event marked by "predestination," taking place on a day "still fierce 'mid many a day struck calm," an image of epiphany. The book was found "Twixt palace and church,— Riccardi where they lived, / His race, and San Lorenzo where they lie" —that is, another place intermediary between life and death, the extremities of existence. It was found "precisely" on a step meant for the Medici to lounge on, but which now served for the re-vending of wares, just as Browning is re-vending the story of the fallen nobleman Franceschini. It was picked out luckily from among other books—a love tale, a schoolboy classic, and several saints' lives—as superior to them in importance. Finally, in reading it, Browning grasped the "whole truth" therein, a momentary suggestion that the book itself contained some kind of "whole truth." Since all of these circumstances lead us to associate the book with the Etruscan circlets, we are left with a defective metaphor: the ring still imitates the circlets, but since the Old Yellow Book has become likened to God's reality as symbolized by the circlets, nothing is left to identify with the ring as imitating that reality.

The gap is filled in the realignment which takes place in the paragraph beginning with line 141, where Browning finally suggests the true ring figure which has been evolving slowly. With some surprise, we find that the book is reduced to the status of mere gold in the process of ring making:

> Now, as the ingot, ere the ring was forged
> Lay gold (beseech you, hold that figure fast!)
> So, in this book lay absolutely truth,
> Fanciless fact. . . .
>
> (141–44)

He has had to tell us here to "hold that figure fast," because he has not yet given us sufficient information to make the identification at all. Yet at last the final state of the metaphor is suggested. For if the Old Yellow Book is to be compared with the gold in the ring-making process, then the poem itself must supply the gap to become the object which imitates reality just as the ring imitates the circlets. And at this point we are finally in a position to look for analogues to the other three elements in ring making which have been described for us in the first paragraph.

The confusions we have seen in the evolution of the final metaphor should be regarded as a deliberate strategy. I have noted above that, according to the fiction of the poem, the materials which Browning used are all supposed, in some way, to be *in* the Old Yellow Book and nowhere else; it is only through this book that the poet has access to the ultimate reality of God's creation. As objective poet, he understands the situation he views better than ordinary readers, and selects from the whole only the facts which make an intelligible picture; as subjective poet, he places the whole in the context of the "universal significance," "intensifying the import of details and rounding the universal meaning" (*ES*, 1009). So here, in line 143, we are told that the gold of "Fanciless fact" is merely *in* the book, not necessarily identical with it. Though the Old Yellow Book is analogous to the gold in the metaphor, it still retains its old associations as symbolic of God's reality. Indeed, everything is *in* the Old Yellow Book, though it takes the poet's own nature to draw it out. It is as though the grand Ring of God's creation, through the passage of time, has simply lost its original "soul" and has been reduced to a mere mass of crude gold; the poet must "find an ember yet unquenched, / And, breathing, blow the spark to flame" (XII, 828–29). The ring is an imitation, not merely of an object, but of the art process by which the circlets were made; so too the poem imitates, not just the facts of the Old Yellow Book as an object, but the truth secreted from the "hearts" and "brains" when the characters were alive, and now lying behind the facts. The Old Yellow Book, therefore, in its role as providing access to "truth," is analogous to the Etruscan circlets; in its proper and final role as one element in the making of a ring, however, it functions as the pure gold of fact, with which Browning fuses his "live soul" as the agent for making such truth alive in the poem.

II

In its character as "mere fact," the Old Yellow Book ("gold") is the subject of the next section of the poem (141–363). We learn little about the ring figure except the now explicit statement seeming to identify the book with the ingot. But since we are told that the "truth" so far is "Fanciless fact," we should note that what follows is not a narrative of the events which took place before the trial. It is a deliberately pedestrian, factual description of the contents of the Old

Yellow Book, which is merely a record of the trial; all the information
there takes the form of arguments by lawyers or their representatives,
and "summaries" by anonymous contributors. These, not the events
of the story, are the "facts" of the Old Yellow Book. Earlier, we called
them the primary facts; although in the order of historical occurrence
the events came first, yet they become secondary facts in the order of
poetic re-creation, since they must be inferred from the trial records.
While the judges more or less accidentally stumbled onto the right
decision in the case, the seer, by a process he describes later, will show
us why it was right. In the Old Yellow Book we have merely "a cry
with an echo" (214); the pleas, the counterpleas, etc. Only later do
we encounter the "Uproar *in* the echo" (834; italics mine), the real life
which contains "truth."

Browning's long treatment of the first element in the ring metaphor
is terminated in the section beginning with line 364:

> This is the bookful; thus far take the truth,
> The untempered gold, the fact untampered with,
> The mere ring-metal ere the ring be made!
>
> (364–66)

What follows is surely the most convincing argument against the position that Browning is merely presenting us in this poem with an objective description of the events, asking us to form our own conclusion in
the case. He first asks whether the "truth" in the Old Yellow Book was
sufficient to stand on its own;[42] if so, he says ironically, he will throw
his poem into the flames: "You know the tale already: I may ask, /
Rather than think to tell you, more thereof" (377–78). But it soon
emerges that what he is after is the ethical truth in the events. Anyone
reading the Old Yellow Book can memorize the mere facts: but about
Caponsacchi, "his strange course /I' the matter, was it right or wrong
or both?" (387–88). Or about the Comparini, "What say you to the
right or wrong of that . . . ?" (392). The answer is obvious, as the
irony turns sarcastic: "you know best" (403). Clearly the poet sees
more deeply than we, who are dependent on him for a full interpretation of the rights and wrongs in the case. After reminding us that this
truth would have been lost had it not been for the poet, Browning
introduces us to the two most controversial elements in the ring metaphor: the alloy and the craftsmanship. It is significant that he does not

introduce them separately, as he does the gold, since they reflect two
powers of the poet himself.

III

Having tried "truth's power / On likely people" (423–24) in Rome,
Browning is scoffed at and apparently denied the aid of anyone connected with the Roman Church. His unsympathetic auditors ask a
question which strikes at the heart of Browning's poetry:

> Do you tell the story, now, in off-hand style,
> Straight from the book? Or simply here and there,
> (The while you vault it through the loose and large)
> Hang to a hint? Or is there book at all,
> And don't you deal in poetry, make-believe,
> And the white lies it sounds like?
>
> (451–56)

The reply is Browning's first explicit statement of his own role in the
poem's creation:

> Yes and no!
> From the book, yes; thence bit by bit I dug
> The lingot truth, that memorable day,
> Assayed and knew my piecemeal gain was gold,—
> Yes; but from something else surpassing that,
> Something of mine which, mixed up with the mass,
> Made it bear hammer and be firm to file.
> Fancy with fact is just one fact the more;
> To-wit, that fancy has informed, transpierced,
> Thridded and so thrown fast the facts else free,
> As right through ring and ring runs the djereed
> And binds the loose, one bar wthout a break.
> *I fused my live soul and that inert stuff,*
> *Before attempting smithcraft,* on the night
> After the day when,—truth thus grasped and gained,—
> The book was shut and done with and laid by. . . .
>
> (457–72; italics mine)

The first and obvious interpretation of these lines is that the "something of mine" which the poet "mixed up with the mass" of gold may
be termed either "fancy" or "soul," and that it simply makes possible
the "smithcraft." Indeed, most critics, by ignoring the term "soul" altogether, apparently assume that the "fancy" must simply be a faculty

of the "soul," and that Browning therefore uses the terms interchange-
ably. But such an imprecise confusion of terms is not acceptable. It
provides two terms in the poem to correspond to the gold in the ring-
making process; it appears to give the alloy a double function; it provides no term in poem making to correspond with the "smithcraft"; and
most important, it ignores the real distinction which Browning built
into his description of the two terms. *Only* the "live soul" is said to have
been "fused" with "that inert stuff"; and whatever is meant by Browning's description of the role of fancy, it certainly is not clear that this
faculty merely prepares the way for the poetic art in the way that an
alloy prepares the way for smithcraft. It will not do to say that Browning here merely gives weightier substance to the "fancy" by associating
it with "soul." That could have been done easily enough without introducing the confusion caused by the five difficult lines dealing with
fancy, which form a complete period by themselves, and which make
sense even without the particular context surrounding them, or as an
"aside." Omission of the lines would certainly have made the meaning
clear, and nothing would have been lost but the simile of the djereed.
The text would then read as follows:

> Something of mine which, mixed up with the mass,
> Made it bear hammer and be firm to file.
> I fused my live soul and that inert stuff
> Before attempting smithcraft. . . .

Fancy could then be introduced in its proper place, after the fusion of
soul and the "inert stuff." The lines are where they are, however, and
with a poet so sensitive to ambiguity as Browning, we must be prepared to regard them as an intentional interruption within the passage.
The most satisfactory solution comes about if we hold fast to the distinction between fancy and soul as two separate faculties. In such a
reading, what would be lost by the omission of the five lines is Browning's careful attention to the contributions of both the subjective and
the objective faculties within the same poem. The fancy, which has
"informed," "transpierced," and "thridded" the facts, is responsible for
the selection of details, for the intelligibility, and for the unity of the
whole; these may be regarded as the art or as "smithcraft," the business
of the objective poet, who is so far in sympathy with the event in its
"narrower comprehension" that he is able to select "no other materials
than it can combine into an intelligible whole" (*ES*, 1008). In the
Essay on Shelley, an objective poem, which Browning describes as a

"particular exercise" of the poet's power, becomes "the fact itself." In *The Ring and the Book,* therefore, it is not surprising to find that "Fancy with fact" may be called "just one fact the more." Browning is here regarding the poem chiefly in its objective aspect. The subjective poet, however, "rounds the universal meaning," which he grasps only "in his own soul as the nearest reflex of that absolute Mind. . . ." He fuses his "soul" with the Old Yellow Book (or gold), and seeks to reveal "the truth *thus* grasped and gained." In spite of Browning's high regard for "fact" in the poem, it seems reductive to apply the term to the work of the soul. In the passage under discussion, Browning is carrying out his explanation of the ring metaphor by introducing us both to the alloy and to the craftsmanship, the subjective and the objective aspects, which are here fused in equal proportion.

In this simultaneous introduction of the objective and the subjective elements, the ambiguity again is deliberate and functional. As Browning defines the two in the *Essay on Shelley,* the distinction between them tends to be chiefly a logical one, useful for analysis, but not quite strictly applicable to reality. Only in excessively rare instances, he says, may either one be found in a condition that is even comparatively "pure"; usually the two exist together, though one or the other is emphasized and gives its character to the poetry. Like the faculties of "mind" and "emotion," the two may be held distinct for the purpose of discussion, but they are always found together in a single personality, where they interact constantly. Furthermore, in a poem which attempts perfectly to fuse the two in equal balance, the "objective" portrayal of the historical event and the "subjective" location of that event according to a universal meaning must, after all, fuse into the "miracle" of an "eventual unity" (1363–64), and it is appropriate that the texture of the poem should reflect the complexity of the aim. And ultimately, the art is there in order to present the ethical as a possible imperative, so that the reader's own effort draws him into the poem. The eye of the reader may pass from one aspect to the other as each reveals itself in the poem, or it may miss the subjective altogether without losing the objective sense of the poem. Since no one can "save the soul" without the owner's cooperation, the existential communication depends on the willing self-activity and appropriation of the recipient. The poem is there for all to see; the truth which "whatever lives should teach" is reserved for those who have eyes to see (XII, 842), a characteristic of parabolic ambiguity.

IV

In terms of the ring figure, one other important function is effected by the ambiguity surrounding "fancy" and "soul": since they are introduced simultaneously, what is said of the alloy tends also to rub off onto the craftsmanship, not logically, but by process of association. Both of these contributions came from the same poet, and both could equally be described as a "something of mine." This idea becomes extremely important in Browning's treatment of the acid, the fourth element in the ring's manufacture, and the section under discussion (457–678) is a masterful preparation for that moment. Browning has begun the section by explicitly introducing the "fancy" and the "soul" in such a way that the distinction between them is there, yet somewhat ambiguous. In the final four lines of the passage quoted above (469–72), a subtle transition is effected (at line 470) between the explicit statement of the idea and the time when the process he describes took place. The rest of the section is a long and powerful illustration, partly by the technique of imitative form, of the process by which his fancy and his soul at that time worked together on the mere facts, so that he actually saw in his mind's eye the scene, the action, and the meaning of the drama, conveying to us the excitement of discovery. The passage illustrates the process by which the poem was later created.

Insufficient attention has been given to the deliberate variations in tone and poetic diction which Browning employs in certain sections of *The Ring and the Book*. The section under discussion is actually a continuation of the narrative dropped at line 141, where Browning has just finished reading his newly purchased book. The interruption at that point introduces a description of the factual, legal nature of the Old Yellow Book, together with an address to the British Public; accordingly, the poetry is given the same prosaic quality that one might expect in legal documents. In resuming the narrative now (the transition occurs at line 470), Browning illustrates how he re-created the story for himself, so that we get a synoptic view of certain events in the story, not merely a description of the legal records which make up the Old Yellow Book. Since the subjective poet is now involved, the poetry itself is heightened in tone to correspond with the new subject matter; the scene is again surrounded with the kind of religious imagery we noted in the opening of the narrative concerning the "Etrurian circlets" and then the miraculous discovery of the book. His rapt absorption in the Old Yellow Book, so great that he had "to free myself

and find the world" (478), is an image of devout religious meditation
symbolized by the chanting monks of "Felice-Church" (482), and his
vision of the truth in the Old Yellow Book reflects divinity by a metaphor linking the flame falling from the clouds (489) to the gold snow
of Jove (490), another image of epiphany. The presence of the "busy
human sense beneath my feet" (493) is similar in function to the
"Buzzing and blaze" of the opening narrative; it further links his reading of the dead past to the living present, so that he can bring to bear
on the Old Yellow Book the "human sense" of the present. As he proceeds, the description turns from that of present surroundings to the
imaginary scene; the mood deepens as the verb changes from "I looked"
(497) to "I felt" (500). The sense of utter absorption in the imagination is increased as he then says that he actually "fared" towards Rome
by "feeling my way" (506). His explanation of how "The life in me
abolished the death of things, / Deep calling unto deep" (520–21),
together with the claim that he finally saw the whole scene "with my
own eyes" (523), is an image of the fusion of his own soul with the
materials of the Old Yellow Book. The scene he describes is clearly
not limited to the facts in that book; even while he looks, the vision of
his soul departs and dwindles back down to that mere book, from
which he says he could "calculate . . . the lost proportions of the
style" (677–78). He has illustrated in little, through imitative form,
the process of the poem's creation.

                                    V

One further aspect of this passage ought to be mentioned here, even
at the risk of an apparent digression; it will be seen to have some bearing on the subjective/objective structure of the poem, and it illustrates
an aspect of Browning's use of allusion which has seldom been noted
by critics. In dealing with the relationship between "One Word More"
and *The Ring and the Book* (above), I mentioned the importance of
the dedication to Elizabeth Barrett Browning, whom the poet addresses
at the end of Book I and again at the end of the poem, thus giving a
circular, or ring-like form to the poem itself. "O lyric Love," in fact, is
more than just a dedication; it is a reflection of the intimacy of their
love, and an admission of her influence on his poetry. First of all, it
was he who first called her from the "heaven" of isolation into an active
life in the world, his voice which

> Reached thee amid thy chambers, blanched their blue,
> And bared them of the glory—to drop down,
> To toil for man, to suffer or to die. . . .

(398–400)

In return, God best taught him the art of poetry through the instru-
mentality of his wife, who has a role in all of his poetry:

> Never may I commence my song, my due
> To God who best taught song by gift of thee,
> Except with bent head and beseeching hand—

(1403–5)

The personal and the religious are here brought in to suggest the subjective theme which underlies the poem. Just as in the *Divine Comedy*
Beatrice (in the image of Christ) is the instrument of Dante's salvation, so here we may infer that Elizabeth Barrett Browning is the instrument of the poet's salvation and the primary "cause" of his poetry.
Furthermore, since the ring which provides the opening metaphor
was hers, we are to think that her spirit particularly informs the whole
of *The Ring and the Book;* we might also suspect that the many parallels, pointed out by DeVane and others, between Browning's own
romance and the conduct of Pompilia and Caponsacchi, are not merely
autobiographical, but reflect a profound intention in the poem.

Near the opening of Book I, Browning inserts a parenthesis (l. 92)
emphasizing that the month of his discovery of the Old Yellow Book
was June. He names the month again, somewhat more insistently, in
the passage we have been discussing, just before he re-creates the story
for us in his imagination. He has come out into his terrace and sees
the window of the church opposite him,

> Whence came the clear voice of the cloistered ones
> Chanting a chant made for midsummer nights—
> I know not what particular praise of God,
> It always came and went with June.

(484–87)

The emphasis may simply have reference to Elizabeth Barrett Browning, who died on June 29, 1861. In that case, when Browning wonders
in Book XII whether the public will judge that his poem is "composite
as good orbs prove, or crammed / With worse ingredients than the
Wormwood star" (11–12), we are also reminded of his wife's fears:
"What an omen you take in calling anything my work!" "If it is my
work, woe on it—for everything turns to evil which I touch." Accord-

ing to Betty Miller, Elizabeth constantly reminded her husband of "the law of my own star, my own particular star, the star I was born under, the star *Wormwood*."[43] All of this gives point to the final lines of the poem, which occur just after Browning expresses his intention to "suffice the eye and save the soul beside":

> And save the soul! If this intent save mine,—
> If the rough ore be rounded to a ring,
> Render all duty which good ring should do,
> And, failing grace, succeed in guardianship,—
> Might mine but lie outside thine, Lyric love
> Thy rare gold ring of verse (the poet praised)
> Linking our England to his Italy!
>
> (XII, 864–70)

His poem may fail to save the souls of others, but he will nonetheless save from the Star Wormwood (an image of Satan, incidentally) the woman whom he had summoned to "drop down, / To toil for man, to suffer or to die," so that she will be immortalized not only in her own poetry, but in his as well.

In the passage under discussion, however, Browning gives conspicuous attention to the particular "chant" which he hears from the "cloistered ones," and which has clearly drawn his attention quite often before; it is a "chant made for midsummer nights," and it "always came and went with June." Such deliberate insistence on these matters, especially in a scene which obviously includes only significant details, should make the reader suspicious. One might even suspect that Browning is here illustrating his explicit theory that certain poets work by "intensifying the import of details and rounding the universal meaning" (*ES*, 1009). At any rate, since he has nevertheless provided all the clues necessary to identify the chant, his ironic and elaborate "confession" that he is ignorant of its nature becomes an invitation to investigate the matter for ourselves. In view of Browning's interest in musical history, it seems particularly unlikely that he would be unfamiliar with the famous hymn *Ut queant laxis*, which in the thirteenth century provided for the musical scale the nomenclature which is still in use today.[44] (The combined first syllables of each phrase in the first verse, sung on succeeding notes on the scale, were ut, re, mi, fa, sol, la, si.) Browning describes the Church of San Felice as "fringed for festival"; significantly, this hymn is sung at the Vesper services on the Vigil of the Nativity of St. John the Baptist (June 23), and again

on the day of the Feast itself (June 24), the only such important feast
which occurs during the month of June. In Browning's day, it would
also have been sung at least twice more during the Octave of the Feast
(on June 27 and June 30); it would not have been sung, however, on
July 1, even though that day celebrates the end of the Octave.[45] The
hymn, therefore, "always came and went with June"; and since June
24 was considered to be the summer solstice, or midsummer, Browning
really secures the identification of the chant for us by saying that it
was one "made for midsummer nights."

As I have noted above, the scene in which this passage occurs is filled
with symbolic associations. Just a little earlier, the poet has told us
how he discovered the Old Yellow Book ("Mark the predestination!");
he then described the factual nature of that legal record. Here he
pauses momentarily to tell us how he fused his "live soul" with "that
inert stuff" even before he began writing the poem, and he will soon
illustrate that fusion by recreating the story in his imagination. The
present scene is a transition to that important narrative, and even his
situation is symbolic; he has emerged from inside the house, where he
finished reading the Old Yellow Book, and stepped onto the "narrow
terrace" which is built over the street, giving him a position between
the "busy human" scene below him and the glowing sky reminiscent
of the "gold snow Jove rained on Rhodes." Such a location, compre-
hending and linking the human and the divine, is a perfect image of
the poet who intends not only to "suffice the eye" but to "save the soul
beside." Like the poet in "How it Strikes a Contemporary," he is fully
a part of the human scene, but sufficiently above it to interpret it for
his readers; yet his business, as Browning once remarked of poets, is
also with God.[46] In such a situation, when Browning stresses so deliberately the "chant made for midsummer nights," it seems clear that he
is associating his own mission with that of St. John the Baptist, who is
celebrated in this "summer Christmas" as the Precursor of Christ, or as
a herald of the Christian message. We shall see in a moment that
Browning later directly associates himself with Christ; here he is telling us what to look for in a poem written according to his own aesthetic
theory, which involves the poet's divine mission. Two of the "lessons"
recited during the Second Nocturne on the Feast of St. John the Baptist
are taken from St. Augustine's twentieth sermon, and express the typological significance of John: "John was a figure of the old Testament,
and typified the law in himself; and therefore John foretold the Savior,

just as the law preceded grace."⁴⁷ A further passage more closely
describes Browning's situation: "John, lying in prison, directs his
disciples to Christ. This event represents the law sending to the
Gospel." It should be remembered that Browning attacks law throughout the poem, and that such characters as Caponsacchi repeatedly link
law and Gospel as if to suggest that the law must be fulfilled by the
Christian message of love; certainly the movement from law to love
is at the basis of meaning in the poem. In view of his desire to "save
the soul," Browning may even have conceived of himself in the terms
of Lesson VI: "Of him [John] the blessed Evangelist proclaims: He
was a burning and a shining light, that is, he was enkindled by the
fire of the Holy Spirit, that to a world held in the night of ignorance
he might show forth the light of salvation, and amid the thickest darkness of sin might by his ray point out the most resplendent sun of
justice, saying of himself: I am the voice of one crying in the wilderness."

The allusion has even further consequences for the poem. In the
First Vespers recited on the Feast of St. John the Baptist we find a
biblical passage suggesting the typological association of John: "We
shall go before Him in the spirit and power of Elias [Elijah], to prepare unto the Lord a perfect people" (Luke 1:17). I have said above
that Browning, describing himself at a point before he began writing
the poem, identifies symbolically with John as the Precursor of Christ.
The reference to Elijah, however, reminds us that it was Elisha who
assumed the mantle of Elijah; and Elisha was traditionally regarded
as a type of Christ, performing the miracle of restoring a dead child
to life. This is the miracle with which Browning in Book I compares
his own efforts in "resuscitating" the "inert stuff" of the Old Yellow
Book. It should be noted that Browning also compares his mission
with that of Christ at the end of Book XII, where he says that he came
"in the fulness of the days" (826), an allusion to St. Paul's phrase in
Gal. 4:4, referring to Christ as having been sent "in the fulness of the
time." In this allusion, Browning imagines himself first (before creating the poem) as a herald of Christ and then as a type of Christ, fulfilling his own prophesy.

Browning insists that he found the Old Yellow Book in a Florentine
bookstall on a day in June. If that was in fact the month, then Browning more than ever must have regarded his "find" as "predestinated."
But even if he simply assigned the date in order to make it coincide

with the month of his wife's death, he would nonetheless have regarded it as providential that the same month introduced the Feast
of the Precursor of Christ, whose message is basic to the poem. It seems
clear that Browning, in this single allusion, drew together the three
aspects of his intention in the poem: the deep involvement of his own
love for his wife, the message of the validation of human love through
the Incarnation, and the sense of his own divine mission in "saving the
soul."

VI

After illustrating his re-creation of the story behind the Old Yellow
Book, Browning now moves to a second explicit statement of the
fancy/soul problem which occasioned this narrative part of the section. Here the ambiguity is nearly cleared up:

> This was it from, my fancy with those facts,
> I used to tell the tale, turned gay to grave,
> But lacked a listener seldom; such alloy,
> Such substance of me interfused the gold
> Which, wrought into a shapely ring therewith,
> Hammered and filed, fingered and favoured, last
> Lay ready for the renovating wash
> O' the water.
>
> (679–86)

Again, the first two clauses (the second beginning "such alloy") may
be read as referring only to the fancy, the second in apposition to the
first, and the word "such" having the same referent as "this." A more
clear and satisfactory interpretation, however, is that each clause refers
to a different faculty. The soul is the substance which "interfused the
gold," while the fancy provided the techniques used "to *tell* the tale";
it "hammered and filed, fingered and favoured" the combined gold and
alloy, adding the structure and the art. This interpretation of the soul
as the only alloy is finally enforced by the next section of the poem
(698–772), which is certainly at the center of meaning in Book I. As
if to assure us that there has been a problem all along, Browning first
asks us whether we have solved it:

> What's this then, which proves good yet seems untrue?
> This that I mixed with truth, motions of mine
> That quickened, made the inertness malleolable
> O' the gold was not mine,—what's your name for this?
>
> (700–703)

The question is rhetorical, however. The next sixty-five lines define the function of his soul alone, which he "commissions forth" as his essential alloy, finding "body" in the gold of the book which is not his, and presented to the British Public in the form of art.

VII

We may now return to the passage in which Browning deals explicitly with the final element in the ring's manufacture, the acid. The passage is unfortunately brief and gives us few clues for interpretation. We have just been told that the operations of the fancy and the soul have been completed, and the "ring" is now ready for "the renovating wash / O' the water." He continues:

> "How much of the tale was true?"
> I disappeared; the book grew all in all;
> The lawyers' pleadings swelled back to their size,—
> Doubled in two, the crease upon them yet,
> For more commodity of carriage, see!—

(686–90)

It must first be remembered that Browning does not directly equate his own disappearance with that of the alloy under the "renovating wash" of the acid; we make the judgment only by inference. Browning is here speaking of his description of the story to friends, at a time before he wrote the poem. When they asked him about the "truth" of it, he simply removed himself altogether and referred them to the Old Yellow Book as evidence. But the whole ring metaphor is clearly meant to have reference to the poem itself, and the problem is to find there an apt analogue for the acid. It has been pointed out that the acid does not really remove all of the alloy;[48] if it did, the ring would melt back to the ingot, and by analogy the poem would disappear—or, as Browning truly says, only the Old Yellow Book would remain. Yet if the acid appears to remove only the surface alloy, what is the poetic equivalent of that? Part of the answer may lie in our earlier observation that the craftsmanship (fancy), by association with the alloy (soul) as the "something of mine" contributed by the poet, is in turn also affected by the wash of the acid, just as, for example, the surface color of the ring would also be affected by the removal of impurities. By thus removing himself from the objective technique of the poem, Browning may simply be "hiding the art," a known Horatian virtue.

Still, in the poem the acid clearly affects the alloy itself, and we have no poetic equivalent to that as yet.

I suggest that the Horatian answer is the correct one, adding that the "renovating wash /O' the water" serves also to hide the evidence of the soul, which nevertheless remains in the poem as its informing spirit, sustaining the subjective element. That seems to be the clear meaning of Browning's final statement concerning the ring figure, which occurs nearly at the end of Book I:

> Such labour had such issue, so I wrought
> This arc, by furtherance of such alloy,
> And so, by one spirt, take away its trace. . . .
>
> (1386–88)

We have seen that, as objective poet, Browning is concerned with human actions. What is not always kept in mind, however, is that from the poet's point of view these acts are completed; they have already been submitted to a moral placement "in the lower moral point of view," which the poet does not invent, but merely represents. Wylie Sypher, for example, in his discussion of Guido's first monologue, says at one point: "It is already clear that Browning has passed his own judgment on this man, who has the soul of a wolf."[49] True, Browning has passed judgment, but it is certainly not here that we first discover the fact, and in the first instance it was not Browning who made the judgment. The trial happens to be over: Pompilia is innocent, Guido is guilty, and the poet merely accepts that as a fact of the Old Yellow Book. As if to make sure we understand the point, Browning, in the remainder of Book I, first offers a brief objective narrative of the story (780–823), and then provides us with a catalogue of dramatis personae in which the moral placement is made clear; he seems, in fact, to be substituting narrative for point of view. For if Browning is to reveal the "truth" as he thinks it really exists, then it is vital to his purpose that the action should be rooted in real life and subject to verification. It is important to stress again and again that we are not merely given the "facts" in order to make up our own minds in the trial: for that, we would need no more than a reprint of the Old Yellow Book. When Browning therefore tells us later that the Pope's judgment in the case is "the ultimate / Judgment save yours" (1220–21), he is by no means enjoining us simply to employ our own point of view. That would be to ignore the nature of his art itself. In making his judgment the Pope is primarily in the situation of the poet, not that of the reader; he sees the documents, not the poem. The "whole poet," who first sees more deeply than the reader and then reflects the divine import, must reveal the exact *quality* of the guilt and the innocence; he must present a just analysis of psychological process; he must even explore the universal moral purpose behind the events; but at least he must show us which of the points of view have to be altered. As Browning points out, the reader's job is simply to understand the poem itself,[50] if he can:

[From an objective poem] we learn only what [the poet] intended we should learn by that particular exercise of his power,—the fact itself,—which with its infinite significances, each of us receives for the first time as a creation, and is hereafter left to deal with, as, in proportion to his own intelligence, he best may. (*ES*, 1008)

As objective poet, of course, he stresses the importance of "mere fact," "pure crude fact." He thus sticks carefully to the Old Yellow Book, so that if one likes he may see only the "objective" psychological exposition of points of view and subject them to his own. That is the first kind of "truth" mentioned in the passage under discussion:

> Lovers of dead truth, did ye fare the worse?
> Lovers of live truth, found ye false my tale?
>
> (696–97)

When the poet delivers his finished product, his "fact," to the public, that act of separation is symbolized by the spurt of acid. As Browning says, for the objective poet, "the thing fashioned, his poetry, will of necessity be substantive, *projected from* himself *and distinct*" (*ES*, 1008; italics mine). If the reader *then* asks "How much of the tale is true?" the poet disappears, "the book" becomes "all in all." Take away the alloy, you have merely the pleadings in the Old Yellow Book, which returns to its status as "pure gold"; that book is the only valid test of the objective or factual truth in the poem, and the poet here invites the comparison. But in the poem also is Browning's soul as the alloy. If you want the "live truth," the something which "whatever lives should teach," you must remember that the acid has removed only the surface alloy; the alloy itself is still part of the substance. This truth comes from the poet's own soul before poetry set in, and that soul is not removed by the acid. For the subjective poet, the "effluence" of his poetry "cannot be easily considered in abstraction from his personality, —being indeed the very radiance and aroma of his personality, *projected from it but not separated*" (*ES*, 1009; italics mine). In the sec-

tion which I have described as central to the meaning of Book I,
Browning emphasizes this objective/subjective duality by claiming
that the poem results from "a special gift, an art of arts, / More *insight*
and more *outsight* and much more / Will to use both of these than
boast my mates" (746–49). Browning seems to feel that the will to use
both faculties is what lacked in poets who heretofore wrote poetry
employing either the one or the other faculty alone. But then their
purpose may not have been to "suffice the eye *and* save the soul
besides."

REFERENCE MATTER

NOTES

BERCOVITCH: HOROLOGICALS TO CHRONOMETRICALS

1 John Winthrop, *A Model of Christian Charity* (1630), in *Puritan Political Ideas, 1558–1794*, ed. Edmund S. Morgan (New York, 1965), pp. 90–91; John Cotton, *Gods Promise to His Plantations* (London, 1630), in *Old South Leaflets* (Boston, [1874–76]), Vol. III, no. 53, pp. 4, 13.

2 Samuel Willard, *Useful Instructions for a professing People* (Cambridge, 1673), p. 12; Winthrop, *Model*, pp. 90–91; Cotton, *Gods Promise*, p. 1; Loren Baritz, *City on a Hill: A History of Ideas and Myths in America* (New York, 1964), p. 31; Jesper Rosenmeier, "VERITAS: The Sealing of the Promise," *Harvard Library Bulletin*, XVI (1968), 33.

3 Herman Melville, *Pierre: or, the Ambiguities*, ed. Henry A. Murray (New York, 1949), pp. 247–50; Newton Arvin, *Herman Melville* (New York, 1950), p. 22. This passage, from Plotinus Plinlimmon's pamphlet, "'EI' . . . Chronometricals and Horologicals," has been variously interpreted. I intend here the simple dichotomy which its author makes explicit, between an idealistic absolutism based on the example of Christ, the perfect "chonometer," and common-sense expediency that takes due account of the defective state of man, the post-lapsarian "horologue." Elsewhere I use the dichotomy in the ironic sense it takes on in the novel as a whole, where Melville seems to ridicule those men who "in their clogged terrestrial humanities" would follow "heavenly ideals," and, at the same time, to admire the enduring imaginative force embodied in that "passionate absolution [to which] Melville himself was particularly prone" (Melville, *Pierre*, pp. 8, 37, 195, 352, 398; Arvin, *Melville*, p. 221).

4 Thomas Shepard, *Election Sermon* (1638), in *New England Historical and Genealogical Register*, XXIV (1870), 363, and *The Parable of the Ten Virgins Opened & Applied* (1636–40), ed. Jonathan Mitchel and Thomas Shepard, Jr. (London, 1695), pt. II, p. 5; Increase Mather, Preface to Eleazar Mather, *A Serious Exhortation to the Present and Succeeding Generations in New-England* (Cambridge, 1671), sigs. A2ᵛ–A3ʳ, and *An Earnest Exhortation* (Boston, 1676), p. 23; Alan Simpson, *Puritanism in Old and New England* (Chicago, 1961), p. 22; Charles Francis Adams, *Massachusetts: Its Historians and its History* (New York, 1893), p. 79; Peter Gay, *A Loss of Mastery: Puritan Historians in Colonial America* (Berkeley, 1966), p. 69; Perry Miller,

title essay of *Errand into the Wilderness* (Cambridge, Mass., 1958), p. 8.

5 Perry Miller, *The New England Mind: From Colony to Province* (Boston, 1961), p. 29, and *The New England Mind: The Seventeenth Century* (Boston, 1961), p. 462; Gilbert Burnet, Preface to *An Abridgement of the History of the Reformation* (London, 1683), sigs. A7ᵛ–A8ᵛ; Cotton Mather, *Magnalia Christi' Americana; or, The Ecclesiastical History of New England*, ed. Thomas Robbins (Hartford, 1853), II, 108. On the jeremiads of fifteenth- and sixteenth-century England, see J. W. Blench, *Preaching in England . . . A Study of English Sermons, 1450–c.1600* (New York, 1964), pp. 228–313, where the themes of lamentation are specifically related to those Gerald R. Owst delineates in his discussions of the medieval ministry, *Preaching in Medieval England* (Cambridge, 1926), and *Literature and Pulpit in Medieval England* (Cambridge, 1933).

6 Clement Cotton, Dedication to John Calvin's *Two and Twenty Lectvres Vpon . . . Ieremiah* (London, 1620), sigs. A2ʳ–A2ᵛ; John Cotton, *The Covenant of Grace* (London, 1655), p. 40, and *A Treatise of the Covenant of Grace* (London, 1659), pp. 18–21; Jean Daniélou, *From Shadows to Reality: Studies in the Biblical Typology of the Fathers*, trans. Dom Wulstan Hibbard (Westminster, Md., 1960), p. 154; Iranaeus, *Against Heresies*, trans. John Kemble (London, 1872), p. 533; Israel Friedlaender, "The Prophet Jeremiah," in *Past and Present: Selected Essays* (New York, 1961), p. 73; Joseph Klausner, *The Messianic Idea in Israel, from its Beginning to the Completion of the Mishnah*, trans. W. F. Stinespring (London, 1956), p. 100; Francis Roberts, *Clavis Bibliorum* (London, 1649), pp. 455, 465; Peter Bulkeley, *The Gospel-Covenant* (London, 1651), p. 416; John Cotton (grandson), *A Sermon Preach'd at the Public Lecture in Boston* (Boston, 1728), pp. 27–28. See also Hugo Gressman, "The Sources of Israel's Messianic Hope," *American Journal of Theology*, XVII (1913), 177.

7 John Calvin, *Commentaries on the Prophet Jeremiah*, trans. and ed. John Owen (Grand Rapids, Mich., 1950), IV, 126–30; Augustine, *City of God* (bk. XVII), in *Works*, trans. Gerald C. Walsh and Daniel J. Honan (New York, 1954), VII, 21; Emil G. Kraeling, *The Old Testament Since the Reformation* (New York, 1955), p. 30 (cf. p. 17 on Luther and "Messianic prophecy"); Ernest L. Tuveson, *Millennium and Utopia: A Study in the Background of the Idea of Progress* (New York, 1964), pp. 15, 26; Gordon L. Keyes, *Christian Faith and the Interpretation of History: A Study of St. Augustine's Philosophy of History* (Lincoln, Neb., 1966), p. 158; Ronald S. Wallace, *Calvin's Doctrine of the Word and Sacrament* (Grand Rapids, Mich., 1957), pp. 44–45; Martin Luther, "Preface to the Prophet Jeremiah," in *Works* (Philadelphia, 1915–32), VI, 409–10 (and see further his exposition of the Book of Daniel: VI, 488–89); T. F. Torrance, *Kingdom and Church: A Study in the Theology of the Reformation* (London, 1956), pp. 147, 100, 116, 155-56, 94–95, 21, 19, 139; George Joyce, Preface to *Jeremy* (Antwerp, 1534), sig. Av verso. All references to the Bible are to the King James version, unless otherwise noted.

8 Gilbert Burnet, *The History of the Reformation of the Church of England* (1679), ed. Nicholas Pocock (Oxford, 1865), II, 666; John Milton, *Areopagitica* . . . (1644), ed. William Haller, in *Works*, ed. Frank Allen Patterson (New York, 1931), IV, 341; John Bale, *The Image of Both Churches* . . . (1548), in *Select Works*, ed. Henry Christmas (Cambridge, 1849), pp. 516, 458, 252, 410; William Haller, *The Elect Nation: The Meaning and Relevance of Foxe's "Book of Martyrs"* (New York, 1963), pp. 85, 109; John F. Wilson, "Another Look at John Canne," *Church History*, XXXIII (1964), 45; A. S. P. Woodhouse, ed., *Puritanism and Liberty* (Chicago, 1951), p. [41]; Leo F. Solt, *Saints in Arms: Puritanism and Democracy in Cromwell's Army* (Stanford, 1959), p. 76; Thomas Beard, *The Theatre of Gods Iudgements* (London, 1597), pp. 460–82; Anon., *The Covenant-Interest and Priviledge of Believers* (London, 1675), pp. 1–2; William Haller, *Liberty and Reformation in the Puritan Revolution* (New York, 1955), p. 18; Thomas Fuller, *The Church History of Britain From the Birth of Jesus Christ Until the Year MDCXLVIII*, ed. James Nichols (London, 1842), I, 7, 2 (Dedication). See also C. A. Patrides, *The Phoenix and the Ladder: The Rise and Decline of the Christian View of History* (Berkeley, 1964), p. 33; and the texts of the "agreements of the people" in *Leveller Manifestoes of the Puritan Revolution*, ed. Don M. Wolfe (New York, 1944), pp. 225–34, and Professor Wolfe's commentary, pp. 223–24, *et passim*.

9 Northrop Frye, "The Typology of *Paradise Regained*," *Modern Philology*, LIII (1955–56), 233; Edmund Calamy, *The Great Danger of Covenant-refusing and Covenant-breaking* (London, 1646), sig. A4ʳ, pp. 12–14, 34; Robert Dowglas, *The Form and Order of the Coronation* (1651), in *A Phenix, or, The Solemn League and Covenant* (Edinburgh, [1662]), pp. 38–39, and, in this tract, *A Phenix*, p. 3; Helmut Richard Niebuhr, "The Idea of Covenant and American Democracy," *Church History*, XXIII (1954), 133; Joseph Mede, *Churches*, in *Works*, ed. John Worthington (London, 1677), p. 370; Kenneth B. Murdock, "William Hubbard and the Providential Interpretation of History," *Proceedings of the American Antiquarian Society*, LII (1942), 17; Herschel Baker, *The Race of Time* (Toronto, 1967), p. 38; French R. Fogle, "Milton as Historian," in *Milton and Clarendon: Two Papers on 17th Century English Historiography presented at . . . the Clark Library* . . . (Los Angeles, 1965), p. 6. See also Leonard J. Trinterud, "The Origins of Puritanism," *Church History*, XX (1951), 41–42, and Tuveson, *Millennium*, p. 27.

10 John F. Wilson, in *Church History*, XXXIII, 34; Edmund S. Morgan, *Visible Saints: The History of a Puritan Idea* (New York, 1963), p. 34; Heinrich Bullinger, *A Hundred Sermons Vppon the Apocalipse of Iesu Christ*, trans. John Daws (London, 1573), p. 32; Rudolf Bultmann, *The Presence of Eternity: History and Eschatology* (New York, 1957), p. 36; John Canne, *A Necessity of Separation from the Church of England Proved by the Nonconformists Principles* (1634), ed. Charles Stead (London, 1849), p. 194; Geoffrey F. Nuttall, *Visible Saints: The Congregational Way, 1640–1660* (Oxford, 1957), pp. 142, 66; John Robinson, *A Justification of Separation* (1610), in *Works*, ed. Robert Ashton (Boston, 1851), II, 116, 126–27, 304, 311, 473. See

also: the anonymous *Saints Apology* (1644), in Woodhouse, *Puritanism and Liberty*, p. 300; Joseph Lecler, *Toleration and the Reformation* (New York, 1960), II, 394; and Richard M. Reinitz, "Symbolism and Freedom: The Use of Biblical Typology as an Argument for Religious Toleration in Seventeenth Century America" (University of Rochester dissertation, 1967), pp. 368 ff.

11 R. V. G. Tasker, *The Old Testament in the New Testament* (London, 1946), pp. 147–48; Baker, *Race of Time*, pp. 55, 53; John Robinson, quoted in the anonymous *An Answer to John Robinson of Leyden by a Puritan Friend* (1609), ed. Champlin Burrage, *Harvard Theological Studies*, IX (Cambridge, Mass., 1920), pp. 74, 17, and "answered," p. 85; J. Robinson, *Justification*, in *Works*, II, 116, 126-27.

12 Haller, *Elect Nation*, p. 249; Charles Chauncy, *Gods Mercy Shewed to His People* (Cambridge, 1655), p. 19; Joy B. Gilsdorf, "The Puritan Apocalypse: New England Eschatology in the Seventeenth Century" (Yale University dissertation, 1964), p. 120; Thomas Shepard and John Allin, *A Defence of the Answer* (1658), quoted in Perry Miller, *Orthodoxy in Massachusetts, 1630–1650* (Boston, 1959), pp. 150–51; Stow Persons, *American Minds: A History of Ideas* (New York, 1960), pp. 89, 41; Peter N. Carroll, *Puritanism and the Wilderness: The Intellectual Significance of the New England Frontier, 1629–1700* (New York, 1969), p. 21; Thomas Hooker, *The Dangers of Desertion* (1633), quoted in Gilsdorf, *Puritan Apocalypse*, p. 133; John Winthrop, *Letters* (May 15, 1629), quoted in Carroll, *Puritanism*, p. 19, and "Conclusions for the Plantation" (1629), in *Old South Leaflets*, Vol. II, no. 60, pp. 3–4, 6; Robert Cushman, *Of the State of the* [Plymouth] *Colony . . .* (1621), in *Chronicles of the Pilgrim Fathers*, ed. Alexander Young (Boston, 1844), p. 256; Joshua Scottow, *A Narrative of the Planting of the Massachusetts Colony* (1694), in *Massachusetts Historical Society Collections*, 4th ser., IV (1858), 287–88. Regarding the exegetical tradition behind the "woman" of Rev. 12, see for example George Fox's *The Great Mystery . . .* [concerning] *Babylon's Merchants* [and] *. . . the Seed of that Woman who hath long fled in the Wilderness* (London, 1659), *passim*, and cf. Henry Burton, *A Vindication of Churches Commonly Called Independent* (London, 1644), p. 31.

13 Stanley Gray, "The Political Thought of John Winthrop," *New England Quarterly*, III (1930), 682; Thomas Hooker, *A Survey of the Summe of Church-Discipline* (London, 1648), pp. 50–51; Richard Mather, *An Apologie of the Churches in New-England for Church-Covenant* (London, 1643), p. 12; William Bartlet, quoted in Nuttall, *Visible Saints*, p. 72; John Cotton, quoted in Increase Mather, *The First Principles of New-England, Concerning . . . Baptism* (Cambridge, 1675), p. 30; Samuel Mather, *The Figures or Types of the Old Testament* (London, 1705), pp. 326, 329; John Milton, *Of Reformation Touching Church-Discipline in England*, ed. Harry M. Ayres, in *Works*, ed. Patterson, III, 4; J. Robinson, *Justification*, in *Works*, II, 134; Samuel Danforth, *The Building Up of Sion*, in *Bridgwater's Monitor* (Boston, 1717), p. 2. Regarding the "city" and the "hill," see further: John Rogers, *The Book of Revelation . . . opened* (Boston,

1720), p. 96; T[homas] H[ooker], *The Unbeleevers preparing for Christ* (London, 1638), p. 4; Samuel Danforth, *A Brief Recognition of New-Englands Errand into the Wilderness* (Cambridge, 1671), pp. 8–12; *A Platform of Church Discipline* (Cambridge, 1649), p. 5; W. O. E. Oesterley, *The Evolution of the Messianic Idea: A Study in Comparative Religion* (London, 1908), pp. 207–212, 240–67.

14 Robert Cushman, *Reasons and Considerations Touching the Lawfulness of Removing . . . into . . . America* (1621), in Young, *Chronicles,* pp. 240–41; J. Robinson, *Justification,* in *Works,* II, 111, 207 (see also *A Just and Necessary Apology,* in *Works,* III, 74–75); Roger Williams, *Complete Writings* (New York, 1963), IV, 403, 181 (*The Bloody Tenent Yet More Bloody* [1652]), I, 76 ("Mr. Cotton's Letter . . . Answered" [1644]), and III, 322 (*Christenings Make Not Christians* [1645]); R. Williams, *The Bloody Tenent of Persecution* (1644), quoted in George H. Williams, *Wilderness and Paradise in Christian Thought: The Biblical Experience of the Desert in the History of Christianity, and the Paradise Theme in the Theological Idea of the University* (New York, 1962), p. 104; S. Mather, *Figures or Types,* p. 332; John Cotton, *The Bloody Tenent washed, And made white in the bloud of the Lambe* (London, 1647), pp. 68, 126, 61–64; Michael McGiffert, "American Puritan Studies in the 1960's," *William and Mary Quarterly,* XXVII (1970), 36–67; Larzer Ziff, *The Career of John Cotton: Puritanism and the American Experience* (Princeton, 1962), p. 171. My essays on this subject, referred to above are: "New England Epic: Cotton Mather's *Magnalia Christi Americana,*" *English Literary History,* XXXIII (1966), 337–50, "Typology in Puritan New England: The Williams-Cotton Controversy Reassessed," *American Quarterly,* XIX (1967), 166–91, and "The Historiography of Johnson's *Wonder-Working Providence,*" *Essex Institute Historical Collections,* CIV (1968), 138–61.

15 John Norton, *The Heart of N-England rent* (Cambridge, 1659), p. 20; Eliphalet Adams, *The Necessity of Judgment* (New London, 1710), p. 37; Jonathan Mitchel, *Nehemiah on the Wall in Troublesom Times* (Cambridge, 1671), p. 9; Cotton Mather, "Biblia Americana" (MS. in Massachusetts Historical Society, Boston), IV, reel 2, s.v. Jer. 30 (used with the kind permission of the Society); Nicholas Noyes, *New-Englands Duty and Interest* (Cambridge, 1698), pp. 1–3, 39–45; William Adams, *Gods Eye on the Contrite* (Cambridge, 1685), p. 1; Urian Oakes, *New-England Pleaded With* (Cambridge, 1673), pp. 19–21; Danforth, *Building,* pp. 5, 9. See further Thomas Parker, *The Visions and Prophesies of Daniel Expounded* (London, 1646), pp. 155–56, and cf. Richard Reinitz, "The Typological Argument for Religious Toleration: The Separatist Tradition and Roger Williams," *EAL,* V (1970), 74–111.

16 Etienne Gilson, *The Christian Philosophy of Saint Augustine,* trans. L. E. M. Lynch (New York, 1960), p. 5 (and see also the same author's "Eglise et Cité de Dieu chez Saint Augustin," *Archives d'Histoire Doctrinale et Littéraire du Moyen Age,* XX [1953], 5–23); Stanley Stewart, *The Enclosed Garden: The Tradition and the Image in Seven-*

teenth-Century Poetry (Madison, 1966), p. 140; Henry Vane, *An Epistle to the Mystical Body of Christ on Earth* (1662), quoted in G. Williams, *Wilderness*, p. 105; Luella M. Wright, *The Literary Life of the Early Friends, 1650–1725* (New York, 1932), p. 137; Rosemund Tuve, *A Reading of George Herbert* (Chicago, 1952), pp. 28 ff.; David D. Hall, "Understanding the Puritans," forthcoming in *The State of American History,* ed. Herbert Bass (Quadrangle Books, Chicago; cited by permission of the author); William Ames, *The Marrow of Theology,* ed. John Eusden (Boston, 1968), pp. 77–78. See further Ernest L. Tuveson, *Redeemer Nation: The Idea of America's Millennial Role* (Chicago, 1968), p. 139, and Charles S. Singleton, *Dante Studies 2* (Cambridge, Mass., 1958), p. 5. The current theological reaction against theories of progress often expresses itself in this Augustinian mode (which of course itself stems from disillusionment with notions of progress). See, for example, the comments of the Catholic Jean Daniélou and the Protestant Theo Priess on "Christian Faith and History" in *Journal of Religion,* XXX (1950), 157–79.

17 Hannah Arendt, *Between Past and Future: Six Exercises in Political Thought* (New York, 1966), p. 66; Werner G. Kümmel, *Promise and Fulfilment: The Eschatological Message of Jesus* (London, 1961), pp. 112, 141, 145 (for further background on the conflict between "realized" and "futurist" eschatology, see respectively Charles H. Dodd, *Parables of the Kingdom* [London, 1936] and Amos N. Wilder, *Eschatology and Ethics in the Teaching of Jesus* [London, 1950]); A. W. Plumstead, ed., *The Wall and the Garden: Selected Massachusetts Election Sermons, 1670–1775* (Minneapolis, 1968), Introduction, p. 16; Robert W. Hanning, *The Vision of History in Early Britain: From Gildas to Geoffrey of Monmouth* (New York, 1966), pp. 26–42; Morton W. Bloomfield, *Piers Plowman as a Fourteenth-Century Apocalypse* (New Brunswick, N. J., 1961), pp. 99, 101; Bultmann, *Presence,* p. 57; Ernst Benz, "Ecumenical Relations Between Boston Puritanism and German Pietism: Cotton Mather and August Hermann Francke," *Harvard Theological Review,* LIV (1961), 173; Norman Cohn, *The Pursuit of the Millennium* (New York, 1957), pp. 104–6; Oakes, *New-England Pleaded With,* p. 46; Michael Walzer, *The Revolution of the Saints: A Study in the Origin of Radical Politics* (Cambridge, Mass., 1965), p. 297; William Perkins, *Workes* (London, 1608–31), I, 10–12; Hall, "Understanding"; Cotton, *Gods Promise,* p. 6; John Cotton and Cotton Mather, quoted respectively in the Introduction to Samuel Mather's *Figures or Types,* ed. Mason I. Lowance (New York, 1969), pp. v, ix, xx, and in Lowance's "Typology and the New England Way: Cotton Mather and the Exegesis of Biblical Types," *EAL,* IV (1969), 30–31; cf. Samuel Torrey, *Man's Extremity, God's Opportunity* (Boston, 1695), pp. 40–52. Professor Lowance (in *EAL,* IV, 32 ff.) distinguishes between Cotton's and Cotton Mather's use of typology, but he notes that the latter "never abandoned his strong faith in the eschatological view of history, in which his doctrine of the types was firmly rooted," and that, in "this context, the new world, New England, and the 'errand into the wilderness' were [for him]

repeated historical episodes in the larger framework of the history of redemption" (pp. 37, 23). Theodor E. Mommsen offers a succinct contrast between Augustine and "Christian progressivists" in "Saint Augustine and the Christian Idea of Progress," *Journal of the History of Ideas*, XII (1951), 346–74.

18 Larzer Ziff, "The Salem Puritans in the 'Free Aire of a New World,'" *Huntington Library Quarterly*, XX (1956–57), 373–84; R. Williams, "Mr. Cotton's Letter . . . Answered," in *Complete Writings*, I, 24; Miller, *Orthodoxy*, pp. 310, 224, and *Seventeenth Century*, pp. 462, 446; Larzer Ziff, "The Social Bond of Church Covenant," *AQ*, X (1958), 455, 462; Morgan, *Visible Saints*, pp. 83–103, *et passim*; R. Mather, *Apologie*, pp. 26, 6; Bulkeley, *Gospel-Covenant*, p. 39.

19 Samuel Hudson, *The Essence and Unitie of the Church* (London, 1645), p. 7; Cawdrey on Owen, quoted in Nuttall, *Visible Saints*, p. 69; Gilsdorf, "Puritan Apocalypse," pp. 127, 75, 77; Miller, *Colony to Province*, p. 70; John Cotton, *A Sermon Delivered at Salem* (1646), in *John Cotton on the Churches of New England*, ed. Larzer Ziff (Cambridge, Mass., 1968), pp. 44–46, 55–56, 58, 65; R. Mather, *Apologie*, pp. 1–3, 31, 27 (Mather of course added that "If men in entring into this Covenant looke for acceptance through any worth of their owne . . . they shew themselves like to the Pharisees . . . and turne the Church-Covenant into a Covenant of workes" [pp. 4–5]). Cf. on the question of New England's mixture of the "utilitarian" and the "idealistic," Daniel J. Boorstin, *The Americans: The Colonial Experience* (New York, 1958), p. 24.

20 William Stoughton, *New-Englands True Interest* (Cambridge, 1670), pp. 8–9; John Norton, *The Evangelical Worshipper* (1663), in *Three Choice and Profitable Sermons* (Cambridge, 1664), pp. 29–30; Thomas Thacher, *A Fast of Gods chusing* (Boston, 1678), p. 14; William Hooke, *New-Englands Sence* (London, 1645), p. 23. For examples of the blurring of spiritual and literal levels in certain key terms ("wilderness," "Israelite," etc.), see R. Mather, *Apologie*, pp. 5–7, Increase Mather, *Heavens Alarm to the World* (Boston, 1681), pp. 4–7, and John Eliot, Preface to *The Christian Commonwealth* (London, [1659]), sig. B4^v.

21 Wallace, *Calvin's Doctrine*, p. 58; John Robinson, *Of Religious Communion*, in *Works*, III, 202–3 (and cf. the speech of True Godliness to Poverty, refusing to "assure thee of worldly good things," in Benjamin Keach's *Travels of True Godliness* [1682], ed. Howard Malcom [Boston, 1831], p. 77); Tuveson, *Millennium*, p. 85; Thomas Brightman, *Apocalypsis Apocalypseos* (1609) translated as *The Revelation of S. Iohn, Illustrated* (3rd ed.; Leyden, 1616), p. 173; E. Adams, *Necessity of Judgment*, p. 37; Mede, "Discourse XLIV," in *Works*, p. 250; William Williams, *The Great Duty of Ministers to Advance the Kingdom of God* (Boston, 1726), p. 10; John Higginson, The *Cause of God, and his People in New-England* (Cambridge, 1663), p. 10; Mede, *Works*, pp. 252–53; Danforth, *Building*, p. 28; John Davenport, *A Sermon Preached at the Election* (Cambridge, 1669), p. 16; James Keith, *A Case of Prayer*, in *Bridgwater's Monitor* (Boston, 1717), pp. 22, 6, 2, 7; John Cotton (grandson), *A Sermon Preach'd At the Publick*

Lecture (Boston, 1728), p. 16; Bulkeley, *Gospel-Covenant*, p. 292; Richard Mather and William Tompson, *An Heart-Melting Exhortation* (London, 1650), p. 7. Cf. William Bradford's picture of how, in the early Plymouth experience, material "plenty did come in, / From his hand only who doth pardon sin" ("A Description and Historical Account of New England" [n.d.], *Collections of the Massachusetts Historical Society*, III [1794], 77; Solomon Stoddard, *The Way for a People to Live Long in the Land that God Hath given them* [Boston, 1703], *passim*), and Francis Higginson's description of how "*Iosephs* encrease in *AEgypt* is outstript here," in *New Englands Plantation*, in *Tracts and Other Papers . . .* , ed. Peter Force (Washington, 1836–46), Vol. I, no. 12, p. 6.

22 Norman Pettit, *The Heart Prepared: Grace and Conversion in Puritan Spiritual Life* (New Haven, 1966), pp. 19, 219; Bulkeley, *Gospel-Covenant*, pp. 17, 35, 361, 314–15, 326–27. The duality discussed above is often made explicit; I choose Bulkeley's work as a central reference point because in it the covenant theory, as Pettit notes (*Heart Prepared*, pp. 114–15), appears in its "full flowering" and "purest form"; see also Babette Levy, *Preaching in the First Half Century of New England* (New York, 1967), p. 30. The elitist nature of early New England preaching has been stressed by several scholars. The problem, as Professor Morgan states it, was: "How would the gospel be spread to the heathen . . . with a church designed [as it was in New England] only for the saved? . . . John Cotton, for example . . . could only ask of his critics: ' . . . when an Indian or unbeleever commeth into the Church, doe not all the prophets . . . apply their speech to his conviction and conversion?' The honest answer . . . was probably no" (*Visible Saints*, pp. 122–23).

23 Cotton, *Covenant of Grace*, p. 48; Bulkeley, *Gospel-Covenant*, p. 100; T. Hooker, *The Saints Dignitie and Dutie* (London, 1651), p. 38; Bulkeley, *Gospel-Covenant*, pp. 105, 390, and Shepard's Preface to this work, sig. B1^r.

24 Cotton, *Sermon at Salem*, pp. 53–54; John Robinson, *New Essays*, in *Works*, I, 117 (italics mine); Bulkeley, *Gospel-Covenant*, pp. 29–30, 325, 75, 373, 411, 102; Ursula Brumm, "Edward Johnson's *Wonder-Working Providence* and the Puritan Conception of History," *Jahrbuch für Amerikastudien*, XIV (1969), 143 (cf. Samuel C. Chew's discussion of Truth and Time in *The Virtues Reconciled: An Iconographic Study* [Toronto, 1947], p. 88); Pettit, *Heart Prepared*, p. 219; Ziff, Introduction to *Cotton on the Churches*, p. 28; Edmund S. Morgan, *The Puritan Family: Essays in Religion and Domestic Relations in Seventeenth Century New England* (Boston, 1944), pp. 90, 94, and *Visible Saints*, pp. 122–23 (and Cotton, quoted on p. 103 of this study); Bulkeley, *Gospel-Covenant*, pp. 276, 279, 281, 383, 420. Cf. John F. Frederick, "Literary Art in Thomas Hooker's *The Poor Doubting Christian*," *American Literature*, XL (1968), 7 ff., with Solomon Stoddard, *The Efficacy of the Fear of Hell* (Boston, 1718), pp. 9–12. On the question of democracy, cf. Theodore Hornberger's comments on Cotton's "idea of equality," in "The Enlightenment and the American Dream," in *The American Writer and the European Tradition*,

ed. Margaret Denny and William H. Gilman (Minneapolis, 1950),
pp. 20–21, with Coleridge's gloss on Cotton's view that only saints
"should have the rights of citizens," quoted in David Davies,
"Coleridge's Marginalia in Mather's *Magnalia,*" *Huntington Library
Quarterly,* II (1938–39), 237.

25 Thomas Shepard, *The Sincere Convert* (London, 1669), pp. 110, 178,
180, and Preface to Bulkeley, *Gospel-Covenant,* sig. B2ʳ; John Cotton,
Gods Mercie Mixed with His Justice (1641), ed. Everett H. Emerson
(Gainesville, 1958), pp. 17–19, and *Covenant of Grace,* pp. 34, 102;
Thomas Shepard, *The Soules Preparation* (London, 1638), pp. 10–11,
31, 132–33, and *The Saitns* [*sic*] *Jewel* (London, 1669), p. 187 (and
see also his argument on p. 201 of this tract on why "not to believe
and lay hold on the Promise is a sin of unbelief"); Bulkeley, *Gospel-
Covenant,* pp. 75, 373, 411, 102.

26 Shepard, Preface to Bulkeley, *Gospel-Covenant,* and sig. B2ᵛ, pp.
425–26.

27 J. Higginson, *Cause of God,* p. 19; Thomas Hooker, *The Soules
Implantation* (London, 1637), pp. 188–90 (and see further his discussion of the "Liberties and Priviledges . . . we enjoy in *New-England,*"
in *The Application of Redemption . . .* [London, 1659], IX, 248);
Stoughton, *New-Englands True Interest,* pp. 16–17. Lessons on the
meaning of grace often form an intrinsic part also in the Artillery
Election Sermons: e.g., Urian Oakes, *The Unconquerable, All-Con-
quering, & more-than-Conquering Soldier* (Cambridge, 1674), pp.
1–4. This interrelationship between the covenant of grace and the
federal covenant may well have been influenced by Johann Cocceius'
application of typology to covenant theory: see Perry Miller's notes to
Jonathan Edwards, *Images or Shadows of Divine Things,* ed. Miller
(New Haven, 1948), p. 142; John T. McNeill, *The History and
Character of Calvinism* (New York, 1954), pp. 266, 434; and Charles
S. McCoy, "Johannes Cocceius: Federal Theologian," *Scottish Journal
of Theology,* XVI (1963), 352–70.

28 William DeLoss Love, *The Fast and Thanksgiving Days of New Eng-
land* (Boston, 1895), p. 221; Richard Mather, *A Farewel-Exhortation*
(Cambridge, 1657), p. 23; Increase Mather, *David Serving His Gen-
eration* (Boston, 1698), p. 22, and *The Times of Man are in the
Hand of God* (Boston, 1675), p. 19; Cotton Mather, *Wonders of the
Invisible World* (Boston, 1693), p. 9, *Parentator* (1724), quoted in
Williston Walker, *The Creeds and Platforms of Congregationalism*
(New York, 1893), p. 410, and *A Pillar of Gratitude* (Boston, 1700),
pp. 13–14; Samuel Willard, *The Perils of the Times Displayed* (Boston,
1700), pp. 40, 53; Samuel Torrey, *An Exhortation Unto Reformation,
Amplified* (Cambridge, 1674), p. 10; E. Mather, *Serious Exhortation,*
p. 11; W. Adams, *Gods Eye,* pp. 1, 37.

29 R. Mather, *Farewel-Exhortation,* pp. 15–16; Increase Mather, Preface
to Torrey, *Exhortation,* sig. A2ᵛ; Oakes, *New–England Pleaded With,*
pp. 13, 27; John Whiting, *The Way of Israel's Welfare* (Boston, 1686),
p. 7; John Oxenbridge, *New-England Freemen, Warned and Warmed*
(Cambridge, 1673), p. 18; Ebenezer Pemberton, *A Sermon Preached
in the Audience of the General Assembly* (Boston, 1706), p. 10;
Norton, *Evangelical Worshipper,* p. 35; William Williams, *The Great*

Salvation Revealed and Offered (Boston, 1717), pp. 29, 132–33;
Willard, *Useful Instructions*, p. 3; John Davenport, *Gods Call To His
People* (Cambridge, 1669), p. 18. See further Samuel Willard's
description of how Jeremiah "brings in God as clothed with human
affection," in *The Only Sure Way to Prevent Threatned Calamity*
(Cambridge, 1682), p. 5.

30 Bulkeley, *Gospel-Covenant*, p. 16; Samuel Torrey, *A Plea For the Life
of Dying Religion* (Boston, 1683), p. 42; John Wilson, *A Seasonable
Watch-Word* (Cambridge, 1677), p. 9; Miller, *Colony to Province*,
p. 33; Stoughton, *New-Englands True Interest*, p. 27; Samuel Hooker,
Righteousness Rained from Heaven . . . (Cambridge, 1677), p. 17;
Cotton Mather, *The Everlasting Gospel* (Boston, 1700), pp. 71–72;
W. Williams, *Great Salvation*, pp. v, 1.

31 Cotton Mather, *The Serviceable Man* (Boston, 1690), pp. 13–14,
Things to be Look'd for (Cambridge, 1691), pp. 57, 59–60, and
The Present State of New England (Boston, 1690), p. 25; Thomas
Shepard, Preface to Danforth's *Brief Recognition*, sig. A2^r; Mitchel,
Nehemiah, pp. 25, 33; Increase Mather, *An Historical Discourse
Concerning the Prevalency of Prayer* . . . (Boston, 1677), p. 19;
Torrey, *Plea*, pp. 28, 40–41 (and cf. Samuel Wakeman, *Sound Repen-
tance* [Hartford, 1685], p. 42). Regarding the importance of Nehemiah
as type in the election sermon, from before Mitchel's *Nehemiah*
(preached in 1667) through the Revolution, see Lindsay Swift, "The
Massachusetts Election Sermons," *Publications of the Colonial Society
of Massachusetts*, I (1892–94), 411.

32 Alan C. Charity, *Events and their Afterlife: The Dialectics of Christian
Typology in the Bible and Dante* (Cambridge, 1966), p. 78; J.
Higginson, *Cause of God*, p. 24; Willard, *Only Sure Way*, p. 187;
William Hubbard, *The Happiness of a People* (Boston, 1676), p. 53;
Davenport, *Gods Call*, pp. 24, 27; Torrey, *Exhortation*, p. 29; William
Adams, *The Necessity of The pouring out of the Spirit from on High*
(Boston, 1679), p. 13; Samuel Willard, *The Duty of a People* (Boston,
1680), p. 13. Cf. Increase Mather, *Renewal of Covenant* (Boston,
1677), pp. 5–6, 12–16, 20, and *Returning unto God the great concern-
ment of a Covenant People* (Boston, 1680), p. 18 (and see the Covenant-Renewal Declaration appended). See also Peter Folger's satirical
verse-comments on how the settlers looked to "the Prophet *Jeremy*"
for assurance that "god will afflict us no more," in *A Looking Glass
for the Times* (1676), in *Rhode Island Historical Tracts*, XVI (1883),
p. 16. Regarding Zerubbabel as a figure of Christ, see, for example,
Joseph Sarachek, *The Doctrine of the Messiah in Medieval Jewish
Literature* (New York, 1932), p. 11; regarding the meaning of the
candlestick, see my comments on "Hilda's Seven-Branched Allegory,"
EAL, I (1966), 5–7. A lucid description of the historiographic view
behind the use of both Zerubbabel and the candlestick appears in
Thomas Goodwin, *Zerubbabels Encouragement* (London, 1642), esp.
pp. 3, 12, 14.

33 Kenneth Silverman, "Introduction to the Colonial Elegy," *Colonial
American Poetry*, ed. Silverman (New York, 1968), pp. 128–29;
Michael Wigglesworth, *God's Controversy With New-England* (1662),

in *The Puritans: A Sourcebook of their Writings*, ed. Perry Miller and Thomas H. Johnson (New York, 1963), II, 616; *The Necessity for Reformation . . . Agreed upon by the Elders . . . in the Synod at Boston . . . Sept. 10, 1679* (Boston, 1679), p. v. (cf. Walker, *Creeds and Platforms*, pp. 410 ff.); Stoughton, *New-Englands True Interest*, pp. 24, 29, 33; James Allin, *New-Englands Choicest Blessing* (Boston, 1679), p. 13.

34 Mitchel, *Nehemiah*, p. 32; Samuel Willard, *The Checkered State of the Gospel Church* (Boston, 1701), p. 193, cited in Gilsdorf, "Puritan Apocalypse," p. 193; Oxenbridge, *New-England Freemen*, pp. 19, 47; Whiting, *Israel's Welfare*, p. 16; J. Higginson, *Cause of God*, p. 5; Torrey, *Plea*, pp. 18, 42, 7, 45 (see also Davenport, *Gods Call*, pp. 16, 20, Danforth, *Brief Recognition*, p. 9, and Edward Johnson, *The Wonder-Working Providence* [1654], ed. J. Franklin Jameson [New York, 1910], pp. 159–60); Oakes, Preface to Increase Mather, *The Day of Trouble is near* (Cambridge, 1674), sigs. A1ʳ–A1ᵛ, and *New-England Pleaded With*, pp. 15, 63.

35 Gurdon Saltonstall, *A Sermon Preached Before the General Assembly* (Boston, 1697), p. 55; Hubbard, *Happiness*, p. 60; Wakeman, *Sound Repentance*, p. 11; Chauncy, *Gods Mercy*, p. 8; Thomas Thacher, Preface to Thomas Shepard, *Eye-Salve, Or A Watch-Word From our Lord* (Cambridge, 1673), sig. A2ᵛ; Increase Mather, *Ichabod* (Boston, 1701), pp. 83–84; Allin, *New-Englands Choicest*, p. 14; Joseph Rowlandson, *The Possibility of Gods Forsaking a People* (Boston, 1682), p. 15; I. Mather, *Earnest Exhortation*, p. 21.

36 John Winthrop, *Conclusions for the Plantation in New England*, in *Old South Leaflets*, Vol. II, no. 50, p. 9; John Cotton, "A Reply to . . . Williams," in Williams' *Complete Writings*, II, 131; Stoughton, *New-England's True Interest*, p. 10; Bale, *Image*, p. 295; I. Mather, *Times of Man*, pp. 16, 19–20, *Earnest Exhortation*, p. 5, Preface to *Returning unto God*, sig. A2ʳ, and Preface to Torrey, *Exhortation*, sig. A2ᵛ; John Sherman and Thomas Shepard, Preface to Oakes, *New-England Pleaded With*, sig. A2ʳ; Mitchel, *Nehemiah*, p. 31. See further Jonathan Mitchel's explanation of how "God loves to humble *Instruments* . . . even when they are carrying on his good work" ("Postscript" to I. Mather, *First Principles*), and Increase Mather's discourse on the "*great difference in those temporal judgments, which the wicked and the righteous are subject to in this world*" (*The Righteous Man a blessing . . .* [Boston, 1702], p. 49).

37 Norton, *Heart of N-England*, p. 5; Increase Mather, *The Great Blessing of Primitive Counsellours* (Boston, 1693), p. 9, and *Righteous Man*, p. 49; J. Higginson, *Cause of God*, p. 21; R. Mather and W. Tompson, *Heart-Melting Exhortation*, p. 58; Urian Oakes, *The Soveraign Efficacy of Divine Providence* (Boston, 1682), pp. 23–25.

38 Edmund S. Morgan, *Roger Williams: The Church and the State* (New York, 1967), p. 107; Tuveson, *Redeemer Nation*, p. 8; Haller, *Elect Nation*, p. 245; Calvin, *Commentaries on Jeremiah*, I, 87, and III, 371 (italics mine); I. Mather, *Times of Man*, p. 7; Cotton Mather, *Things for a Distressed People to Think upon* (Boston, 1696), p. 15; Willard, *Useful Instructions*, p. 63. Regarding the continuity of these

parallels to Calvin's doctrine, see, for example, Increase Mather, *The Wicked Mans Portion* (Boston, 1675), p. 14; Samuel Danforth, *The Cry of Sodom Inquired Into* (Cambridge, 1674), p. 9; and Benjamin Colman, Preface to *The Judgments of Providence in the hand of Christ* (Boston, 1727), pp. 7–8.

39 Oakes, *New-England Pleaded With*, p. 63; Cotton, *Covenant of Grace*, pp. 102–9; Thomas Hooker, *The Soules Preparation for Christ* (London, 1632), pp. 131–32; John Norton, *The Believers Consolation*, in *Three Choice . . . Sermons*, p. 26; C. Mather, *Things to be Look'd for*, p. 25, and *Magnalia*, I, 205, 527; Hubbard, *Happiness*, pp. 59–60; Stoughton, *New-Englands True Interest*, p. 19; Increase Mather, *The Mystery of Israel's Salvation* (London, 1669), p. 104; William Williams, *A Plea for God* (Boston, 1719), p. 35. Regarding the continuity of these parallels, compare Calvin's explication of Jer. 2:9—"there was need of many evils . . . because he [God] would heal those wounds which he himself had inflicted" (*Commentaries on Jeremiah*, I, 87)— with Chauncy's *Gods Mercy*, pp. 31–33, I. Mather's *Wicked Mans Portion*, p. 14, Danforth's *Cry of Sodom*, p. 9, and Colman's *Judgments*, pp. 7–8.

40 C. Mather, *Things to Think upon*, p. 27; I. Mather, Preface to Torrey's *Exhortation*, sig. A4ʳ; Danforth, *Brief Recognition*, p. 20; Torrey, *Plea*, p. 45; John Williams, *Warnings to the Unclean* (Boston, 1699), p. 30; Shepard, *Eye-Salve*, p. 14 (Shepard's description here is characteristic in that it links Christ's temptations with those of the Hebrews and the New Englanders; the image of affliction as a method of "purgation" is also pervasive); J. Higginson, *Cause of God*, p. 18; C. Mather, *Serviceable Man*, p. 45; I. Mather, *Times of Man*, p. 5; Keith, *Case of Prayer*, p. 20; Mitchel, *Nehemiah*, pp. 16–17; Oakes, *New-England Pleaded With*, p. 21.

For analogues to the above images in the discourses on grace, see, for example, Norton, *Believers Consolation*, in *Three Sermons*, p. 27.

41 I. Mather, *Day of Trouble*, pp. 4–5, 12–15, 18, 26–28. Regarding the importance of this sermon in Increase's career, see Miller, *Colony to Province*, p. 30, and Kenneth B. Murdock, *Increase Mather, the Foremost American Puritan* (Cambridge, Mass., 1926), p. 102. Increase's sermon was preached just before the outbreak of King Philip's War.

42 W. Williams, *Plea*, p. 34; Cotton Mather, *The Way to Prosperity* (Boston, 1690), p. 23; Torrey, *Exhortation*, p. 6; Charles L. Sanford, *The Quest for Paradise: Europe and the American Moral Imagination* (Urbana, 1961), p. 83; Darrett B. Rutman, "God's Bridge Falling Down: 'Another Approach' to New England Puritanism Assayed," *William and Mary Quarterly*, XIX (1962), 416; Mason I. Lowance, Jr., "Images and Shadows of Divine Things: Puritan Typology in New England from 1660 to 1750" (Emory University dissertation, 1967), p. 44; Warren I. Susman, "History and the American Intellectual: Uses of a Usable Past," in *The American Experience*, ed. Hennig Cohen (New York, 1968), pp. 85–87. Regarding the mutual commendations in the jeremiads, see Oxenbridge, *New-England Freemen*, p. 19; W. Adams, *Gods Eye*, p. 27; Whiting, *Israel's Welfare*, sig. A4ʳ; Allin,

New-Englands Choicest, p. 9; I. Mather, Preface to Torrey, *Exhortation,* sigs. A3ʳ–A3ᵛ; Increase Mather, *A Discourse Concerning the Danger of Apostasy* (Boston, 1685), pp. 57, 81, 109; and cf. Swift, *Pub. Col. Soc. Mass.,* I, 396.

43 Norton, quoted in I. Mather, *First Principles,* p. 17 (see also the statements by Hooker and Cotton, on pp. 9–10, 13); Morgan, *Puritan Family,* p. 103; Increase Mather, *A Discourse Concerning the Subject of Baptism* (Boston, 1675), pp. 7–8, 26, *Pray for the Rising Generation* (Cambridge, 1678), p. 11, and *The Duty of Parents to Pray for their Children* (Boston, 1703), pp. 15–16; and see also his *Divine Right of Infant-Baptisme* (Boston, 1680), pp. 9–14.

44 Cotton Mather, *The Duty of Children* (Boston, 1703), p. 28; I. Mather, *Divine Right,* p. 2; Thacher, *A Fast,* p. 15; Cotton Mather, *Parentalia, An Essay Upon the Blessings and Comforts, Reserved for Pious Children* (Boston, 1715), p. 26, Preface to *The Wayes and Joyes of Early Piety* (Boston, 1712), sig. A3ʳ, *Parentator, Memoirs of . . . the Ever-Memorable Dr. Increase Mather* (Boston, 1724), pp. 40–48, *A Family Well-Ordered* (Boston, 1699), pp. 35–36, and *Successive Generations* (Boston, 1715), pp. 19–39; Bulkeley, *Gospel-Covenant,* p. 36; R. Mather, *Farewel-Exhortation,* p. 12; J. Cotton, *Covenant of Grace,* p. 56; Miller, *Colony to Province,* p. 211; Peter Y. De Jong, *The Covenant Idea in New England Theology, 1620–1847* (Grand Rapids, Mich., 1945), p. 38; E. S. Morgan, quoted in Silverman, *Colonial Poetry,* p. 44; Persons, *American Minds,* p. 17; John Penry, *An Exhortation unto the Governours and People* (1588), in *Three Treatises Concerning Wales,* ed. David Williams (Cardiff, 1960), p. 70; I. Mather, *Discourse Concerning Apostasy,* p. 65, and *Pray,* pp. 14–15. Regarding the "excessively tangled" and "thorny" views on baptism among the English congregationalists, see Nuttall, *Visible Saints,* pp. 118 ff., 135.

45 C. Mather, *Duty of Children,* pp. 49, 22, 32; Shepard, *Eye-Salve,* p. 2; I. Mather, *Duty of Parents,* pp. 15–16. Cf. Increase Mather's Preface to *Solemn Advice to Young Men* (Boston, 1695), *passim.*

46 J. Higginson, *Cause of God,* p. 12; Scottow, *Narrative,* pp. 311, 305; Allin, *New-Englands Choicest,* p. 14; Stoughton, *New-Englands True Interest,* pp. 19, 33; Oxenbridge, *New-England Freemen,* pp. 9, 30; James Fitch, *An Holy Connexion* (Cambridge, 1674), pp. 12–13; William Hooke, *New Englands Teares for Old Englands Feares* (London, 1641), p. 21; C. Mather, *Magnalia,* II, 579, and *Wonders,* p. 10. Cf. Cotton Mather, *The Bostonian Ebenezer* (1698), in *Old South Leaflets,* Vol. III, no. 67, p. 17; *Necessity,* p. iii. Many of the phrases in which the fathers are described refer to apocalytic texts: the opening reference, for example (from Scottow), to the sun and moon comes from Rev. 12, where "this woman . . . the true Christian church . . . [is] decked with the shining Sun of righteousness" and the moon signifies that "All moveable things hath the Lord subdued unto her" (Bale, *Image,* p. 404).

47 John F. Wilson, in *Church History,* XXXII, 43; Gerald R. Cragg, *Puritanism in the Period of the Great Persecution* (Cambridge, 1957), p. 258. Perez Zagorin, *A History of Political Thought in the English*

Revolution (London, 1954), p. 97; Simpson, *Puritanism*, p. 98 (cf. Nuttall, *Visible Saints*, p. 147); Haller, *Elect Nation*, p. 249; C. Mather, *Magnalia*, I, 42; Mommsen, in *JHI*, XII, 361; Samuel Sewall, *Phaenomena quadem Apocalyptica . . .* (Boston, 1967), pp. 2, 40; Mitchel, *Nehemiah*, p. 9; Increase Mather, *A Discourse Concerning Faith and Fervency in Prayer* (Boston, 1710), p. 17. Regarding the phrase "ends of the earth," see further Shepard, *Eye-Salve*, p. 24; Johnson, *Wonder-Working Providence*, p. 54; and Saltonstall, *Sermon*, p. 59.

48 Gilsdorf, "Puritan Apocalypse," p. 48; Erwin Panofsky, *Early Netherlandish Painting* (Cambridge, Mass., 1958), I, 135; John Goodwin, *Imputatio Fidei* (1642), quoted in Woodhouse, *Puritanism and Liberty*, p. [46]; Bale, *Image*, pp. 598, 252; Robert Burton, *Anatomy of Melancholy*, cited in Baker, *Race of Time*, p. 68; Sewall, *Phaenomena*, pp. 2, 40.

49 Sewall, *Phaenomena*, sig. A2ᵛ; François Wendel, *Calvin* (New York, 1963), p. 285; Torrey, *Exhortation*, p. 1; James P. Martin, *The Last Judgment in Protestant Theology from Orthodoxy to Ritschl* (Grand Rapids, Mich., 1963), p. 65; Tuveson, *Millennium*, p. 86; C. Mather, *Things to be Look'd for*, p. 24, and *Things to Think upon*, pp. 32–33, 35–36, 38, and *Magnalia*, I, 331; I. Mather, *Mystery*, pp. 163–64, 169, and *Morning Star*, appended to *Righteous Man*, p. 81; John Cotton, Preface to John Norton, *The Answer to the Whole Set of Questions of . . . Apollonius* (1648), trans. Douglas Horton (Cambridge, Mass., 1958), p. 14. See further Tuveson, *Millennium*, pp. 24, 52, on Luther's attitude toward the Book of Revelation and on King James' "meditations" on it.

50 C. Mather, *Magnalia*, II, 8; Cotton Mather, *Pillar of Gratitude* (Boston, 1700), pp. 5–6; Wakeman, *Sound Repentance*, p. 18; C. Mather, *Way to Prosperity*, pp. 9–12; Allin, *New-Englands Choicest*, p. 2; Increase Mather, *A Call from Heaven* (Boston, 1685), pp. 60–61; C. Mather, *Bostonian Ebenezer*, in *Magnalia*, I, 103, 93, 95 (also reprinted in *Old South Leaflets*, Vol. III, no. 67). An interesting analysis of the Exodus as primarily an Old Testament type appears in David Daube, *The Exodus Pattern in the Bible* (London, 1963). For some further American Puritan renderings of this theme, see: I. Mather, *Ichabod*, p. 63, Preface to Torrey, *Exhortation*, sig. A2ᵛ, and Preface to E. Mather, *Serious Exhortation*, sig. A3ᵛ; Oxenbridge, *New-England Freemen*, pp. 17–21; Willard, *Useful Instructions*, pp. 15, 61; J. Williams, *Warnings*, p. 47 (but cf. pp. 57–60); W. Adams, *Gods Eye*, p. 25; Torrey, *Plea*, pp. 10, 18; Oakes, *New-England Pleaded With*, pp. 11–14.

51 C. Mather, Preface to *Serviceable Man*, sig. A2ᵛ; Danforth, *Cry of Sodom*, p. 9; Stoughton, *New-Englands True Interest*, pp. 22, 8 (see also pp. 9–11); John Norton, *Sion the Out-Cast*, in *Three Choice and Profitable Sermons* (Cambridge, 1664), p. 4; Thomas Hooker, *The Soules Implantation* (London, 1637), p. 85; Thomas Browne, *Religio Medici*, ed. James Winny (London, 1963), p. 13; Hooker, *Survey*, p. 70; I. Mather, Preface to *Serman Shewing That the present Dispensations of Providence declare that wonderful Revolutions in the*

World are near at Hand (Edinburgh, 1710), sig. A3ᵛ; R. Mather, *Farewel-Exhortation*, p. 3; Jens G. Møller, "The Beginnings of Puritan Covenant Theology," *Journal of Ecclesiastical History*, XIII–XIV (1962–63), 47; Joye, Preface to *Jeremy*, sig. Aiiʳ; Calvin, *Commentaries on Jeremiah*, III, 141; J. Higginson, *Cause of God*, p. 13. On the Jewish typology of the vine, see Rachel Wischnitzer, *The Messianic Theme in the Paintings of the Dura Synagogue* (Chicago, 1948), pp. 96–98.

52 Eliot, Preface to *Christian Commonwealth*, sig. B4ᵛ; George Boas, "Joachim of Florus," *Essays in Primitivism and Related Ideas in the Middle Ages* (New York, 1966), p. 206; Sidney G. Sowers, *The Hermeneutics of Philo and the Hebrews: A Comparison of the Interpretation of the Old Testament in Philo Judaeus and the Epistle to the Hebrews* (Zurich, 1965), p. 127; Noyes, *New-Englands Duty*, pp. 24–25; C. F. Adams, *Massachusetts*, p. 59; Daniel Boorstin, "The Puritan Tradition: Community Above Ideology," *Commentary*, XXVI (1959), 294; William Tyndale, *A Pathway to the Holy Scripture*, in *Works*, ed. Gervasi Duffield (Appleford, 1964), I, 15.

53 Edward Taylor, *Christographia*, ed. Norman S. Grabo (New Haven, 1962), pp. 53–54; Daniélou, *Shadows to Reality*, pp. 155–56; Johann Hofmann, paraphrased in Rudolf Bultmann, "Prophecy and Fulfillment," trans. James C. G. Grieg, in *Essays in Old Testament Hermeneutics*, ed. Claus Westermann (Richmond, Va., 1963), p. 56 (see further with regard to Bultmann's position, the comments in this volume by Gerhard von Rad on p. 20, Walter Zimmerli on pp. 116–20, Claus Westermann on pp. 124–28, Walter Eichrodt on pp. 233–35, and Wolfhart Pannenberg on pp. 321–25); John Cotton, *Brief Exposition with Practical Observations Upon the whole Book of Canticles* (London, 1655), p. 9; I. Mather, *Morning Star*, p. 80; Danforth, *Brief Recognition*, pp. 5–7; Norton, *Evangelical Worshipper*, p. 37; C. Mather, *The Wonderful Works of God* (Boston, 1690), p. 3; Danforth, *Building*, p. 20; Mitchel, *Nehemiah*, p. 9.

54 Parker, *Visions of Daniel*, pp. 155–56; Oakes, *New England Pleaded With*, pp. 21, 44; I. Mather, *Sermon Shewing Dispensations*, p. 13; C. Mather, *Duty of Children*, p. 4; Perry Miller and Thomas H. Johnson, *The Puritans* (New York, 1963), I, 89; Johnson, *Wonder-Working Providence*, pp. 271, 237–39, 256, 203. Cf. Helen Gardner, *The Business of Criticism* (Oxford, 1959), pp. 142–43. Karl Keller points out that Sewall wrote his *Phaenomena* in order "to document what he doggedly believed to be a 'synchronisme' between the Old Jerusalem of the Jews, the Christian Kingdom of God, and New Zion in America . . . the final Garden of Eden. . . . In the 'cognations' which he sees between the Old Testament types and New Testament antitypes, Sewall finds room for New England as further antitype" ("'The World Slickt Up in Types': Edward Taylor as a Version of Emerson," *EAL*, V (1970), 128, 131. It is in this sense above all that the Puritans throughout the century saw their plantation as "destined to be the nucleus not only of a holy but of a *millennial* people" (Tuveson, *Redeemer Nation*, p. 25).

55 Scottow, *Narrative,* pp. 286–87; Torrey, *Exhortation,* pp. 7, 31–32;
Gilsdorf, "Puritan Apocalypse," p. 125; I. Mather, *Day of Trouble,*
p. 27 (italics mine); Oakes, *New-England Pleaded With,* pp. 17, 20,
23 (see also pp. 44–45); I. Mather, Preface to Torrey, *Exhortation,*
sig. A2ʳ; Mitchel, *Nehemiah,* pp. 19, 8; C. Mather, *Magnalia,* II, 8;
I. Mather, *Ichabod,* p. 67; Willard, *Useful Instructions,* p. 15; Shepard,
Eye-Salve, pp. 13–14; Torrey, *Exhortation,* pp. 31–32; Samuel Wil-
lard, *Impenitent Sinners warned of their Misery* (Boston, 1698),
p. 23. See also Richard Mather, *Church-Government and Church-
Covenant* (London, 1643), p. 34; Saltonstall, *Sermon,* pp. 59–60;
Hubbard, *Happiness,* p. 8; C. Mather, *Serviceable Man,* pp. 41–42.
56 Tuveson, *Redeemer Nation,* p. 98; G. Williams, *Wilderness,* p. 58;
Hubbard, *Happiness,* p. 61; Martin, *Last Judgment,* p. 23; Shepard,
Eye-Salve, p. 10 [i.e., p. 11]; E. Adams, *Necessity of Judgment,* p. 35;
Cotton, quoted in C. Mather, *Magnalia,* I, 325; Gilsdorf, "Puritan
Apocalypse," pp. 97, 99.
57 Norton, *Evangelical Worshipper,* p. 37; Shepard, *Eye-Salve,* p. 10
[i.e., 11]; E. Adams, *Necessity of Judgment,* p. 35; Miller and Johnson,
Puritans, I, 81; Allin, *New-Englands Choicest,* p. 13; I. Mather,
Discourse Concerning Apostasy, p. 77, Preface to Torrey, *Exhortation,*
sig. A2ʳ, and Introduction to C. Mather's *Johannes in Eremo,* in *Mag-
nalia,* I, 248; Oakes, *New-England Pleaded With,* pp. 21, 23; C.
Mather, *Serviceable Man,* p. 28; Sewall, *Phaenomena,* p. 2. Cf.
Increase Mather, *A Brief History of the Warr* . . . (Boston, 1676),
p. 51, and Benjamin Colman, *The Earth devoured by the Cursed*
(Boston, 1727), p. 83. Regarding the apocalyptical import of the
"harvest" image (pervasive in the political sermons) see Bloomfield,
Piers Plowman, p. 106. The double vision of the jeremiads is noted by
A. W. Plumstead, Introduction to *Wall and Garden,* pp. 25, 27; for
dissenting views, see the reviews of the book in *American Literature,*
XLI (1969), 613–17, by Louis P. Simpson, and in *William and Mary
Quarterly,* XXVI (1969), 313–15, by Jesper Rosenmeier. See also
George Williams on the Creation-Eden-New Jerusalem motif ("Endzeit
gleicht Urzeit"), in *Wilderness,* p. 10n., *et passim,* Sowers, *Hermeneutics,* p. 89n., and Karl Löwith, *Meaning in History* (Chicago,
1957), p. 148.
58 Isidore Koplowitz, *The Mosheeach or Messiah* (Athens, Ga., 1907),
p. 8; Erich Auerbach, "*Figura,*" trans. Ralph Manheim, in *Scenes from
the Drama of European Literature* (New York, 1959), p. 8 (and cf.
p. 38); Cotton Mather, *The Joyful Sound Reaching to Both the
INDIA'S,* pt. I of *India Christiana* (Boston, 1721), pp. 47–48;
Bulkeley, *Gospel-Covenant,* pp. 9–10, 13–16, 18–20. See further, for
example, Arise Evans, *Light for the Jews* (London, 1656), and John
Dury, *Israels Call* (London, 1646).
59 I. Mather, *Pray,* p. 6; Abba Hillel Silver, *A History of Messianic Spec-
ulation in Israel, from the First through the Seventeenth Centuries*
(New York, 1927), pp. 151–52, 173, 4, 150–51, 164; Julius H.
Greenstone, *The Messiah Idea in Jewish History* (Philadelphia, 1906),
pp. 203, 206.
60 Louis B. Wright, *Middle-Class Culture in Elizabethan England*

(Ithaca, 1958), p. 326; J. H. Adamson, "The War in Heaven: Milton's Version of the *Merkabah*," *Journal of English and Germanic Philology*, LVII (1958), 691; Baker, *Race of Time*, p. 58; John Milton, *Paradise Regained*, bk. III, ll. 429, 419, 433–35, in *Complete Poems and Major Prose*, ed. Merritt Y. Hughes (New York, 1957); Silver, *History*, pp. 150–64; Joseph Saracheck, *The Doctrine of the Messiah in Medieval Jewish Literature* (New York, 1932), p. 13.

61 Gorton, quoted in Sanford, *Quest*, p. 82; Increase Mather, Preface to *A Discourse Concerning Faith and Fervency in Prayer, and the Glorious Kingdom of the Lord . . . Now Approaching* (Boston, 1710), p. i, and Preface to E. Mather, *Serious Exhortation*, sig. A3ᵛ; Sewall, *Phaenomena*, pp. 27–28; C. Mather, *Things to be Look'd for*, pp. 3, 10; Johnson, *Wonder-Working Providence*, p. 271; Davenport, quoted in C. Mather, *Magnalia*, I, 331; David E. Smith, "Millenarian Scholarship in America," *AQ*, XVII (1965), 539; Louise F. Brown, *The Political Activities of the Baptists and Fifth Monarcy Men in England During the Interregnum* (Washington, 1912), p. 15; Thomas Shepard, *The Clear Sun-shine of the Gospel Breaking Forth upon the Indians in New-England* (London, 1648), p. 30; I. Mather, *Mystery*, pp. 177, 171, 52; Bulkeley, *Gospel-Covenant*, pp. 23–24.

62 Mitchel, Preface to Shepard, *Parable*, sigs. A3ʳ–A3ᵛ (the parable itself, of course, according to traditional interpretation, speaks of the Parousia); John Cotton, *A Briefe Exposition of the whole Book of Canticles* (London, 1648), pp. 182, 200; Johnson, *Wonder-Working Providence*, pp. 30, 238–39, 255, 268; Wilbur M. Smith, "The Prophetic Literature of Colonial America," *Bibliotheca Sacra*, C (1943), 76; Charles Evans, *American Bibliography* (New York, 1941), I, 28; I. Mather, *Mystery*, p. 37; Johan J. Chydenius, *The Typological Problem in Dante: A Study in the History of Medieval Ideas* (Helsingfors, 1958), pp. 112–17; Cotton Mather, *A Midnight Cry* (Boston, 1692), p. 59; see also Mather's pun on "*Columba*," or "dove," for America-Columbia, in *Magnalia*, I, 581; and for the apocalyptic meaning of this reference to Cant. 2:14, see Theodore Beza, *Sermons Vpon the Three First Chapters of the Canticle of Canticles*, trans. John Harmer (Oxford, 1587), and Joseph Hall, *Columba Noah* (London, 1623). For the importance of *Midnight Cry*, see Thomas J. Holmes, *Cotton Mather: A Bibliography* (Cambridge, Mass., 1940), II, 680. I. Mather's use of the parable of the ten virgins (from Matt. 25) is discussed by W. G., Preface to *Mystery*, [p. 3]; regarding the widespread popularity of this treatise, see Froom, *Prophetic Faith*, III, 128.

63 I. Mather, *Pray*, p. 6, *Day of Trouble*, p. 20, *Mystery*, pp. 80, 90, and *Discourse Concerning Prayer*, pp. 22, 29; C. Mather, *Duty of Children*, p. 4, and *Present State*, p. 5; W. Williams, *Great Duty*, p. 2; Keith, *Case of Prayer*, p. 30; Calvin, Commentary on Mat. 24:30, quoted in Torrance, *Kingdom and Church*, p. 123.

64 Torrey, *Man's Extremity*, pp. 55–56; Mitchel, *Nehemiah*, p. 19; J. Cotton, *Sermon at Salem*, p. 51; Bloomfield, *Piers Plowman*, pp. 176–77.

65 William Manson, "Eschatology in the New Testament," *Scottish Journal of Theology, Occasional Papers*, no. 2 (1953), pp. 4–5; Charity,

Events and their Afterlife, pp. 78–79, 75–76, 32–33; Klausner, *Messianic Idea*, p. 94; H. H. Rowley, *The Relevance of Apocalyptic: A Study of Jewish and Christian Apocalypses from Daniel to the Revelation* (New York, 1964), p. 170; Gilsdorf, "Puritan Apocalypse," p. 142; Oakes, *New-England Pleaded With*, p. 25; Willard, *Perils*, p. 78; I. Mather, *Discourse Concerning Prayer*, p. 96; C. Mather, quoted in Miller, *Colony to Province*, p. 188.

66 Miller, *Colony to Province*, pp. 187–88; Ola E. Winslow, *John Eliot: "Apostle to the Indians"* (Boston, 1968), pp. 167–68; Anon., *Indian Narratives . . .* (Claremont, N.H., 1854), p. 29; Douglas E. Leach, *Flintlock and Tomahawk: New England in King Philip's War* (New York, 1966), p. 160; Cotton Mather, *Decennium Luctuosum* (1699), in *Narratives of the Indian Wars, 1675–1699*, ed. Charles H. Lincoln (New York, 1913), p. 184.

67 I. Mather, *Historical Discourse*, p. 11, *Discourse Concerning Baptism*, p. 7, *Brief History*, p. 51, and *Renewal of Covenant*, p. 13; Miller, *Colony to Province*, p. 116; Thacher, *Fast*, p. 7. The covenant-renewal ceremonies show in effect an interesting similarity to Catholic appeals for confession in pre-Reformation England; see Blench, *Preaching*, pp. 246–47.

68 C. Mather, *Midnight Cry*, p. 52; I. Mather, *Earnest Exhortation*, p. 12; I. Mather, *Returning Unto God*, p. 18 (and see the covenant-renewal declaration appended); W. Adams, *Necessity*, p. 13; I. Mather, *Renewal of Covenant*, p. 7, and *Times of Man*, p. 2; Torrey, *Man's Extremity*, pp. 16–17, 35, 38, 45–46; Oakes, *Soveraign Efficacy*, pp. 5 ff.; C. Mather, *Duty of Children*, p. 20.

69 C. Mather, *Things to Think upon*, p. 53, and *Way to Prosperity*, p. 12; Scottow, *Narrative*, p. 330; I. Mather, *Renewal of Covenant*, pp. 7, 15–16, 4, 3, 20, and *Earnest Exhortation*, p. 13; W. Williams, *Plea*, p. 40 (cf. pp. 7, 21–22, 33–34); C. Mather, *Serviceable Man*, p. 14; W. Adams, *Necessity*, p. 14; I. Mather, *Returning unto God*, p. 7; Torrey, *Plea*, pp. 1–2, 25; C. Mather, *Everlasting Gospel*, p. 28; I. Mather, *Pray*, p. 22; W. Adams, *Necessity*, p. 40; Keith, *Case of Prayer*, pp. 25, 22; I. Mather, *Discourse Concerning Prayer*, p. 79 (cf. W. Williams, *Plea*, p. 36, and Wakeman, *Sound Repentance*, p. 42); Miller, *Colony to Province*, p. 214; W. Adams, *Gods Eye*, p. 35 (cf. pp. 5, 19); Willard, *Duty*, p. 13; C. Mather, *Things to Think upon*, p. 60; Saltonstall, *Sermon*, pp. 59, 53; Increase Mather, *A Sermon Wherein is shewed that the Church of God is sometimes a Subject of Great Persecution* (Boston, 1682), pp. 23–24 (cf. pp. 20–21). See also, I. Mather, *Heavens Alarm*, p. 14; Thacher, *Fast*, pp. 1, 8; C. Mather, *Present State*, p. 1, and *Midnight Cry*, pp. 12–14; I. Mather, *Pray*, p. 11 (on material-spiritual blessings).

70 Keith, *Case of Prayer*, pp. 7–8; C. Mather, *Magnalia*, II, 571; I. Mather, *David Serving*, p. 4; Keith, *Case of Prayer*, p. 4; I. Mather, *Historical Discourse*, title page, and *Duty of Parents*, p. 5 (see also p. 43); C. Mather, *Duty of Children*, pp. 7, 61 (see also pp. 49, 52); Thacher, *Fast*, p. 15; Danforth, *Exhortations to All*, in *Wall and Garden*, ed. Plumstead, pp. 157–60, 166–69, 172, 176.

71 W. Adams, *Necessity*, p. 34 (see also p. 18); Josiah Torrey and Samuel

Flint, Preface to Adams, *Necessity*, sigs. A3ʳ–A3ᵛ. See also, I. Mather, *Discourse Concerning Prayer*, p. 89; C. Mather, *Midnight Cry*, pp. 47–49; and S. Hooker, *Righteousness Rained*, p. 6.

72 Miller, *Colony to Province*, p. 117; I. Mather, Preface to *Returning Unto God*, sig. A3ʳ, *Duty of Parents*, p. 20, and *Divine Right*, p. 8; Adams, *Gods Eye*, p. 5; C. Mather, *Wonderful Works*, p. 43, and *Things to be Look'd for*, p. 51; I. Mather, *Discourse Concerning Prayer*, pp. 84, 31, and *Sermon Shewing Dispensations*, p. 20; Noyes, *New-Englands Duty*, p. 63 (see also pp. 60–62); Danforth, *Building*, p. 25; Torrey, *Plea*, p. 23; I. Mather, *Sermon Shewing Dispensations*, pp. 20, 13, and *The Glorious Throne* (Boston, 1702), pp. 117, 121; Adams, *Gods Eye*, p. 20; W. Williams, *Great Duty*, p. 2; C. Mather, *Things to be Look'd for*, p. 44. See further, C. Mather, "Biblia Americana," Vol. IV, reel 2, s.v. Isa. 62.

73 Torrey, *Man's Extremity*, *passim*; John Norton, *Sion the Out-Cast healed of her Wounds*, in *Three Sermons*, pp. 6–7; Danforth, *Brief Recognition*, pp. 19–21. On the relation between rhetoric and "systems of thought," see David Levin's review of William R. Smith, *History as Argument: The Patriot Historians of the American Revolution* (New York, 1966), in *William and Mary Quarterly*, XXV (1968), 312.

74 Norton, *Sion the Out-cast*, pp. 6–7; W. Adams, *Necessity*, pp. 32–33; Torrey and Flint, Preface to Adams, *Necessity*, sig. A2ʳ; I. Mather, *First Principles*, p. 15; Torrey, *Exhortation*, p. 6.

75 W. Adams, *Necessity*, p. 6 (on the representative quality of this sermon for its times, see Love, *Fast and Thanksgiving Days*, p. 214); S. Hooker, *Righteousness Rained*, p. 12; Torrey, *Exhortation*, p. 10, and *Man's Extremity*, pp. 2–3; Oxenbridge, *New-England Freemen*, p. 30; I. Mather, *Great Blessing*, p. 21.

76 Oakes, *New-England Pleaded With*, pp. 22, 25, and *Soveraign Efficacy*, pp 17, 19; Higginson, *Cause of God*, p. 24; Whiting, *Way of Welfare*, p. 18; Noyes, *New-Englands Duty*, pp. 77, 63–64; Torrey, *Man's Extremity*, pp. 56–59.

77 David Levin, Introduction to Cotton Mather, *Bonifacius: An Essay upon the Good*, ed. Levin (Cambridge, Mass., 1966), p. xvi (cf. Cotton Mather, *Theopolis Americana. An Essay . . . of Better Things to be yet seen in the AMERICAN World* [Boston, 1710], p. 43; John Cotton, *The Churches Resurrection* [London, 1642], pp. 14–15; Miller, *Colony to Province*, p. 188; Edward R. Lambert, *History of the Colony of New Haven* [New Haven, 1838], p. 50); Sewall, *Phaenomena*, p. 2; I. Mather, *Mystery*, p. 154; C. Mather, *Midnight Cry*, p. 63, and *Things to be Look'd for*, pp. 26, 33; I. Mather, *Discourse Concerning Prayer*, pp. 33, 57; Increase Mather, *A Sermon Shewing . . . that Wonderful Revolutions in the World are near at hand* (Edinburgh, 1710), p. 13, and *Glorious Throne*, pp. 117–19.

78 Miller, *Colony to Province*, p. 189; Cotton Mather, *Wonderful Works*, pp. 4, 40–41, *Things to be Look'd for*, pp. 3, 31, 33–34, *Midnight Cry*, pp. 29–33, 22, 24, *Eleutheria* (London, 1698), pp. 87, 27, and *Magnalia*, I, 44, 46, 302, 653–54; C. Mather, quoted in Woody, *EAL*, IV, 18–19, 40–46. For echoes of the phrases cited above in the *Magnalia*, see, for example, I, 46, and II, 447, 470, 579.

79 Daniel J. Boorstin, *The Genius of American Politics* (Chicago, 1953),
    p. 57; C. Mather, *Magnalia*, I, 330–31, 27, 79, 237, 509, and II, 8,
    57; Haller, *Elect Nation*, p. 100; Gilsdorf, "Puritan Apocalypse," pp.
    49–50; Shepard, *Parable*, II, 8; Thacher, Preface to Shepard, *Eye-
    Salve*, sig. A2ʳ; Allin, *New Englands Choicest*, p. 5; Increase Mather,
    The Surest Way to Greatest Honour (Boston, 1699), p. 24.
80 Cotton Mather, *Diary*, ed. Worthington C. Ford (New York, 1957),
    I, 358 (July 4, 1700); Willard, *Useful Instructions*, p. 58; Norton,
    Sion the Out-Cast, p. 6; Stoughton, *New-Englands True Interest*, p.
    21; I. Mather, Preface to Torrey, *Plea*, sig. A2ʳ; C. Mather, *Magnalia*,
    I, 36, 27 (see also, I, 603).
81 Darrett B. Rutman, "Local Freedom and Puritan Control," in *Puritan-
    ism in Seventeenth-Century Massachusetts*, ed. David D. Hall (New
    York, 1968), p. 118; David D. Van Tassel, *Recording America's Past*
    (Chicago, 1960), pp. 22–23; Harvey Wish, *The American Historian*
    (New York, 1960), p. 29; Joseph Morgan, *The History of the Kingdom
    of Basaruah* (1715), ed. Richard Schlatter (Cambridge, Mass., 1946),
    pp. 110, 88–99, 116, 133, 151, 158–59; Alan E. Heimert, *Religion
    and the American Mind, from the Great Awakening to the Revolution*
    (Cambridge, Mass., 1966), p. 60; David E. Smith, in *AQ*, XVII, 540;
    Carl Bridenbaugh, *Mitre and Sceptre: Transatlantic Faiths, Ideas,
    Personalities, and Politics* (New York, 1962), p. 175; Thomas Prince,
    A Chronological History of New-England in the Form of Annals
    (Boston, 1736), I, Dedication, sigs. A2ʳ–A2ᵛ, pp. 170, 104, 98, 103,
    199, and Preface, p. iii. Prince makes an exception among his predeces-
    sors as New England historians of the rationalist David Neal, who in
    The History of New England (1620) "pleased both with his Spirit,
    Style and Method" (Preface to *Chronological History*, p. iii); Neal's
    History of the Puritans, his next important work, was published in the
    next decade (1632–38). Regarding the jeremiad background of J.
    Morgan's *History*, see specifically Cotton Mather's election sermon of
    1689, which discusses America's prospects through an allegory (or
    pseudo-historic parable) of the "*Fighting City*" and the "Godly City"
    (*Way to Prosperity*, p. 31).
82 Prince, *Chronological History*, p. 1; Thomas Prince, *The People of
    New England* (1730), in *Wall and Garden*, ed. Plumstead, pp. 199,
    219, 205, 220; Susman, "History and the American Intellectual," p. 89;
    Darrett B. Rutman, *Winthrop's Boston: Portrait of a Puritan Town,
    1630–1649* (Chapel Hill, 1965), pp. 278–79 (see also pp. 21–22, 274,
    289); Thomas J. Holmes, "Cotton Mather and His Writings on Witch-
    craft," *Bibliographical Society of America, Papers*, XVIII (1924), 41;
    Otto T. Beall, Jr. and Richard H. Shryock, *Cotton Mather: First Signifi-
    cant Figure in American Medicine* (Baltimore, 1954), p. 123 (see
    also p. 94).
83 David E. Smith, in *AQ*, XVII, 537.
84 Heimert, *Religion*, pp. 287 (italics mine), 284 (quoting John Barnard,
    1766), 288 (paraphrasing Daniel Shute, 1768), 288 (quoting Samuel
    Williams, 1765), 350, 438–39 (paraphrasing William Smith); William
    Smith (1775) quoted on the flyleaf of Clinton Rossiter, *Seedtime of
    the Republic: The Origin of the American Tradition of Political*

Liberty (New York, 1953), in Heimert, *Religion*, p. 266, and in Perry Miller, "From the Covenant to the Renewal," in *Nature's Nation* (Cambridge, Mass., 1967), p. 102 (see also p. 111); Thomas Frink, *A Sermon Preached before His Excellency* (Boston, 1758), pp. 1, 30, 38, and *A Sermon Delivered at Stafford* (Boston, 1757), pp. 4–6, 8; David Freneau and Hugh Henry Brackenridge, "A Poem, On the Rising Glory of America," in *Colonial Poetry*, ed. Silverman, pp. 438, 442–43.

85 Rossiter, *Seedtime*, p. 40; Miller, "Covenant to Revival," *Nature's Nation*, p. 102 (see also p. 97); Sanford, *Quest*, pp. 118–20 (on Franklin), 171–72; Merrill Jensen, *The New Nation* (New York, 1962), p. 90; Baritz, *City*, pp. 96–101; Heimert, *Religion*, pp. 493, 454 (paraphrasing Timothy Dwight and Nathaniel Niles), 284, 409–10 (quoting Samuel Sherwood's "characterization of American war aims"); Tuveson, *Redeemer Nation*, p. 169 (quoting Humphreys); Jacob Duché, *The American Vine* (Philadelphia, 1775), p. 17; Samuel Sherwood, *The Church's Flight into the Wilderness* (New York, 1776), p. 23; Jacob Duché, *Observations on a Variety of Subjects* (Philadelphia, 1774), pp. 103, 107, and *American Vine*, p. 27.

86 Miller, "Covenant to Revival," *Nature's Nation*, pp. 95, 103, 105–6 (quoting Brackenridge, Cooper, Stiles, West, and Williams); Tuveson, *Redeemer Nation* (quoting Dwight, Humphreys, and others); Timothy Dwight, *A Discourse on the National Fast* (New York, 1812), pp. 54–56, and *A Discourse on Some Events of the Last Century* (New Haven, 1801), pp. 39–40, 42–43; Joel Barlow, *The Columbiad* (Philadelphia, 1809), IV, 435, 332; Timothy Dwight, *The Conquest of Canaän* (Hartford, 1788), I. 1–3, and XI. 254. On the Washington-Moses-Joshua parallel, see further, Thomas Baldwin, *A Sermon Occasioned by the Death of Washington* (Boston, 1799). What might appear in the pairing of Eden and the chiliad by Timothy Dwight to be an "inconsistent version of America" (Tuveson, *Redeemer Nation*, p. 107), becomes entirely clear within the typological historiography of the New England Puritans, where *"Urzeit gleicht Endzeit"* —beginning and end meet in harmony—in accordance with the doctrine of the "Sabbatism," espoused by ministers from John Cotton through Cotton Mather to Jonathan Edwards (see also James Sloan, quoted in Heimert, *Religion*, p. 101).

87 Tuveson, *Redeemer Nation*, pp. 53–54, 171; Miller, "Covenant to Revival," *Nature's Nation*, p. 119; Helmut Richard Niebuhr, *The Kingdom of God in America* (Hamden, Conn., 1956), pp. 154 (on reform movements as "evidences of the consummation of God's plan"), 154–55 (on the intimate connection between "the anticipated . . . kingdom-to-come [and] . . . the progress of industrialism and capitalism," and on evangelical groups, such as the Campbellite movement which felt itself to have "been stationed by Providence on a sublime eminence, from which [to] . . . behold the fulfillment of illustrious prophecies"); David E. Smith, in *AQ*, XVII, 544–45 (on utopian experiments); Perry Miller, *The Life of the Mind in America, From the Revolution to the Civil War* (New York, 1965), pp. 55–56 (quoting Batchelder and Williams; see also his comments on p. 79 concern-

ing William Cogwill's *Harbinger of the Millennium*); George M. Frederickson, *The Inner Civil War: Northern Intellectuals and the Crisis of the Union* (New York, 1965), p. 195 (on Christian Socialism); Niebuhr, *Kingdom of God*, p. 158; C. Mather, "Joyful Tidings," in *India Christiana*, pp. 47–48; Robert Meredith, *The Politics of the Universe: Edward Beecher, Abolition, and Orthodoxy* (Nashville, 1968), p. 165 (quoting Parker and Edward Beecher; see also pp. 135–36); Niebuhr, *Kingdom of God*, p. 157 (on Theodore Weld); Frederickson, *Inner Civil War*, p. 2 (see also p. 82); Tuveson, *Redeemer Nation*, p. 195 (see also on p. 88 Tuveson's comments on the "echo of the theories of . . . Joachim of Flora" in this period); Frederic I. Carpenter, *American Literature and the Dream* (New York, 1955), p. 12; Quentin Anderson, "Henry James and the New Jerusalem," *Kenyon Review*, VII (1946), 517; Frederickson, *Inner Civil War*, pp. 118, 68, 7; Lincoln, quoted in Edward M. Burns, *The American Idea of Mission: Concepts of National Purpose and Destiny* (New Brunswick, N. J., 1957), p. 14. See further Tuveson on Hollis Read's *The Coming Crisis of the World* (1861): "does this trial [Hollis asks] indicate that God in judgment is casting off the chosen people? The answer is unhesitating. God 'hath made us his modern Israel . . . and yet in many respects, more abundantly [than before].' . . . God who has promised the world salvation will not 'give up the heritage, which he has cherished and watched over with such . . . care' " (*Redeemer Nation*, p. 195).

88 George Hochfield, ed., *Selected Writings of the Transcendentalists* (New York, 1966), pp. xx, xi, xxvii; the quotations from Alcott and Brownson appear on pp. 93, 143, 155–56, 175–76, 252–53 of this volume (see also on pp. 74–75 Sampson Reed's discussion of time); Ralph Waldo Emerson, *Complete Works*, ed. Edward W. Emerson (Boston, 1903–4), XI, 299, and *Journals*, ed. William H. Gilman (Cambridge, Mass., 1960), II, 4–5, 72, 116. Cf. Charles H. Nichols, *Many Thousand Gone* (Leiden, 1963), p. 204.

89 Emerson, *Complete Works*, I, 156; Hochfield, Introduction to *Transcendentalists*, pp. xi, xvi; Baritz, *City*, p. 207; Tuveson, *Redeemer Nation*, pp. 121–22, 169 (discussing Lyman Beecher's *Plea for the West*, Humphreys' "combination of the westward and the millennialist techniques," and Freneau's vision of the West as "Arcadia realized"); G. Williams, *Wilderness*, p. 9 (on John Mason Peck's *Guide to the West*; see also on pp. 118 ff., Professor Williams' comments on the Mormons of 1830, a "new Israel . . . in the wilderness, moving westward under the compulsion of both persecution and a phantom promise" of the Holy Land); Albert K. Wineberg, *Manifest Destiny: A Study of Nationalist Expansion in American History* (Gloucester, Mass., 1958), pp. 243, 284, *et passim*; Emerson, quoted and paraphrased in Leo Marx, *The Machine in the Garden: Technology and the Pastoral Ideal in America* (New York, 1964), pp. 231, 236, 239; Frederickson, *Inner Civil War*, pp. 235–37, on Henry James, Sr., who is quoted in A. N. Kaul, *The American Vision: Actual and Ideal Society in Nineteenth-Century American Fiction* (New Haven, 1963), pp. 261–68; Tuveson, *Redeemer Nation*, p. 125; O'Sullivan, quoted in

Julius W. Pratt, "The Origin of 'Manifest Destiny,'" *American Historical Review*, XXXII (1926–27), 797; Norman A. Graebner, ed., *Manifest Destiny* (Indianapolis, 1968), p. xv; Robert C. Winthrop, quoted by Pratt, in *American Historical Review*, XXXII, 797; Harry S. Truman and Walter Lippmann, quoted in Burns, *American Idea*, pp. 10–11.

90 Heimert, *Religion*, pp. 57–60, 123–30; Niebuhr, *Kingdom of God*, p. 143; Alan Heimert, Introduction to Edwards' *Humble Inquiry*, in *The Great Awakening: Documents Illustrating the Crisis and Its Consequences*, ed. Alan E. Heimert and Perry Miller (New York, 1966), p. 424. On the parallels between the Separates of this period and (for example) Roger Williams, see "A Letter from the Associated Ministers . . . of Windham" (1745), in *Great Awakening*, ed. Heimert and Miller, which uses "the Parable of the Tares" as Williams did to show the "plain Difference between the World and the Church" with the concomitant requirement "that all the Converted should be separated from the Unconverted." It may be well to note here that despite my disagreements with Professor Heimert I am deeply indebted to his study of the Great Awakening and its consequences; if in the following pages I select his work as a central reference point against which to present my own view of Edwards' debt to the jeremiad, I do so precisely because I consider *Religion and the American Mind* an authoritative examination of Edwards' thought and of the Calvinist movement in general. Peter Gay discusses Edwards' *History of Redemption* and provides a good bibliographical discussion on the scholarship to 1966 (*Loss of Mastery*, pp. 68–117, 153–57).

91 Tuveson, *Redeemer Nation*, p. 51; David E. Smith in *AQ*, XVII, 539; Heimert, *Religion*, pp. 105, 74; Tuveson, *Redeemer Nation*, p. 34; Perry Miller, *Roger Williams* (New York, 1953), pp. 34–35, and *Jonathan Edwards* (New York, 1949), p. 320; Kai Erikson, *Wayward Puritans: A Study in the Sociology of Deviance* (New York, 1966), p. 68; David E. Smith in *AQ*, XVII, 539, 541–42. See further, on the question of premillenarianism and postmillenarianism, Heimert, *Religion*, pp. 61, 86–87. Professor Smith notes that "the starting point for postmillenarianism in America . . . may be seen in the hopeful expectation of Sewall, Cotton Mather, Morgan and others" (*AQ*, XVII, 546)—though by "others" he presumably means members of the last period of the orthodoxy. Though Tuveson also portrays Edwards' postmillenarianism as a radical departure, he observes that "by the end of the seventeenth century, the . . . idea that history is moving toward a millennial regeneration of mankind became not only repectable but almost canonical" (*Redeemer Nation*, p. 17); see also Lee M. Friedman, "Cotton Mather and the Jews," *American Jewish Historical Society Publications*, XXV (1918), 201.

92 Jonathan Edwards, *A History of the Work of Redemption* (1774), ed. John Erskine, in *The Works of President Edwards* (New York, 1849), I, 354 (italics mine); David Austin, Notes to Jonathan Edwards, *A History of the Work of Redemption* (New York, 1793), p. 149n.; Edwards, *History of Redemption*, in *Works*, I, 511–12, *A Humble Attempt to Promote Explicit Agreement and Visible Union of God's*

People in Extraordinary Prayer, in *Works,* III, 492, and *History of Redemption,* I, 510; Heimert, *Religion,* pp. 67–68, 64; Cambridge Platform, quoted in C. C. Goen, "Jonathan Edwards: A New Departure in Eschatology," *Church History,* XXVIII (1959), 32 (italics mine); Bridenbaugh, *Mitre and Sceptre,* p. 172; Heimert, *Religion,* p. 60; Martin, *Last Judgment,* p. 82; Joseph Bellamy, *The Millennium* 1758), in *Great Awakening,* ed. Heimert and Miller, p. 617; Edwards, *History of Redemption,* in *Works,* I, 481–82, 486; Bellamy, *Millennium,* in *Great Awakening,* ed. Heimert and Miller, pp. 617–18; Jonathan Parsons, *Wisdom Justified of Her Children* (Boston, 1742), p. 49; Thomas Foxcroft, Preface to Jonathan Dickinson, *The True Scripture Doctrine* (Boston, 1741), p. ii. The reference to the "army with banners" (from Cant. 6:10) remains popular throughout the colonial period and carries the same apocalyptic reference to Gog and Magog for the revivalists as for the Puritans: see Cotton, *Brief Exposition of Canticles,* p. 180. Edwards' view of God's intent in delaying America's discovery is "that the new and most glorious state of God's church on earth might commence there . . . the *new heavens and the new earth*" (Edwards, quoted by Goen, in *Church History,* XXVIII, 28).

93 John J. Zubly, quoted by Miller, "Covenant to Renewal," *Nature's Nation,* p. 96; Heimert, *Religion,* p. 96; Martin, *Last Judgment,* p. 7; Heimert, *Religion,* pp. 108–9, 470n., 98 (see also p. 85); Jonathan Edwards, *Thoughts on the Revival in New England,* in *Works,* III, 316, 308–9, 311, 313, 319, and *History of Redemption,* in *Works,* I, 468–69. See further, Edwards, *Humble Attempt,* in *Works,* III, 443, and *Distinguishing Marks,* in *Works,* I, 555 (on the discovery of America); and cf. Heimert, *Religion,* p. 332, on the question of Edwards' and the Calvinists' sense of "nation."

94 Heimert, *Religion,* p. 68; *Edwards, History of Redemption,* in *Works,* I, 486, 490–91, 493–94, 488, and *Thoughts on the Revival,* in *Works,* III, 299. Regarding the "poor negroes," see further David Austin's plea for "our age and nation to liberate . . . these miserable outcasts of mankind," in his Notes on Edwards' *History of Redemption,* p. 515n.; and Samuel Davies on the "salutary influences to the poor *African Negroes*" promised by the millennium, in his *Mediatorial Kingdom and Glories of Jesus Christ* (Bristol, 1783), p. 43. (Austin's hope is not unlike that which Edwards expresses for the Jews: see his *Humble Attempt,* in *Works,* III, 129, 444, 492–93, and especially his *History of Redemption,* in *Works,* I, 487.)

95 Heimert, *Religion,* pp. 64–66; Edwards, *Thoughts on the Revival,* in *Works,* III, 291, and *History of Redemption,* in *Works,* I, 483; Buell, quoted in Heimert, *Religion,* p. 236; Edwards, *Humble Attempt,* in *Works,* III, 492; Heimert, Introduction to Bellamy's *Millennium,* in *Great Awakening,* ed. Heimert and Miller, p. 610, and *Religion,* p. 236; Edwards, *Thoughts on the Revival,* in *Works,* III, 334.

96 Edwards, *History of Redemption,* in *Works,* I, 481, 469, 487, *Humble Attempt,* in *Works,* III, 461, 458, 460–61; Samuel Davies, *The State of Religion . . . in Virginia* (1751), in *Great Awakening,* ed. Heimert

and Miller, p. 387; Edwards, *Thoughts on the Revival,* in *Works,* III, 316 (see also Goen, in *Church History,* XXVIII, 30); Sewall, *Phaenomena,* p. 51; Edwards, *Thoughts on the Revival,* in *Works,* III, 316, 322–24. On Edwards' use of the type of the Babylonian captivity, see Ursula Brumm, *Religiöse Typologie im Amerikanischen Denken* . . . (Leiden, 1963), pp. 75–78; on Edwards' "remarkable" view of the Conversion of the Jews, see Goen, in *Church History,* XXVIII, 28.

97 C. Mather, *Everlasting Gospel,* pp. 61, 60; Heimert, *Religion,* p. 80; Samuel Wigglesworth, *An Essay for Reviving Religion* (1733), in *Great Awakening,* ed. Heimert and Miller, pp. 7, 5; Gordon, quoted by Miller, "Covenant to Revival," *Nature's Nation,* p. 99; Edwards, *Humble Attempt,* in *Works,* III, 458–59, and subtitle; cf. Jonathan Parsons, "Account of the Revival . . . at Lynne . . ." (1744), in *Great Awakening,* ed. Heimert and Miller, p. 37. On the parallel between Mather and Edwards, see Heimert, *Religion,* p. 359 (with respect to the *Magnalia*) and p. 163, on Edwards' biography of Brainerd as "the Calvinist *Manuductio ad Ministerium*"; and compare Mather's well-known comments in the *Manuductio* on the School of Halle with those of Edwards in *History of Redemption,* in *Works,* I, 469–70.

98 Heimert, *Religion,* p. 55; Edwards, *Thoughts on the Revival,* in *Works,* III, 410, 417–18, 424, *History of Redemption,* in *Works,* I, 482, *Humble Attempt,* in *Works,* III, 431, 433, *History of Redemption,* in *Works,* I, 487, and *Humble Attempt,* in *Works,* III, 457, 454; C. Mather, *Magnalia,* I, 43, 42; David Austin, "Advertisement" to Edwards, *History of Redemption,* p. iv. Edwards' "typical" use of Samson is many times foreshadowed in the jeremiads, which similarly compare the settlers to Samson "when hee had broken the Covenant" and so "became weake as another man" (though "virtually" remaining of course one of "God's faithfull ones"): see Higginson, *Cause of God,* p. 18; C. Mather, *Serviceable Man,* p. 45; I. Mather, *Times of Man,* p. 5; Keith, *Case of Prayer,* p. 20; Mitchel, *Nehemiah,* pp. 16–17; Oakes, *New-England Pleaded With,* p. 21.

99 Heimert, *Religion,* p. 92 (see also pp. 208–9); Jonathan Mayhew, *A Sermon Preach'd* (1754), in *Wall and Garden,* ed. Plumstead, p. 291; Jeremiah Dummer, quoted in Heimert, *Religion,* pp. 245–46; Charles Chauncy, *Seasonable Thoughts on the State of Religion in New England* (1743), in *Great Awakening,* ed. Heimert and Miller, p. 299; Channing, quoted in Niebuhr, *Kingdom of God,* p. 144; Chauncy, *Seasonable Thoughts,* in *Great Awakening,* ed. Heimert and Miller, pp. 302n., 302–3; Heimert, *Religion,* p. 114; Duché, *American Vine,* p. 26; Winthrop, Duffield, and Sloan, quoted in Heimert, *Religion,* pp. 396, 493–94, 543. For further aspects of the contrast described above, see Plumstead's Introduction to Samuel Danforth's election sermon of 1714, in *Wall and Garden,* ed. Plumstead, p. 145, and Heimert, *Religion,* pp. 98, 156 (on the contrast between Edwards' *Thoughts on the Revival* and Franklin's *Proposal for Promoting Useful Knowledge*); cf. Frank H. Foster, "The Eschatology of the New England Divines," *Bibliotheca Sacra,* XLIII (1886), esp. 6–20 (Edwards), 20–21 (Bellamy), 299–302 (Dwight), 711–26 (Hopkins). For

other specific images and scriptural phrases, see, for example, Tuveson, *Redeemer Nation*, p. 49, and Heimert, *Religion*, pp. 95, 149, 546 (on Europe, the Temple, and Christ's Army).

100 Lionel Trilling, "Reality in America" (1940, 1946), in *The Liberal Imagination* (New York, 1957), pp. 7–8; Richard Chase, *The American Novel and Its Tradition* (New York, 1957), pp. 7, 27–28; Marx, *Machine*, p. 364; Roy Harvey Pearce, *The Continuity of American Poetry* (Princeton, 1961), pp. 41–42, 430–31; Susman, "History," in *American Experience*, ed. Cohen, p. 93; see also Richard Hofstadter's contrast between popular American thought and the intellectual tradition which reaches back to the Puritan clergy, in *Anti-Intellectualism in American Life* (New York, 1963), pp. 59, 62, 399.

101 Newton Arvin, Symposium in *Partisan Review*, XIX, 286; Kaul, *American Vision*, p. 34.

102 Henry Adams, *The Education of Henry Adams*, ed. James Truslow Adams (New York, 1931), pp. 232, 459, 343, 5, 280, 92 (italics mine), and James Truslow Adams's Introduction, p. ix.

103 C. Mather, *Magnalia*, I, 103, and II, 181; Adams, *Education*, pp. 328–29, 12–14, 21, 313, 308; Edwards, paraphrased in Heimert, *Religion*, p. 67.

104 Adams, *Education*, pp. x, 21, 19, 343, 383, 238, 505. See further, on the question of Adams's nationalism versus his sense of failure and isolation, J. C. Levenson, *The Mind and Art of Henry Adams* (Cambridge, Mass., 1957), pp. 165–67, 376–79, Ernest Samuels, *Henry Adams: The Major Phase* (Cambridge, Mass., 1964), pp. 341–56, 548–49, and Sayre, *Examined Self*, p. 198.

105 Marx, *Machine*, p. 252; Henry Thoreau, *Walden and Other Writings*, ed. Brooks Atkinson (New York, 1950), pp. 182, 20, 19, 7, 33; Walt Whitman, *Democratic Vistas*, in *Leaves of Grass and Selected Prose*, ed. Sculley Bradley (New York, 1962), pp. 494, 506, 495, 516, 496, 489, 506, 514, 544.

106 Thoreau, *Walden*, p. 185; Alcott, quoted in F. O. Matthiessen, *American Renaissance: Art and Expression in the Age of Emerson and Whitman* (New York, 1941), p. 79n.; Whitman, *Democratic Vistas*, pp. 489, 513; Marx, *Machine*, pp. 253, 265; Edwin Fussell, *Frontier: American Literature and the American West* (Princeton, 1965), pp. 184, 189, 194, 221, 224, 229. See further in *Walden* Thoreau's comments on the Puritans (pp. 34–35), on time and eternity (pp. 80–81), on the "fabulous landscape of my infant dreams" and the aims of America (pp. 141, 148, 177, 218), on the "Golden Age" and the conflict between "sacred" and social laws (pp. 279–81, 287; and cf. pp. 13, 29, 195).

107 Johnson, *Wonder-Working Providence*, pp. 29, 52, 159–60 (cf. Increase Mather, *A Discourse Concerning Earthquakes* [Boston, 1706], pp. 129–30); C. Mather, "Joyful Sound," in *India Christiana*, pp. 32–33; Edwards, *Thoughts on the Revival*, in *Works*, III, 316; see further David Austin, *The Dawn of Day, Introductory to the Rising Sun* (New Haven, 1800), and Sewall's argument in *Phaenomena*, p. 29, that "as *Jerusalem* was to the westward of Babylon; so *New-Jerusalem* must be to the westward of Rome"; Duché, *Observations*, p. 107; Thoreau, "Walk-

ing," in *Walden and other Writings*, ed. Atkinson, pp. 609, 612, 608, and *Walden*, p. 279. See also J. Sullivan Cox's 1846 statement that "the scriptural prophecies are confirmation of the hopes obscurely represented by secular utopias throughout the centuries; these latter are, as it were, intuitions of the divine plan" embodied in America (quoted in Tuveson, *Redeemer Nation*, p. 126).

108   Richard Chase, *Walt Whitman Reconsidered* (New York, 1955), pp. 157, 160; Sanford, *Quest*, p. 202; Whitman, *Democratic Vistas*, pp. 495, 509, 490, 513, 544, 488, 514. The reference to "fire in his bones" is from Norton's description of Jeremiah (cited above) who, "looking at his sufferings he will speak no more, but looking at Gods promise . . . he cannot but speak" of the splendid things to come.

109   Chase, *Whitman*, p. 162; Whitman, *Democratic Vistas*, p. 539, *Walt Whitman's Workshop*, ed. C. J. Furness (Cambridge, Mass., 1928), pp. 127–28, and "Preface to the 1855 Edition of *Leaves of Grass*," in *Complete Poetry and Selected Prose*, ed. J. E. Miller, Jr. (Boston, 1959), p. 411; Pearce, *Continuity*, pp. 82, 170, 173. See also: Wright Morris, *The Territory Ahead* (New York, 1963), p. 71; James Miller, Jr., *A Critical Guide to "Leaves of Grass"* (Chicago, 1957), pp. 174–86; Roger Asselineau, *L'Evolution de Walt Whitman* (Paris, 1954), pp. 478–92; and especially Charles Feidelson's description of "the link between [Whitman's] poems and American life," in *Symbolism and American Literature* (Chicago, 1953), pp. 17 ff.

110   Pearce, *Continuity*, p. 170; Chase, *Whitman*, p. 160; Gay, *Loss of Mastery*, p. 65; C. Mather, *Magnalia*, I, 34–37; Austin Warren, "Grandfather Mather and his Wonder Book," *Sewanee Review*, LXXII (1964), 102; Whitman, quoted in Pearce, *Continuity*, pp. 168, 166, "Eidólons," in *Poetry and Prose*, ed. Miller, pp. 8–9, and *Democratic Vistas*, pp. 491, 525. Regarding the (widespread) notion of the American poet as priest, cf. Lanier's comments on this "new dispensation," in *Sidney Lanier: Centennial Edition*, ed. Paul F. Baum (Baltimore, 1945), II, 5–6.

111   Hofstadter, *Anti-Intellectualism*, pp. 64, 67; Heimert, *Religion*, pp. 153, 114, 67; Susman, "History," p. 93; R. W. B. Lewis, *The American Adam: Innocence, Tragedy, and Tradition in the Nineteenth Century* (Chicago, 1959), pp. 165, 173; David W. Noble, *Historians Against History* (Minneapolis, 1965), pp. 4, 16–17, 23–24, 30, 118, 177–78. See also, Ola E. Winslow, *Jonathan Edwards* (New York, 1961), pp. 200–47, and David Levin, *History as Romantic Art: Bancroft, Prescott, Motley, and Parkman* (Stanford, 1959), p. 97, *et passim*.

112   Sanford, *Quest*, p. 192; Stephen Whicher, "Emerson's Tragic Sense," *American Scholar*, XII (1953), 290–91; Baritz, *City*, pp. 258, 260, 265–66; Frederickson, *Inner Civil War*, pp. 176–78. See also Stephen Whicher, *Emerson and Fate: An Inner Life of Ralph Waldo Emerson* (Philadelphia, 1953), pp. 46–49, 60–65, 123–53.

113   Kaul, *American Vision*, p. 133; James Fenimore Cooper, *The Heidenmauer*, in *Works* (New York, 1901). XXIX, p. iv, *The Crater*, in *Works*, XV, 408, 164, 412, 199–200, and *The Pioneers*, in *Works*, III, 506; Leo Marx, "Mr. Eliot, Mr. Trilling, and Huckleberry Finn," *American Scholar*, XII (1953), 439; Lionel Trilling, "Huckleberry Finn," in *Liberal Imagi-*

nation, pp. 106, 104; James Fenimore Cooper, *The Prairie,* in *Works,* V, 453–61. See also, Henry Nash Smith, *Mark Twain's Fable of Progress: Political and Economic Ideas in "A Connecticut Yankee in King Arthur's Court"* (New Brunswick, N.J., 1964), *passim;* Charles S. Holmes, "A Connecticut Yankee in King Arthur's Court: Mark Twain's Fable of Uncertainty," *South Atlantic Quarterly,* LXI (1962), 462–72, and my "Huckleberry Bumppo: A Comparison of *Tom Sawyer* and *The Pioneers,*" *Mark Twain Journal,* XIV (1968), 1–5.

114 Lawrence Ferlinghetti, *A Coney Island of the Mind* (Norfolk, 1955), p. 49 (italics mine); F. Scott Fitzgerald, *The Great Gatsby* (New York, 1953), pp. 23, 178, 99, 182; Dotson Rader, *I Ain't Marchin' Anymore* (New York, 1969), pp. 166, 158, 139, 158, 101, 86, 8, 101, 2, 102. One view of dissent in America suggests an anti-Establishment line from the first colonial "heretics." Thus Richard Reinitz ("Symbolism," p. 193) sees in the Cotton-Williams controversy a prototype for our times: the Puritan theocrat, regarding "New England society as the New Jerusalem . . . [was] the first of many American leaders to adopt such an attitude. . . . Williams, insistently . . . rejecting American exceptionalism," foreshadowed the current student rebels. Rader's book, and many other similar documents, abundantly reveal that Cotton's rhetoric has continued to influence leaders and rebels alike. The tradition of dissent has not been studied as a whole from this perspective, but for a partial view, see, for example, Arthur Mann, *Yankee Reformers in the Urban Age* (Cambridge, Mass., 1954), and James Dombrowski, *The Early Days of Christian Socialism in America* (New York, 1936).

115 Rader, *I Ain't Marchin' Anymore,* pp. 101–12; James Baldwin, "Mass Culture and the Creative Artist: Some Personal Notes," *Daedalus,* LXXIX (1960), 376; Alfred Kazin, "The Trouble He's Seen," *New York Times Book Review* (May 5, 1968), p. 2; Jack Behar, "History and Fiction," *Novel,* III (1970), 260–63; Norman Mailer, *The Armies of the Night: History as the Novel, The Novel as History* (New York, 1968), pp. 194, 320, 172, 177, 68.

116 Kazin, in *New York Times Book Review* (May 5, 1968), pp. 1–2; Mailer, Symposium in *Partisan Review,* XIX, 299, and *Armies of the Night,* pp. 211, 179; Rader, *I Ain't Marchin' Anymore,* pp. 7, 101. See further John W. Aldridge, *After the Lost Generation: A Critical Study of the Writers of Two Wars* (New York, 1951), pp. 133–56, and cf. Melvin Maddock's review of *Armies of the Night* (portraying "our holy fool," Mailer, as the national "spokesman for the apocalypse"), "Norm's Ego Is Working Overtime for You," *Life* (May 10, 1968), p. 8.

117 Marx, *Machine in Garden,* pp. 317, 306; Melville, *Pierre,* pp. 8, 37, 195, 352, 298, and *White-Jacket,* ed. Hennig Cohen (New York, 1967), pp. 399–400, 145, 149; Arvin, *Melville,* pp. 275, 221; Herman Melville, *Moby-Dick; or, The Whale,* ed. Charles Feidelson (New York, 1964), p. 80. See also: Walter E. Bezanson, Introduction to Herman Melville, *Clarel,* ed. Bezanson (New York, 1960), p. cvi; Baritz, *City,* p. 273; Kaul, *American Vision,* pp. 183, 213; Sanford, *Quest,* p. 184; and my "Melville's Search for National Identity: Father and Son in *Redburn, Pierre,* and *Billy Budd,*" *College Language Association Journal,* X (1967), 217–29.

118 Melville, *Moby-Dick*, p. 145; Nathalia Wright, *Melville's Use of the Bible* (Durham, 1949), pp. 147, 82 (see also pp. 84–88, on the similarity between Jonah, Ahab, and Jeremiah, and pp. 87–88 on Melville's interest in Jeremiah's prophecies about the salvation of Israel from Babylon through the Exodus pattern, and cf. T. Walter Herbert, Jr., "Calvinism and Cosmic Evil in *Moby-Dick*," *PMLA*, LXXXIV [1969], 1613–19). The contrast between Puritan logic and poetic speech should perhaps be stated more fully, since it forms a basis for the present study. Perry Miller writes that the Puritans "strove with might and main to chain their language to logical propositions, and to penetrate to the affections of their auditors only by thrusting an argument through their reason"; therefore, "any criticism which endeavors to discuss Puritan writings as part of literary history . . . is approaching the materials in a spirit they were never intended to accommodate" (Miller, *Colony to Province*, p. 12, and *Seventeenth Century*, p. 362). William Haller contends that "the strength of the Puritan pamphleteers did not lie . . . in a greater power of lucid and coherent thought but in their command of the art of suggestive, provocative, poetic speech" (*The Rise of Puritanism* [New York, 1957], p. 256).

1 Robert Langbaum, *The Poetry of Experience* (New York, 1957), p. 109.
2 Wylie Sypher, Introduction to *The Ring and the Book* (New York: Norton Library, 1961), pp. xvi–xvii.
3 In writing to Ruskin, Browning said: "I *know* that I don't make out my conceptions by my language: all poetry being a putting of the infinite within the finite." (Quoted in W. G. Collingwood, *Life and Work of John Ruskin* [London, 1893], p. 164.)
4 For example, he rejects the comparison of his achievement with that of Faust, who formed an alliance with the Devil, and associates it with that of Elisha in restoring the dead to life (760–72). But his association with the divine is omnipresent in Book I and in the appropriate places in Book XII as well.
5 Langbaum, *"The Ring and the Book*: A Relativist Poem," in *Poetry of Experience*, pp. 9ˆ–128. (*Browning's Roman Murder Story* [Chicago, 1968], by Richard D. Altick and James F. Loucks II, is a massive literary analysis which does not, however, touch on Browning's aesthetic theory.) Since my essay was written, several other studies of the poem have appeared which I could not include in my text. In my opinion, the best of these is the section entitled "The Union of the Subject and the World," in D. David Shaw's *The Dialectical Temper: The Rhetorical Art of Robert Browning* (Ithaca, 1968), pp. 235–307. Shaw employs Browning's poetic theory and certain ideas of Kierkegaard in ways quite different from my own. A polemical treatment of the poem, centering largely on Browning's religious views, is the chapter entitled *"The Ring and the Book*: Browning's Concept of Truth," in Norton B. Crowell's *The Convex Glass: The Mind of Robert Browning* (Albuquerque, 1968), pp. 182–224.
6 Langbaum, *Poetry of Experience*, p. 104.
7 Ibid., p. 135.
8 Since some readers will nevertheless find such a comparison as this irrelevant, I should say here that I do not mean to prove that an idea is "in" a poem by Browning simply because it is in a book by Kierkegaard. It is unlikely that Browning had read any of the early German translations of Kierkegaard. Of greater interest to me than a possible direct influence, however, is recognition that the similar ideas of the two writers reflect a certain current of the age. For an interesting comparison between

Kierkegaard and Dostoevsky, see the chapter entitled "The Breakdown of Autonomy," in Geoffrey Clive's *The Romantic Enlightenment* (New York, 1960), pp. 96–131.

9 Altick and Loucks, *Browning's Roman Murder Story*, p. 82n.

10 William Clyde DeVane, *A Browning Handbook*, 2d ed. (New York, 1955), p. 47.

11 See, for example, Roma A. King, *The Bow and the Lyre* (Ann Arbor, 1957), p. 132.

12 Betty Miller, *Robert Browning: A Portrait* (London, 1952), pp. 10–12 and elsewhere. Mrs. Miller's use of psychology is legitimate, but she necessarily employs the poetry in order to trace the psychological origins of the ideas. Whether or not this particular idea arose precisely in the way she claims, the fact that it was psychological illustrates Browning's point. Mine is that in a reading of the poetry the belief must also be regarded as an idea; and for that purpose the psychological aspect takes on a different role. Unfortunately, its relevance tends to be obscured when the idea is found to have occurred to others (Mrs. Miller, on p. 11, quotes Browning as recognizing it in Schopenhauer).

13 A. H. Hallam gives an interesting contemporary expression to a similar idea in his review of an Italian translation of Milton: "It is the consciousness of intellectual power, not the possession of right opinions, which agitates beneficially the spirit of a nation, and prepares it for intellectual discovery. Feeling is the prime agent in this, as in other human operations. . . ." In a note he explains the idea succinctly: "The work of intellect is posterior to the work of feeling." (T. H. Vail Motter, ed., *The Writings of Arthur Henry Hallam* [New York and London, 1943], p. 241.)

14 Kierkegaard says that the job of the existential thinker is to "penetrate existence with thought," and illustrates the process on pp. 147–61 of the *Postscript*.

15 Thomas J. Collins, *Robert Browning's Moral-Aesthetic Theory, 1833–1855* (Lincoln, Nebraska, 1967).

16 DeVane, *Browning Handbook*, pp. 577–80; Philip Drew, "Browning's Essay on Shelley," *Victorian Poetry*, I (1963), 1–6. On other matters, Collins disagrees with both DeVane and Drew.

17 Collins, *Browning's Moral-Aesthetic Theory*, p. 113.

18 Ibid., p. 117.

19 Ibid.

20 The echoes of Shelley's *The Cenci* in *The Ring and the Book* (DeVane, *Browning Handbook*, p. 320) reflect only the objective side of the poem.

21 Collins, *Browning's Moral-Aesthetic Theory*, p. 114.

22 Collins does not quote Milsand's comments on the subjective and objective elements in the book, but the French writer's views are illuminating: "Mr. Browning sympathizes equally with both sources of inspiration, and I am inclined to think that his constant endeavor has been to reconcile and combine them, so as to be, not in turn, but simultaneously, lyrical and dramatic, subjective and objective. . . . His poetry would have us conceive of the inner significance of things by making us see the exteriors." (Quoted by DeVane, *Browning Handbook*, p. 211.)

23 Collins, *Browning's Moral-Aesthetic Theory*, p. 125.
24 Ibid.
25 Collingwood, *John Ruskin*, p. 166.
26 Since the facts, however, are the only materials through which he can employ the subjective faculty, such a theory as this may help to resolve one element in the controversy regarding Browning's attitude towards fact in the Old Yellow Book (cf. the "symposium" in Numbers 15, 16, and 17 of *Victorian Newsletter*; see note 39 below). Browning in his discovery of the Old Yellow Book was ecstatic not only because it gave him a perfect chance to express and to illustrate his theory in a single work, but also because in it he could show how his theory related to real life, not just to the world of poetic invention.
27 *Essay on Shelley*, p. 1009: "There is a time when the general eye has, so to speak, absorbed its fill of the phenomena around it, whether spiritual or material, and desires rather to learn the exacter significance of what it possesses than to receive any augmentation of what is possessed." Browning here is speaking of the transition from the objective to the subjective eras of poetry. In giving the objective poet a concern for the spiritual, he seems to contradict the earlier passage, quoted in the text above, in which he distinguished between the subjective and the objective poets by assigning the spiritual to the subjective: "The spiritual comprehension may be infinitely subtilized, but the raw material it operates upon must remain." But the analysis of a spiritual condition is not the same as placing it within the context of a universal meaning, which is the business of the subjective poet.
28 In his *Essay on Shelley* (p. 1012), Browning says that an ordinary youth, having found that his idealism is unable to cope with practical matters, would give up the attempt: "Wanting words to speak," he thus never makes "a fool of himself by speaking." But "in Shelley's case, the early fervor and power to *see* was accompanied by as precocious a fertility to *contrive*; he endeavored to realize as he went on idealizing; every wrong had simultaneously its remedy, and, out of the strength of his hatred for the former, he took the strength of his confidence in the latter—till suddenly he stood pledged to the defense of a set of miserable little expedients, just as if they represented great principles."
29 Hodell points up the role of the poet in discerning the truth, though he does not recognize the objective/subjective intent of the poem: "The deeper spiritual meaning of the three major characters and of their play upon one another is purely a part of the Poet's vision. They are hopelessly obscured to ordinary sight in the Book." (Quoted in DeVane, *Browning Handbook*, p. 339.)
30 Langbaum, *Poetry of Experience*, p. 109.
31 It is in this sense that the "whole truth" (I, 117) may be said to exist in the Old Yellow Book, though it requires the poet to infer it and the poetic imagination to express it.
32 He claims to have done this, for example, in Book XII, lines 9–10, when he speaks of Guido: "you have seen his act, / By my power."
33 Walter Lowrie discusses Kierkegaard's relationship to Romanticism in his *Kierkegaard* (New York, 1962; a partial revision of the 1938 edition), I, 100–115. Kierkegaard's definition of the aesthetic category of existence,

from one point of view, seems to be similar to the Victorian reaction against such poets as Shelley and Byron as imperfectly cognizant of reality. The unhappiness, moodiness, and attitudinization of the Byronic hero are especially important attributes of the Kierkegaardian ideal aesthete. It is interesting to note, therefore, that Byron and Shelley are the only two English poets whose works Kierkegaard possessed in his personal library. See Niel Thulstrup, *Søren Kierkegaards Bibliotek* (Copenhagen: Munksgaard, 1957), p. 91, items 1868–70 and 1898.

34 I agree here with Hodell's description of the relationship between the poem and the Old Yellow Book, as summarized in brief by DeVane: "Here [Hodell] shows that the poet has lifted the whole action of the major characters of the poem to a higher and more significant level than the actions and personages of his source—just as the Greek dramatist exalted human nature by magnifying it in tragedy. Guido is a far more consummate villain in Browning's poem. . . . Caponsacchi, a daredevil of gallantry in the Yellow Book, is given the subtle and tender spirit of a soldier-saint. . . . Pompilia in the poem . . . is glorified far beyond the patient, devout, outraged girl of the narrative in the Yellow Book" (*Browning Handbook*, p. 339).

35 See David F. Swenson, *Something About Kierkegaard* (Minneapolis, 1941), pp. 123–26.

36 A. H. Hallam expresses this idea in his treatment of the roles of idea and emotion: "[The work of feeling] lies at the foundation of the Man; it is his proper self, the peculiar thing that characterizes him as an individual. No two men are alike in feeling, but conceptions of the understanding, when distinct, are precisely similar in all" (Motter, *Writings of A. H. Hallam*, p. 241).

37 See Swenson, *Something About Kierkegaard*, p. 124.

38 Cf. XII, 864: "And save the soul! If this intent save mine. . . !"

39 The reader will see for himself the various points of relevance between this paper and those in the "symposium" in Numbers 15, 16, and 17 of the *Victorian Newsletter* (Paul A. Cundiff, "Robert Browning: 'Our Human Speech,'" no. 15 [1959], pp. 1–9; Donald Smalley, "Browning's View of Fact in *The Ring and the Book*," no. 16 [1959], pp. 1–9; Paul A. Cundiff, "Robert Browning: 'Indisputably Fact,'" no. 17 [1960], pp. 7–11; Robert Langbaum, "The Importance of Fact in *The Ring and the Book*," ibid., pp. 11–17). Again, while I most often side with Langbaum's view, many points of difference are introduced by Browning's objective/subjective theory. I cannot, for instance, agree with the view that "we are more impressed by the gold or fact in the Ring metaphor than by the alloy of fancy" (Langbaum, p. 12), simply because both poetic faculties are given equal importance, though greater honor is perhaps due to the subjective as belonging to the "soul," which is the real alloy.

I agree with Langbaum's suggestion that in many ways Browning was doing the historian's job, but it is also instructive to note that he was doing more than that. The historian's speculative imagination is within the province of the poet's objective faculty, though in re-creating his historical characters the poet may draw upon his subjective faculty as well. But in addition to the "historical source" (Langbaum, p. 14), the "whole poet" has also the "evidence" of his own "soul," the alloy in the poem. Browning's attitude towards the Higher Criticism as expressed in *Christmas-Eve*, for example, suggests that he would reject any quest for the historical Jesus. He would be more likely, I think, to accept Kierkegaards view that speculative history, in having to assign rational connections between cause and effect, must necessarily read both God and the human soul out of history. In *The Ring and the Book* it is precisely by employing his "soul" viewed as the subjective faculty that Browning says he can resuscitate the corpse and find God in the facts.

40 Such a transference of the ring metaphor from art to life is warranted by the Pope's doing so in reference to Guido:

> could he know
> The mercy of a minute's fiery purge!
> The furnace-coals alike of public scorn,
> Private remorse, heaped glowing on his head,
> What if,—the force and guile, the ore's alloy,
> Eliminate, his baser soul refined—
> The lost be saved even yet, so as by fire?
>
> (X, 707–13)

41 Quoted in E. T. Cook, *A Popular Handbook to the Greek and Roman Antiquities in the British Museum* (London, 1902), p. 570.

42 I therefore read line 372 as introducing a second question: it does not merely ask (Langbaum, *VNL*, no. 17, p. 14) whether the story itself lived in memory (to restore that is the objective poet's job), but also whether the "truth" therein was "of force" (the subjective poet's business). The irony in the statement that "You know the tale already" (377) lies not in the poet's statement that he will "add nothing to the events," but in the audience's apparent conviction a few lines later that the poet is not needed to reveal the moral meaning in the events. Langbaum appears to hold that the Pope's judgment was accepted as "truth" until the memory of it was lost, but clearly the Pope's judgment was not unanimously accepted.

43 Miller, *Robert Browning*, p. 86.

44 In response to an assignment in a graduate seminar on Browning, one of my students, Mr. Patrick Segedy, first suggested to me that this might be the "chant made for midsummer nights." I have taken some of the liturgical information which follows from a 1945 edition of the *Saint Andrew Daily Missal*.

45 I have verified his information in an 1859 edition of the *Breviarium Romanum;* quotations are taken from a modern translation. For help in interpreting the regulations affecting the Divine Office, I am indebted to my two colleagues, Professors Bernard S. Levy and Jack Carey.

46 See, for example, Collingwood, *John Ruskin*, p. 166.

47 This and the following quotations may be verified in any modern English translation of the Breviary published before the recent changes.

48 See Paul A. Cundiff, "The Clarity of Browning's Ring Metaphor," *PMLA*, LXIII (1948), 1276–82. I should add that, according to jewellers I have consulted, an acid bath would remove only the impurities, not

the alloy itself. Cundiff provides a useful summary of work done on the metaphor to 1948, though I disagree with his claim that Browning had a low regard for the "gold" (facts) in this poem. For an extremely sensitive and skilfully presented recent treatment of the ring figure, see George Wasserman, "The Meaning of Browning's Ring-Figure," *MLN*, LXXVI (1961), 420–26. It will be seen that Wasserman, in his own terms, touches on some points which I have here discussed in terms of the *Essay on Shelley*.

49 Sypher, Introduction to *The Ring and the Book*, p. ix.
50 My reading of lines 1220–21 is confirmed, I think, by Browning's apparent repetition of the idea in Book XII:

> you have seen his [Guido's] act,
> By my power—may-be, judged it by your own,—
> Or composite as good orbs prove, or crammed
> With worse ingredients than the Wormwood Star.
>
> (9–12)

If Browning simply meant the reader to assess Guido's guilt or innocence according to his own judgment, then the qualifying "may-be" can only be taken as a rather silly suggestion that some strange reader may have refused to make up his mind. But the meaning of "judged it" is at least ambiguous. If "his act" is what has been "judged," then "may-be" suggests that the reader is perhaps only under the illusion that he has done so. But we may also take it to mean that the reader has judged the "act" only as that may be seen through the poet's power; that is, he has judged the poem. Then "may-be" takes on a more serious meaning, in view of Browning's caution that the poet can only "obliquely" try to bring home truth to those who have eyes to see and yet are blind (XII, 842). Lines 11–12 above involve another ambiguity which follows from the first one. The "composite" orb seems at first to refer only to "his act," according to the literal syntax of the passage. But the orb may equally be that which was produced "By my power"; and in fact, that is the comparison worked out in a simile near the end of Book XII, where the Star Wormwood is associated with the whole tale itself, which has been revived in subjective/objective fulness by the poet:

> so
> Did the Star Wormwood in a blazing fall
> Frighten awhile the waters and lie lost:
> So did this old woe fade from memory,
> Till after, in the fulness of the days,
> I needs must find an ember yet unquenched,
> And, breathing, blow the spark to flame.
>
> (823–29)

These ambiguities can be resolved most successfully, I think, by keeping in mind the objective/subjective theory. Browning seems to mean that objectively the reader may accept Guido's guilt as that is seen in the poem; but "may-be" he has also fallen under the power of the subjective element, which brings him into relation with the absolute by evoking his own ethical activity, thus "saving the soul."

INDEX

Abraham, 40, 51n, 53, 58, 129
Adams, Henry, 92–94, 99, 122
Adams, William, 50
Altick, Richard, 131–34, 216, 217
Arminians, 22–23, 82, 85
Arnold, Matthew, 132
Arvin, Newton, 91
Aspinwall, William, 69
Augustine, St., 15–16, 178–79
Austin, David, 89

Baldwin, James, 103
Bale, John, 9, 43
Bancroft, George, 99
Barlow, Joel, 78
Baptism, 39–41, 111–12
Bellamy, Joseph, 86
Bradstreet, Anne, 116–17
Brightman, Thomas, 21
Brook Farm, 79
Browning, Elizabeth Barrett, 143–44, 175–77
Browning, Robert: relativity in poetry of, 127, 131, 170; reputation as a thinker of, 131, 134; anti-intellectualism of, 131–35; and myth, 132–33, 134, 135; emphasis on love by, 134, 135, 140, 152, 161, 179; emphasis on action by, 145–48, 149–50, 153–54
———, poetics: "truth" in, 127, 130, 134–35, 144, 147, 159–61, 165, 168, 169, 170, 182–83, 218, 220; role of persona in, 127–28; ethical and religious aspect of art and, 127–34 passim, 147–54 passim, 152–54, 156, 157, 160–61, 170; and the poet in, 128, 136–37, 137–39, 143, 147, 152–53, 157, 158, 160, 164, 165, 169, 171–72, 173, 177, 178, 180–83, 221; and ex-

istential communication, 128–29, 131, 147, 154–58, 159–60, 164; objective/subjective, 129, 133, 134, 136–39, 140, 141, 143–44, 145–64 passim, 165, 169, 173, 183, 217, 218, 221; role of fact in, 145, 146, 150, 151, 152, 169–70, 173, 182, 218, 219; liturgical allusion in, 175ff.
———, works of: *Christmas-Eve*, 134; *Easter-Day*, 134; "One Word More," 134, 139, 143, 175; *Essay on Shelley*, 135–39, 141, 144, 145–64 passim, 172–73, 183, 218, 221; "Bishop Blougram's Apology," 139; *Men and Women*, 139, 140, 144; "Fra Lippo Lippi," 140; "Transcendentalism: A Poem in Twelve Books," 140, 141; "How it Strikes a Contemporary," 140–42, 143, 178; *Sordello*, 145
Bulkeley, Peter, 24, 52
Burnet, Gilbert, 6

Calvin, John: and typology, 21; and the Book of Revelation, 44; on affliction, 63, 198; on covenant, 109–10
Canaan and New Canaan, 21, 88
Castellani family, 166–67
Channing, William E., 89
Charity, Alan, 58
Chase, Richard, 91
Chauncy, Charles, 12, 35
Clarke, Samuel, 90
Collingwood, W. G., 216, 218, 220
Collins, Thomas J., 135–39, 217, 218
Congregationalists, 8–11
Cooper, James Fenimore, 100–101, 123
Cotton, John, 4, 5, 14–15, 23, 35, 39, 56, 82, 105
Covenant: national, 4, 6, 8, 44; of grace

223